T0366604

Stanzas in Meditation

Stanzas in Meditation

The Corrected Edition

Gertrude Stein

Edited by **Susannah Hollister** *and* **Emily Setina**

With an Introduction by **Joan Retallack**

Yale UNIVERSITY PRESS

NEW HAVEN & LONDON

In association with the Beinecke Rare Book and Manuscript Library

Stanzas in Mediation is a co-publication of Yale University Press and the Beinecke Rare Book and Manuscript Library.

Published with assistance from the foundation established in memory of James Wesley Cooper of the Class of 1865, Yale College.

Yale University Press books may be purchased in quantity for educational, business, or promotional use. For information, please e-mail sales.press@yale.edu (U.S. office) or sales@yaleup.co.uk (U.K. office).

Designed by Mary Valencia.
Set in Adobe Caslon type by Keystone Typesetting, Inc.
Printed and bound by CPI Group (UK) Ltd, Croydon, CR0 4YY

Library of Congress Control Number: 2011924246
ISBN 978-0-300-15309-5 (paperback : alk. paper)

A catalogue record for this book is available from the British Library.

10 9 8 7 6 5 4 3 2 1

Contents

Preface

John Ashbery wrote in 1957 that reading Gertrude Stein's *Stanzas in Meditation* comes to seem like "living a rather long period of our lives with a houseful of people."[1] In the summer of 2009, the more intense than long period we spent preparing the poem for this edition, we inhabited not a house but a basement room of Yale University's Beinecke Rare Book and Manuscript Library. Our company consisted of Gertrude Stein, present through her large, loose, looping handwriting in manuscript notebooks; Alice B. Toklas, present through her typescripts and neat handwritten edits; Joseph Addison, painted in 1716, present in the portrait hanging on the south wall of our windowless room; Louis Mayer Rabinowitz, painted in 1953, present in the portrait hanging on the west wall; and each other. On the other side of the south wall was an empty space where Francis Picabia's 1933 portrait of Stein, painted soon after the composition of *Stanzas*, usually hangs in the main reading room, though the portrait was off-site that summer for reasons we never learned.

We came to that room, and joined that company, for the story of textual revision and romantic jealousy that led to *Stanzas'* multiple versions. The story, uncovered by Ulla Dydo and presented at length in her *Gertrude Stein: The Language That Rises, 1923–1934* (2003), goes as follows: Stein began writing the poem in the summer of 1932 and ultimately filled six notebooks with its text. Toklas prepared a first typescript of *Stanzas* from Stein's manuscripts, their typical working method, later that year. Then, in December 1932, Toklas read Stein's early fictional work *Q.E.D.*, the manuscript of which had resurfaced in Stein's studio during an April visit by Bernard Fäy and Louis Bromfield. Based on a past love affair, the text brought to light Stein's relationship with May Bookstaver, a relationship Stein had omitted from the disclosures she and Toklas had pledged to each other early on. This late revelation prompted a quarrel between the two that continued through 1935. In the process of preparing a second typescript of *Stanzas* in December 1932 and early 1933, Toklas noticed its recurrent use of the word "may," as both verb and noun, and insisted that Stein make substitutions. The revisions that resulted, which most frequently turned "may" to "can," took dramatic form: changes made by hand black out instances of "may" entirely, indenting and sometimes even tearing through the typescript paper; silent changes typed into lines remove all evidence of both the original "may"s and the work of revision; in one of the last pages of the second typescript, a typed line goes so far as to format the manuscript's "may be" as a name, "May B." (later altered by hand to "can be")—an especially convincing piece of evidence for Dydo's account of the poem's revision.

This story that so dramatizes the repercussions of word choice struck us as a strong argument for accurate texts of Stein's works and, in the particular case of *Stanzas,* for an edition of the poem that follows the manuscript and also records its variants. Our presentation of these multiple versions of *Stanzas* aligns our editorial approach to the poem with a movement in textual scholarship over the past forty years away from the ideal of a single, "correct" text and towards the variety of works in their multiple, distinct forms. This principle guides Donald Reiman's call for "versioning," an alternative to "editing" that reproduces variant texts in their entireties. Where earlier, mid-century editors, following the principles influentially articulated by W. W. Greg and Fredson Bowers, sought an authoritative text (usually defined as the final stage of a work as prepared by the author), newer approaches to textual editing have been skeptical of the concept of an authoritative text, let alone an editor's ability to distinguish such a text among multiple versions. Beginning in the 1970s, alternate approaches have paid greater attention to processes of composition and conditions of production. Editions prepared according to these principles reflect greater interest in the interpersonal and, after Jerome McGann, cultural and institutional factors that shape texts; such editions account for (as Valerie Eliot's 1971 facsimile edition of *The Waste Land* does) further hands in composition or make visible (as Robin Schulze's 2002 *Becoming Marianne Moore* does) a text's evolution across its multiple appearances in print.

Our edition presents *Stanzas* as it changed through stages of revision and early publication; to do so, it prints a single version of the poem in full, using notes to record, in complete lines, variants in the poem's other versions. Providing a continuous reading of the poem required choosing one of its versions as the basis for the text presented here. We maintain that the manuscript has some authority as the single text Stein herself prepared; in Peter Shillingsburg's distinction, we cannot determine from any text her "intention to mean," but the manuscript best captures her "intention to do—to record a specific sequence of words and punctuation."[2] Typescript 1, while ostensibly a clean version of the manuscript, introduced numerous changes that may be accidents of Toklas's transcription and not Stein's poetic choices. Our reasons for choosing the manuscript as our copy text come also from our commitment to allowing the comparison of variants. Both typescript 1 and typescript 2 seem to have been transcribed from the manuscript; both are more consistent with the manuscript than with each other. The variants entered the typescripts in relation to the manuscript, and choosing the manuscript as the copy text lets us preserve that relation. That is, by privileging the manuscript we follow elements of the Greg/ Bowers approach, but we do so to present in the clearest manner the textual history that has been the focus of more recent editors. Stein scholarship has benefited from this turn in textual study, chiefly through Dydo's account of Stein's composition practices; this edition allows readers to follow line by line the revisions of a poem especially remarkable in its material record.

As we spent more hours with Stein and Toklas in that basement room, the process of preparing this edition came to seem appropriate to Stein's poetics; the convergence between the story of the poem, as we encountered it, and the poem itself emerged as another reason for the project. Our work focused our attention on the poem's most consistent features: the movement between pattern and instance and a generic vocabulary that demands and refuses interpretation. Reading aloud each version of the poem, punctuation marks and all, judging marks difficult to decipher, noting revisions and tracing variants, we had an experience of *Stanzas* unique to our role as editors. But the features of the poem we emphasize are available—even unavoidable—to other readers as well, whether following a single version of the poem from Part I through Part V or working across versions through the notes included here in Appendix D. Repetition and generality define *Stan-*

zas in both theme and style and make it one of Stein's most thorough acts of poetic innovation.

These two reasons, biographical and poetic, for the edition inform each other. Though prompted by events beyond the poem, the revisions seem to have grown out of the concerns it makes central: not just the word "may" but the principle of choice that provides Stein's main subject and guides her poetics. She confronts her reader again and again with the multiplicity of options, for a romantic partner (often through play among the numbers one, two, and three, and the repeated word "mine") at the level of theme, for a pronoun's noun (through the insistent "it"s, "we"s, "they"s, "one"s) at the level of style—and Stein's pronouns are so often personal in this poem that this pattern of language continues her theme. The poem, as a result, refuses powerfully the ideal of a singular, certain choice, either of a companion or of a meaning.

A principle of accuracy operates in the poem, though, not through narrowness of reference but through the careful choice and placement of even generic words. Preparing this edition had us following Stein's advice to read—or, better yet, copy—a text "word by word." In *The Geographical History of America* (1936), she vouches that if "you use your glasses as a magnifying glass and so read word by word reading word by word makes the writing that is not anything be something . . . one at a time, oh one at a time is something oh yes definitely something."[3] Reading, as Stein presents it, is a creative activity; through deliberate focus on literary particulars, it transforms "not anything" to "something." The "something" that reading creates is not meaning in a conventional sense but the very experience of a work in its smallest units; the singular focus on one word as the reader takes it in, "one at a time," itself forms the "something," the product of deliberate readerly attention. One reader who benefited from encountering Stein's writing in this way, according to Stein, was Ernest Hemingway. Stein's references to Hemingway's copying of *The Making of Americans* (1925) show her concern with carefulness, her commitment to the scale of the individual word even in her longer works. In *The Autobiography of Alice B. Toklas* (1933), Toklas explains that Hemingway both copied and corrected works of Stein's, and she describes his editorial duties through reference to domestic work: "Correcting proofs is . . . like dusting, you learn the values of the thing as no reading suffices to teach it to you. In correcting these proofs Hemingway learned a great deal and he admired all that he learned."[4]

Among those things that Hemingway did *not* admire, this picture of himself as housekeeper-apprentice must have had a place. Though he praises, in *A Moveable Feast* (1964), Stein's talent for meaningful repetition, he singles out for criticism her refusal to revise: "She disliked the drudgery of revision and the obligation to make her writing intelligible."[5] Hemingway's account of Stein's bad textual housekeeping has seemed to be the one to triumph: indeed, she herself advanced it, in claiming not to revise. But the manuscript and typescripts of *Stanzas* demonstrate that, at least in this poem, one she valued especially, Stein did return to her writing and make rounds of changes.

Our own reading of *Stanzas* word by word, as editors, meant reading with a responsibility for every detail in Stein's papers—and it meant reading actively, exercising judgment to determine what Stein's messiest lines said and which marks, especially in the manuscript, constituted revisions. Did our reading, as Stein claims that Hemingway's did, "like dusting" teach us "the values of the thing as no reading suffices to teach it"? Certainly it heightened our attention to aspects of the text that, we argue, make it distinct. We had the luxury and the necessity of intensity, of reading and rereading the poem over stretches of days within a compressed period of weeks. Read in this way, the poem quickly became familiar. Initially, proper names and words like "Spanish," "peas beans and raspberries strawberries," or "Picabia" felt like a relief, a specificity that as Joan Retallack notes in her introduction anchors other of Stein's difficult works. But as we continued, those moments came to feel like exceptions (delightful ones) to a different kind of familiarity the poem offers, not of the recognizable world but of the poem's internal vocabulary and rhythms—a feature that seemed appropriate enough to our setting in a basement room that also excluded most of the recognizable world. Repeated words, phrases, and full lines suggest variants even within the manuscript's first state. Those rhythms of Stein's repetitions—to Hemingway's judgment the "valid and valuable" discovery of her work[6]—make revision an element of poetic style.

"A whole thing," Stein insists in *The Geographical History*, "is not interesting because as a whole well as a whole there has to be remembering and forgetting."[7] Working together as a pair—one person reading aloud one of the typescripts or published texts of the poem as the other checked it silently against our transcription of the manuscript, noting all variants—we made the various texts simultaneous. The act of reading joined with the memory of reading that the annotated text preserves. Such a method, we believe, supports our view of the poem as necessarily comprised of its multiple versions, the manuscript in its first state as well as the typescripts and revisions.

The active work of reading *Stanzas,* as Retallack describes it, shares much with the work of editing it. Though the poem begins in the simple past, its true tense is the present; the short lines and absence of referential content keep readers in the immediate present of the line before them, reading, as we did, word by word. Over the course of the poem, those instances repeat often enough to provide a sense of familiarity. Each instance, though, still requires readers' attention to its particulars, much as each version of the poem required ours. Retallack explains that each reader of *Stanzas* must develop a poesis, a way of reading, that involves not only or primarily making meaning but also finding patterns. That work calls on the capacity to detect, a capacity we relied on to learn Stein's handwriting and decipher her less legible words. Our editorial method compelled us to read *Stanzas* over long, unbroken stretches, a reading practice that came to seem especially suited to the poem. Through sustained, continuous reading, the poem reveals its patterns—that is, it facilitates the reader's work. The five parts increase in length as the poem proceeds, providing more and more poetic context for any given line; later stanzas echo the vocabulary and syntax of previous ones. The stanzas form patterns together rather than dividing the poem into pieces to excerpt (excerpted though sections often are). Stein herself excerpted sections for publications (noted here in Appendix A), and the very different effect those pieces have shows the advantages of reading the complete sequence cumulatively.

To help guide this work of reading, we include three accounts: Donald Sutherland's introduction to the 1956 edition, John Ashbery's 1957 review in *Poetry* magazine, and Retallack's new introduction, written for this edition. The two early pieces presented *Stanzas* to readers at its first publication, and Sutherland and Ashbery, both at the beginning of their careers, saw importance to their own critical and creative projects in what was then an unknown work: Sutherland at the outset of his task wrote to Toklas, "Stanzas in Meditation is going to have a very articulate preface," and after completing a draft, "My language is as ravaged as my nerves"[8]; Ashbery, in characterizing Stein's style as "a general, all-purpose model which each reader can adapt to fit his own set of particulars," formulated language that he later used to describe his own.[9] Retallack's piece offers the insights of one of Stein's most astute contemporary readers and draws on both the poem's textual history (unavailable to Sutherland and Ashbery) and its over fifty years of reception. Whether aiming to establish the poem's reputation or to adjust it, all three acknowledge that *Stanzas* asks to be read differently from other poems, and they (Sutherland and Retallack, especially) spend time developing and presenting ways to approach it. Through that focus on the work of reading, their distinct understandings of the poem come into view: for Sutherland, the internal dynamics of poetry that makes thought its primary element; for Ashbery, the mimesis of experience in the poem's movement in and out of sense; for Retallack, the interplay of poetic effects and the histories (literary and personal) that inform them.

While the unmarked reading text that follows these accounts presents the poem whole, the notes at the back of the volume show the variants, with some explanation of how they entered, to individual lines. We have put together this edition, then, in a way that we hope sustains two kinds of reading: reading the poem as a continuous progression of 164 stanzas and reading the poem as the sum of its versions and the story of its textual history. Either way one proceeds, the possibility of another way matters in this poem, for its essential pair of themes—themes whose resonance is both biographical and textual—is the work of choosing and the persistence of other options.

Notes

1. Ashbery, *Selected Prose*, 11–12.
2. Shillingsburg, 37, 39.
3. Stein, *Writings, 1932–1946*, 429.
4. Stein, *Writings, 1903–1932*, 873.
5. Hemingway, *A Moveable Feast*, 17.
6. Hemingway, *A Moveable Feast*, 17.
7. Stein, *Writings 1932–1946*, 429.
8. Sutherland to Toklas, January 5, 1952; Sutherland to Toklas, December 31, 1954, Gertrude Stein and Alice B. Toklas Papers, 137.3209.
9. Ashbery, *Selected Prose*, 12. Fifteen years after the appearance of his review, Ashbery told an interviewer, of his own poetry: "What I am trying to get at is a general, all-purpose experience—like those stretch socks that fit all sizes. . . . Something in which anybody can see reflected his own private experiences" ("The Experience of Experience," 251).

Works Cited

Ashbery, John. "The Experience of Experience: A Conversation with John Ashbery," by A. Poulin, Jr., 1972, *Michigan Quarterly* 20, no. 3 (Summer 1981): 242–55.

———. *Selected Prose.* Ed. Eugene Richie. Ann Arbor: University of Michigan Press, 2004.

Dydo, Ulla. *Gertrude Stein: The Language That Rises, 1923–1934.* Evanston, IL: Northwestern University Press, 2003.

Eliot, T. S. *The Waste Land: A Facsimile and Transcript of the Original Drafts Including the Annotations of Ezra Pound.* Ed. Valerie Eliot. New York: Harcourt Brace Jovanovich, 1971.

Hemingway, Ernest. *A Moveable Feast.* New York: Scribner, 1964.

McGann, Jerome. *A Critique of Modern Textual Criticism.* Chicago: University of Chicago Press, 1983.

———. *The Textual Condition.* Princeton: Princeton University Press, 1991.

Moore, Marianne. *Becoming Marianne Moore: The Early Poems, 1907–1924.* Ed. Robin Schulze. Berkeley: University of California Press, 2002.

Reiman, Donald. "'Versioning': The Presentation of Multiple Texts." *Romantic Texts and Contexts.* Columbia: University of Missouri Press, 1987. 167–80.

Shillingsburg, Peter. *Scholarly Editing in the Computer Age: Theory and Practice.* Athens: University of Georgia Press, 1986.

Gertrude Stein and Alice B. Toklas Papers, Yale Collection of American Literature. Beinecke Rare Book and Manuscript Library.

Stein, Gertrude. *Writings, 1903–1932.* New York: Library of America, 1998.

——. *Writings, 1932–1946.* New York: Library of America, 1998.

Acknowledgments

The Beinecke Rare Book and Manuscript Library made this proj-
ect possible by providing financial and practical support at its most
crucial stages: our research in the Gertrude Stein and Alice B.
Toklas Papers and publication of this edition. Special thanks go to
the reading room staff, and to curator Nancy Kuhl, who antici-
pated all aspects of our work at the Beinecke and helped facilitate
each one. Our editor at Yale University Press, Jennifer Banks,
entrusted us with a project important to her and saw the value of an
edition of this kind; her vision of how to present the poem im-
proved every part of this edition. Her assistants, Christina Tucker
and Piyali Bhattacharya, made the many steps of bringing the
edition to publication not only efficient but also pleasant. Through
Jack Borrebach's judicious preparation, the manuscript became
more accurate, consistent, and readable. The manuscript also ben-
efited considerably from the care taken by the readers who submit-
ted reports to the Press. Ulla Dydo's work on Gertrude Stein in-
spired this edition; she and Edward Burns gave invaluable support
at the outset and responded to questions only they could decipher,
much less answer, as we proceeded. Edward Burns also gave careful
attention to the manuscript in its near-final form, and we thank
him and the MLA Committee on Scholarly Editions for their
prompt and thoughtful review. Langdon Hammer helped us be-

come better readers of Stein and also helped us step into our roles as editors. Astute guidance from Cristanne Miller sharpened our editorial practices. An ACLS New Faculty Fellows award, with support of the Andrew W. Mellon Foundation, assisted this project. A grant from the Baylor University Office of the Vice Provost for Research allowed us to return to the Beinecke to complete the final stages of our research. Diana and Peter Cooper generously hosted us for that trip. Sarah Stone was our eyes at the Beinecke when we could not be there ourselves. We knew when Joan Retallack accepted our invitation to write an introduction to this edition that *Stanzas in Meditation* would gain a fine piece of scholarship; we could not have known just how fortunate readers and scholars of the poem would be in her contribution. We are grateful to John Ashbery for his interest in the edition and his willingness to see his early review of the poem included in it. Thanks go also to the Estate of Gertrude Stein for granting permission to publish facsimiles of pages from the manuscript and second typescript of the poem, images that show the history this edition exists to present.

On Not Not Reading *Stanzas in Meditation:* Pressures and Pleasures of the Text

JOAN RETALLACK

I.

By now—on the eve of the second decade of the twenty-first century—it's not that Stein scholars disagree about the importance of *Stanzas in Meditation*; it's widely considered one of that energetically idiosyncratic poet's masterpieces. "Masterpiece" is, of course, a word Gertrude Stein liked very much. But she, who truly wanted to give pleasure to her readers—pleasure at least equal to what she experienced in the writing—could not be other than mightily disturbed by the frequent fate accompanying that honorific, particularly among modernist classics: the fate of being first among the great unread, or very little read, except by the minority of ardent devotees and, of course, earnest graduate students toiling on particularly courageous dissertations. It's an exhilarating rite of passage to wrestle with the literary monster (flip side of masterpiece?) in pursuit of something more than career-making CVs. There is the tonic challenge of confronting—embracing!—an ultimate impenetrability of overweening scale and intractable mystery. (The allure of sacred texts is similar.) Think of Pound's *Cantos,* Joyce's *Finnegans Wake,* Zukofsky's *A,* and Stein's *The Making of Americans* and *Patriarchal Poetry* as well as the text we have here, beautifully presented with corrections, unobtrusive textual notes, and variants. All these works, however revered by the valiant few, reliably bring on the furtive question, Have you actually read it, I mean, every word, all the way through? Within more or less self-confidently literate circles, in private conversation among trusted friends, the verdict on the modernist masterpiece bookshelf tends to be "more or less unreadable."

If, as Gertrude Stein claimed, America invented the twentieth century, that development was the logical consequence of its eighteenth-century invention of happiness as inalienable right. An extraordinary concept, transmuted into the pursuit of pleasure with limitless paraphernalia that has become the most abundant and problematic of U.S. exports. Stein herself was a notable export among countless artists and writers seeking the American ideal of the freer, happier life by moving to Paris, with its promise of convivial experimentation in all things cultural and erotic. It's a lovely irony that the life-long expatriate Stein (from 1903 to her death in France in 1946) became the iconic American most identified with the invention of a truly twentieth-century literature. She has been less reliably associated with the pleasure of the text. Which brings us to *Stanzas,* the most obdurately closed—so it has seemed—to even the best intentioned, most diligent readers of Stein. Since its composition in 1932—alongside the enormously popular *Autobiography of Alice B. Toklas*—*Stanzas in Meditation* has conspicuously failed to satisfactorily consummate the readerly act. Or is it the hapless reader who has failed? Either way, the obvious if uneasy question is this: Just what is one to do with yet another "unreadable" modernist "masterpiece"?

The constructive response to this entirely reasonable question is not to malign Stein's purpose or, worse yet, to renounce the pleasure principle. Rather, let's do some rethinking of approaches to this curiously imbricated text. Imbricated with, among other things, crowds of uninhabited pronouns—most notably, the omnipresent "they"s, but also unidentified "she"s, "he"s and "it"s. Only the first-person pronoun is a constant—an "I" that voices the many forms of meditation propelling the stanzas, despite endemic complexity, with an against-the-odds coherence. One way to describe this work (one among myriad possibilities) is as an enigmatically choreographed interaction of pronouns performing to a music of meditation so polyvalent it throws that very word/act into exploratory relief. Hence, to reformulate the question, What does one do with a 192-page wordscape of constantly shifting textual weather (whether), when its tones and moods can appear elusive at the very moment of discernment? Without a spirit of adventure, this could congeal into a rhetorical question, so let's not linger.

II.

. . . it is extremely difficult not to make sense extremely difficult
not to make sense extremely difficult not to make sense and
excuse.[1]

It is also extremely difficult, absent a random word generator, not to make meaning, and not to make meaning extremely difficult if you are Gertrude Stein; that is, to have nothing in or on your mind as you write. Writing is a form of thinking unless clever artifice is systematically employed to sabotage personal associative processes. As far as we know, Stein—who did like to perform methodical experiments as compositional discipline—was the opposite of a randomizer. She did not use any sort of chance operation to locate or compose the vocabularies of her texts. Needless to say, she didn't appropriate language. To the extent that Wordsworthian or Shakespearian echoes emerge in a work like *Stanzas* it is because they came to mind as she composed. The source was her astutely considered, deeply felt experience of the aesthetics and psychological nuances of daily life laced with permutative playfulness. As she might have put it, she was living the writing she was doing, and vice versa.

Among critics who have attempted to render the reader's interaction with *Stanzas in Meditation* less formidable there have been two leading approaches—biographical puzzle solving, and formalist puzzle solving—most often deployed as if they were mutually exclusive. One is dedicated to the discovery of hidden meanings locked beneath the surface of strategic vocabulary clues, and tends to overlook the play of surface word patterns as an integral part of the sense of the piece. With that kind of search warrant in hand, *Stanzas* is no doubt an intriguing puzzle of subtexts and other sorts of oblique, intentionally obfuscated, or hidden and coded material embedding a both conscious and unconscious autobiographical substrate. The danger in this kind of reading—if narrowly executed —is that an equally present surface-poetics of indeterminacy and word-play can be almost entirely overlooked in favor of "underlying" subject matter. What is lost is the significance of language constructs themselves—patterns of pronouns, for instance. The second approach has attempted to make sense of the poem by means of formalist analyses that assume a field of fluidly indeterminate meaning signifying very little in particular, while identifying the material elements of word patterns as the major source of energy and import. Critics espousing this approach have suggested that the search for determinate meaning not only will add to the reader's frustration but is fundamentally inappropriate to the nature of the "abstract" work that *Stanzas* happens to be.[2]

Here are particularly interesting examples of the two approaches. As I think you'll notice, neither one explicitly or in principle rules out attention of other sorts. Elizabeth Fifer in *Rescued Readings: A Reconstruction of Gertrude Stein's Difficult Texts* says this about *Stanzas*:

> While apparently presenting an entirely "proper" and entirely
> banal series of subjects and events, much of the energy of the text
> lies beneath the surface of its difficult style in its parodic play with
> allusions, ambiguity, partial statements, evasions, coding, and
> other techniques of erotic display. For readers who insist on the
> meaninglessness of this text, "Stanzas" must become rough going
> indeed. (109)

Ulla Dydo, in *Gertrude Stein: The Language That Rises, 1923–1934*, suggests that "the disembodied abstract language [of *Stanzas*] rose from internal energy with no external stimulus" (488). "By 1932, contexts almost vanish from Stein's work," Dydo writes, "her language virtually empties out of references" (489). And later,

> Each time I try to grasp a passage, phrase, or stanza, it changes
> shape, dissolving its boundaries and loosening the bounds of
> commentary. In this instability of shape, voice, and meaning lies
> the maddening magnificence of the stanzas. I want to read, not

read into or pin down, the poems. I read aloud, listen to the changing permutations. The more the language empties out of references and antecedents, nouns to pronouns, the more new readings open. (503)

I want to say at this point that these two approaches are not mutually exclusive in the reading strategies they imply. On a formal level there is a lot going on. There is every indication that the same is true on a referential level, and Ulla Dydo's important archival work (discussed below) affirms Stein's multiple compositional intentions and designs. Meanwhile, I doubt that Elizabeth Fifer would deny that "erotic display" in a poem begins with the display of the language itself. What seems perfectly clear to me, even among pervasive impediments to a sense of what and who is being addressed by the author, is that Stein has set a full complement of "language games" in motion.[3] It makes sense to assume that those language games include all the things both Fifer and Dydo mention—"allusions, ambiguity, partial statements, evasions, coding, and other techniques of erotic display" (Fifer) *and* the "evolving verbal landscape" that Dydo is attentive to; one, as she notes, that is given a good deal of its strangely evocative presence as literally "a voice composing words," and song, and parody, that is, "patterns we can hear and see."

The "erotic display" must be evident in the surface pleasures of the language. Meditations, reflections, ruminations on instances of eros and its discontents—couched by means of coded or oblique allusions—are part of what creates the potent atmosphere of this poetic project as well as the intercourse of text and intertext, intratext and subtexts, beginning with the very first line of Part I, Stanza I, "I caught a bird which made a ball." Metrical properties of this line are part of what makes it beguiling even as its charm turns into the jarring image of a (child's?) hand grasping, caressing, squeezing a little bird into a ball. All this and more is only enhanced by knowing that among Stein's pet names for Alice were "birdie," "love bird," "little ball," "lovely ball," "lively ball"—found in Stein's personal love notes to Toklas.[4] None of this exhausts either the gestural qualities of the line or a precise proliferation of meanings that accumulate with additional thought, knowledge, perspectives. (I'll suggest a Wordsworthian aspect below.) Lesbian coding, modernist play, references to everyday life create a poetic puzzle that is also an expressive agon of overdetermination, ironically, paradoxically, leading not only to autobiographical hints and revelations but to a high degree of indeterminacy. Which the formalist in me is happy to say is in no danger of reduction to a bio note. Similarly, all the bio notes in the world will not pave over the potentially generative (with an actively resourceful reading poesis) indeterminacy of *Stanzas in Meditation*. All of which is to say that composed indeterminacy doesn't erase the personal but accommodates it in its complexities and inherent ambiguities (sometimes manifestations of very personal authorial ambivalences).

III.

The impossibility of charting more than a few particulars Stein might have had in mind, or that might have come to mind in the simultaneous eye-brain-hand act of writing as a form of thinking she herself identifies as "meditation," signals the necessity of turning one's readerly mind toward a model of construal more useful than the eternal return of New Critical analysis. I'd like to suggest a dynamic of something like "particulate/wave" complementarity that, when registered in the reader's mind, leads to sense and meaning in the midst of pervasive textual indeterminacy.[5] One of course must ask if there are any discernible patterns of particulars among the liminally associative waves of language Stein composed into stanzas. My assumption is that stanzaic momentum is of course driven by significant particulars that are only intermittently coterminous with specific vocabulary, that is, direct autobiographical references or coding. The enormous quantity of indeterminate pronouns alone suggests that any discursive subtext here is in the form of an intentionally vague *roman sans clef.* And yet, Dydo, by critical temperament a formalist who embraces the indeterminacy of the piece, and who prefers the term "context" to "biography,"[6] has accomplished a major breakthrough in revealing a rare denotative pattern. It's worth noting that Dydo could only have done this through her precise formalist focus on surface structures of the language, in this case astute textual sleuthing among manuscripts and successive typescripts. Had she not been so dedicated to examining specific word constructions by looking closely at revisions from one typescript to another, Dydo would not have noticed a biographical drama lurking in certain vocabulary choices.

The background to that drama begins with the fact that in 1932 Stein, for no doubt overdetermined reasons, decided to once again explore the possibilities of autobiographical writing. I say "once again" because of the sudden reappearance that year (apparently just prior to her beginning work on *Stanzas*) of an unpublished autobiographical manuscript (written in 1903)—a novella she had titled "Quod Erat Demonstrandum," posthumously published as *Q.E.D.* It is a ruminative roman à clef concerning a lesbian love triangle in which Stein had been deeply involved and deeply hurt. The whole thing had not only ended painfully at the time but was to stir upheaval three decades later when the recovered manuscript reentered Stein's life and consciousness and, eventually, Toklas's. Stein admitted to Toklas that the lovers depicted in the novella were directly based on an affair she had with a young woman named May Bookstaver, the sole early love interest she had not disclosed in a reciprocal "confession" she and Toklas undertook at the start of their commitment to one another. Apart from feeling wounded by Stein's secrecy, Toklas had good reason to suspect that thoughts of May may have entered the writing of *Stanzas*. May Bookstaver was indeed linguistically embedded in the text in hundreds of instances of the modal verb "may." When Toklas—who had just recently typed all those "may"s from Stein's handwritten version—realized in hindsight what was going on, her fury led to a spate of substitutions of "can" for "may." The ensuing turmoil caused not only a systematic expulsion of May/"may" from *Stanzas*, it is largely responsible for this new edition.

Dydo's attention to the scores of "may"s inexplicably changed to "can"s revealed the biographical cleansing that Toklas had demanded. Thanks to Dydo's work—pace Toklas—the current edition is full of the original evocations of May.[7] A significant issue of textual integrity was therefore put right, but many more questions arise from knowledge of these fascinating and fraught circumstances. Chief among them: To what extent was the writing of *Stanzas* more generally given to retrospective thoughts and emotions activated by Stein's reacquaintance with her youthful introspections and longings? May Bookstaver in the guise of the novella's character Helen reappeared in Stein's emotional life and thought at a time that was significantly complicated by a subsequent personal history charged with cumulative difficulties.[8] Might "retrospection" (another form of meditation) triggered by the *Q.E.D.* time capsule have affected the project of *Stanzas* more profoundly?

Some intertextual reading is called for here. *Q.E.D.*, written in the year following the 1902 affair with May, was an attempt to understand not only the excitement, angst, guilt, and confusion brought on by her romantic and sexual feelings for May but, more generally, her fear of passion. She wondered whether it was truly love she had experienced toward May while needing to puzzle through more philosophical questions about the nature of love and moral responsibility. *Q.E.D.* is the textual scene of Stein "figuring out" these things, beginning with its long epigraph from *As You Like It* on "what 'tis to love." Adele, Stein's stand-in character, is trying to apply conscientious rational thought to a situation that the beat-by-beat narration makes evident has turned into something of a mess and a torment. Adele, "with a mind attuned to experiment" (62), is challenged by May cum Helen: "Haven't you ever stopped thinking long enough to feel?" Adele replies that she is given to "thinking [as] a pretty continuous process . . . sometimes it's more active than at others but it's always pretty much there" (66). Adele explicitly identifies her thought processes as "meditation," which manifests in the novella as the voice of Adele "thinking aloud" to herself—a voice (and psychological purview) that certainly evolves over Stein's writing life but some of which is nonetheless familiar in her subsequent work, including *Stanzas in Meditation*. Rereading it alongside *Stanzas*, I looked at passages in *Q.E.D.* that are explicitly labeled acts of meditation. Here's a sample:

> Her meditations again took form. "As for me is it another little
> indulgence of my superficial emotions or is there any possibility of
> my really learning to realise stronger feelings. If it's the first I

will call a halt promptly and at once. If it's the second I won't back
out, no not for any amount of moral sense," and she smiled to
herself. "Certainly it is very difficult to tell. The probabilities are
that this is only another one of the many and so I suppose I had
better quit and leave it. It's the last day together and so to be
honorable I must quit at once." She then dismissed it all and for
some time longer found it very pleasant there playing with the
brightness. (64)

After a long pause she began again meditatively, "I wonder if
either of us has the slightest idea what is going on in the other's
head." (65)

There is a climactic moment in this process giving onto a different
form of meditation:

> ... and then she [Adele] stopped thinking. She kept quiet some
> time longer watching the pleasant night. ... "Why" she said in a
> tone of intense interest, "it's like a bit of mathematics. Suddenly it
> does itself and you begin to see. ... I never even thought I saw
> before and I really do think I begin to see. Yes it's very strange but
> surely I do begin to see."
>
> All during the summer Adele did not lose the sense of having
> seen, but on the other hand her insight did not deepen. She
> meditated abundantly on this problem and it always ended with a
> childlike pride in the refrain "I did see a little, I certainly did catch
> a glimpse." (66–67)

As the novella progresses, it's clear that Adele's continuous medi-
tation—thinking and rethinking—becomes increasingly exasperat-
ing to Helen, exhausting to both young women.

In a spirit of intertextual experimentation, let's fast forward to

1932 and see what happens if one reads passages from *Stanzas,* Part I, Stanza XV, alongside these quotations from *Q.E.D.* The bolded "may"s below are restored from the "can"s that Alice insisted upon with Gertrude's agreement. To state the obvious, because typescript 2, the one Toklas "amended," shows that not all "may"s were changed to "can"s, those that were changed are likely to be signposts for scenes of reference (surely involving surrounding text) that had to do with May. If this is the case, it's odd that Toklas didn't demand a greater purge via more thoroughgoing revisions to *Stanzas.* Might Stein have convinced her that the "may"s were simply an ornamental homage? I don't know, but finding mere ornamentation unlikely, I take the altered "may"s to be sites of confession where surrounding text must, in at least some cases, involve considerable intrusion from things past. In reading the *Stanzas* excerpts below, keep in mind that in the passages quoted from *Q.E.D.,* Adele's questions are followed by a declaration of finally "seeing."

> Should they **may** be they might if they delight
> In why they must see it be there not only necessarily
> But which they might in which they might
> For which they might delight if they look there
> And they see there that they look there
> To see it be there which it is if it is
> Which may be where where it is
> If they do not occasion it to be different
> From what it is.
> In one direction there is the sun and the moon
> In the other direction there are cumulus clouds and the sky
> In the other direction there is why
> They look at what they see

They look very long while they talk along
And they **may** be said to see that at which they look
Whenever there is no chance of its not being warmer
Than if they wish which they were.
They see that they have what is there **may** there
Be there also what is to be there if they **may** care
They care for it of course they care for it. (I.XV.1–20)

Six lines down, "reflecting" is used similarly to "meditating" in
Q.E.D. (one of several ways Stein thinks of acts of meditation
throughout *Stanzas*) with the otherwise obvious difference that
personae inhabiting the "they" or "they"s reflected upon are never
identified.

Once again I think I am reflecting
And they **may** be patient in not why now
And more than if which they are reflecting
That if they with which they will be near now
Or not at all in the same better
Not for which they will be all called
By which they will **may** be as much as if wishing
But which each one has seen each one
Not at all now
Nor if they like as if with them well or ordinarily
Should they be more enjoined of which they like
It is very well to have seen what they have seen
But which they will not only be alike.
They are very evenly tired with more of this (I.XV.26–39)

The passage ends, or I should say pauses before the preposition
"For"—call to continue—with an echoing exhaustion. And yet the

stanza goes on for another 44 lines of continuous thinking, reflecting, meditating, rumination . . .

What may come of this intertextual noticing? There is nothing really that I want to assert other than that the subject matter of *Q.E.D.* significantly appears to be one of many subtexts infusing this section of *Stanzas* with its strange constellations of psychological energies and concerns. The meditative atmosphere of *Stanzas,* where meditation is at times an intensely dedicated ratiocination edged with emotion, recalls similar "meditative" passages in *Q.E.D.* The hypothetical "may" in *Stanzas*—surrounded by the many occurrences of "if"—leads me to read this as an ongoing thought experiment analogous to those in which May (Bookstaver), the hypothetical incarnate, is urgently reconceived as Helen. So the intertextual experiment, for this reader, yields analogies of thought processes and atmosphere, that is, complex textual ecologies that seem to share some confluence of sources. This kind of reading leaves the many forms of contingency—determinate and indeterminate—intact.

With this new edition, *Stanzas* goes on undeterred by Toklas's ire much as Stein did in 1932 notwithstanding the reconstructive sprinkling of "can"s. She had, in the writing of *Stanzas,* meditated through things troubling her, reflected on glimpses of beauty, delighted in her wisdom and humor; and even, perhaps, cherished glimpses of glimpses past. At the end of this poetic project—with book contract in hand—Stein was sufficiently flushed of confusions and doubts to recover her humorous zest and ventriloquize Alice B. Toklas into "her own" autobiography as the beloved and sagacious chronicler of Gertrude's genius. The pronouns remain notably unreliable.

IV.

Meanwhile, autobiographical writing *and* subtle coding weren't the only things on Stein's mind as she embarked on *Stanzas*. In a letter the year before, she had written of her "passion" in her youth "for the long dull poems of Wordsworth and Crabbe"—"I want to do a long dull poem too and *a bare one* . . ."[9] After beginning *Stanzas*, she wrote the following to a friend:

> I am working a lot I am trying to write a long dull poem like the
> long ones of Wordsworth and it is very interesting to do I was
> always fond of these long dull poems[10]

The first reference to her interest in Wordsworth's "long dull" poems as models for a project of her own seems to have come before the reappearance of *Q.E.D.* If we put Stein's reconsideration of Wordsworth together with her renewed interest in autobiography, the work that comes to mind is Wordsworth's long (not necessarily so dull) poem *The Prelude*, though she might have been thinking of any of his semi-autobiographical poems.[11] There are a number of outright Wordsworthian lines in *Stanzas*—all the more remarkable for their sparsely scattered presence: "All out of cloud. Come hither. Neither / Aimless and with a pointedly rested displeasure" (I.VI.53–54); "Out from the whole wide wor/l/d I chose thee" (I.VIII.41).[12] While *The Prelude* or other "long dull poems" may have been one initiating inspiration, there is, more significantly, an obvious enterprise in *Stanzas* that is about *not* being Wordsworthian. According to the editors of this volume, "word" in that last quote began as "world"; the change—with stroke of pen—accomplishes an anti-romantic lettristic coup without erasing the lyrical mode/mood of the line. (Since the line in its first iteration, or either for that matter, may well refer to her choosing Toklas as her wife, this is another probable specimen of delightfully overdetermined text.) Ambiguity of intention and tone can be glimpsed in many places throughout *Stanzas,* including the line "I have thought that the bird makes the same noise differently" (I.X.22) where "differently"—no doubt, among other things—crafts the crucial tonal difference of humor.

The opening lines of the first poem in *Stanzas* can be reread (sliding new senses palimpsestically over others) as evocative of the opening section of *The Prelude* with its early childhood scenes and, at greater length, in "Book First, Introduction—Childhood and School-time," where one finds this:

> Free as a bird to settle where I will.
> What dwelling shall receive me? in what vale
> Shall be my harbour? underneath what grove
> Shall I take up my home? and what clear stream
> Shall with its murmur lull me into rest?
> The earth is all before me. With a heart
> Joyous, nor scared at its own liberty,
> I look about; and should the chosen guide
> Be nothing better than a wandering cloud,
> I cannot miss my way. (9–18)

Wordsworth goes on to recount scenes of boys catching birds in the woods, as well as of his early education. Stein's opening could be reread as addressing similar material of youth, education, and choosing as a form of liberty.

> I caught a bird which made a ball
> And they thought better of it.

But it is all of which they taught
That they were in a hurry yet
In a kind of a way they meant it best
That they should change in and on account
But they must not stare when they manage
Whatever they are occasionally liable to do
It is often easy to pursue them once in a while
And in a way there is no repose
They like it as well as they ever did
But it is very often just by the time
That they are able to separate
In which case in effect they could
Not only be very often present perfectly
In each way whichever they chose. (I.I.1–16)

Immediately following line 5, the unstated reference of the pro-
noun "they" seems to change entirely. Most importantly, from the
inception of Stein's poem, "the difference is spreading."[13] Whether
the difference can be usefully marked in relation to Wordsworth's
long poems, Stein's earlier writing, or in relation to almost all
previous poetics, it is passages like these and those below that make
one realize all over again how enormously grateful one is that there
was a Gertrude Stein who did the living and the composing she
was doing when she did. For example, this:

Think birds and ways and frogs and grass and now
That they call meadows more
I have seen what they knew. (I.XI.44–46)

and this, reread through another lens. May/may is present as one
of many moods:

> In one direction there is the sun and the moon
> In the other direction there are cumulus clouds and the sky
> In the other direction there is why
> They look at what they see
> They look very long while they talk along
> And they may be said to see that at which they look (I.XV.10–15)

"The long dull" autobiographical poem was certainly one template for *Stanzas,* as was the poetics of wor/l/d (life and letters) exploration. In the poem itself, Stein twice refers to the *Stanzas* as one of two autobiographical projects. There may as well be a doubling of that double. She could be referring either to the manuscript of *Q.E.D.* or to the other autobiography already on her mind, *The Autobiography of Alice B. Toklas.* In Part IV, Stanza XIII ends with this line:

> This is an autobiography in two instances (IV.XIII.9)

The next stanza has this:

> This is her autobiography one of two
> But which it is no one which it is can know
> Although there is no need
> To waste seed because it will not do (IV.XIV.17–20)

Further down in this stanza Stein could well be referring to the book deal she has been negotiating with her American agent William Bradley: "They mean I like it if she will do it . . . And prepare to share wealth and honors . . . This is why they like me if they think they do" (IV.XIV.23, 36, 58). I've taken these lines from a long series of what seem to be ruminations on the immense publication break that has just come her way. After so many years of disappointment, a major

New York publisher, Harcourt Brace, is on the verge of giving her a lucrative contract for her autobiography, predicting that it will be a great literary and financial success. The next stanza (XV) continues in this vein with Stein wavering between self-confidence and doubt.

Ulla Dydo writes that while reading the notebooks that contain the original manuscript of *Stanzas,* she found that on the "inside cover of the fifth manuscript [notebook], for Part IV, Stein entered, barely legibly, with revisions, a descriptive title." The title was "Stanzas of my ordinary reflections. Stanzas of Poetry." Later, Stein crossed out "of my ordinary" and replaced the words with "of commonplace."[14] Why?—one might ask—on the threshold of the kind of speculation that is a reader's conversation with history. "Commonplace" has a more literary ring to it; moreover, the contents of the "commonplace book" of that time—a collection of noteworthy quotations from other writers—provides substantial personal distance from the material in the work. One begins to see *Stanzas* as a kind of negative (in the photographic sense) of what *The Autobiography of Alice B. Toklas* will become. Or, perhaps, that moving from "ordinary reflections" to "commonplace" presages the long "quotations" of the narrator persona Alice B. Toklas. Something odd was definitely occurring. The commonplace as genre doesn't provide an accurate characterization of *Stanzas in Meditation.* Somewhere in the proliferation of heavily shaded overlaps— the Venn circles that can chart overdetermination—it becomes clear that though the autobiographical poem may well have been the starting point of *Stanzas,* this poetry is both eluding and exceeding that generic descriptor. In so many ways, it may have turned out to be something much more interesting—a somewhat dangerously charged, ex post facto reflection on *Q.E.D.* aspiring toward other, more liberating, forms of meditation.

V.

Meditation can be a sustained practice of considering; it is also a spiritual practice which requires emptying out one's sense of identity and distinct objects of concern. It is a giving over to what is not self possession. *Stanzas* contains hints of this use of meditative practice. The period in which Stein was writing *Stanzas* seems to have been one of dual crisis (troubled mind and turning point); the writing project functioned as location of daily reflection: the act of writing of the reflective mind-in-action as thought—the kind of writing that provides a transitional zone allowing one to do the work of sorting through difficult circumstances. Perhaps, difficult memories as well. The goal is to achieve stillness of mind, receptiveness, presentness in the moment. Here is an example where the language has moved toward meditation as spiritual exercise:

> Curiously.
> This one which they think I think alone
> Two follow
> I think when they think
> Two think I think I think they will be too
> Two and one make two for you
> And so they need a share of happiness
> How are ours about to be one two or not three.
> This that I think is this.
> It is natural to think in numerals
> If you do not mean to think
> Or think or leave or bless or guess
> Not either no or yes once.
> This is how hours stand still (IV.XI.28–41)

VI. CAN THE PRESSURE BE THE PLEASURE?
A VAST HORIZON OF THEYS

Of course then there are pronouns. . . . They represent some one
but they are not its or his name.[15]

Poetry is I say essentially a vocabulary just as prose is essentially
not.[16]

Matters of vocabulary, such as the quantitatively remarkable
presence of unattributed personal and impersonal pronouns in
Stanzas in Meditation, suggest coordinates for the reader's geome-
try of attention. Moving through Stein's wordscape, always along
the rim of occurrence, in serial patterns of denial and disclosure,
there is never enough disclosure to conclude any given trajectory
of occurrence. Not until the very last lines of the last stanza of
the poem, and even then conclusion is not a revelation, or vice
versa. The revelation is elsewhere, in the experience of reading as
poesis (that is, making sense of words composed into forms, sense,
meaning—the very heart of poetry as practice). Readerly poesis in
the case of *Stanzas,* like most of Stein's poetic texts, is an act one
can perform many times over, never exhausting the possibility of
noticing new things. Noticing (exquisite forms of attention) is the
vehicle of a reading poesis.

Could it be, then, that what has been viewed as a kind of depri-
vation—all that abstracted vocabulary—when one attends to, say,
the rippling patterns of "they"s that become a graphic and sonic
medium through which one navigates the wor/l/d of the poem,
is actually what constitutes the pleasure, that is, the sensation-
inducing pressure of the text? I'm not talking about masochism,
but of the pleasures of finding one's knowledge and intuitions

about language fully necessary and fully charged by tantalizing ratios of presence and absence. In the course of exercising these capacities one is making meaning entirely specific to the word-site of the poem. What makes one an avid reader of Gertrude Stein is— in addition to the kinds of things I've quoted—the stimulating effect of puzzling, of figuring one's way through a text that absolutely requires developing a reading poesis specific to the composition and vocabularies that draw one along the rim of occurrence of the poem. As Leslie Scalapino has asserted, in an essay entitled "Writing on Rim," writing on the rim of occurrence is a form of *living* on the rim of occurrence. That is the form of life Stein chose and that we can choose as readers. Scalapino puts it in a way that is evocative of Stein's "This is how hours stand still":

> This eliminates the separation between writing and realistic rim.
>
> Also to push "it" to where even weariness causes it (no difference between weariness and the horizon and writing) to collapse on itself where it's still, visibly flapping.
>
> I wanted to get the writing to the point of being that still.[17]

But what about the pronouns? The "it" that Dydo discusses as so ubiquitous in *Stanzas*,[18] along with the "he," the "she," and—to my mind, most interestingly and disturbingly—the "they," together form other horizons, other perspectival perforations and limiting conditions in the experience of reading this work. Because my essay has had the purpose of demonstrating that a supposedly unreadable "masterpiece" can indeed be read, and many times over, and pleasurably, I'll end with a descriptive analysis of one possible reading of *Stanzas* as poesis in conversation with Stein's language, remembering that poesis, from the Greek, is to literally make something out of the material at hand, which is—as Stein said of all poetry—vocabulary.

I think it can be safely said that nothing has disturbed readers of *Stanzas* more than its putative "abstraction," its "emptiness." These properties have been attributed to what Dydo has called "neutral words—'I,' 'she,' 'they'; 'be there,' 'be here.'" Yet, as Dydo delightfully notes, Stein can compose material enactments from just such words, as she "composes the rain" in these lines:[19]

> That rain is there and it is here
> That it is here that they are there
> They have been here to leave it now (II.I.7–9)

Those monosyllabic neutral words turn into limpid phonemes, clearly sounding as textual rain drops in lieu of adjectives or adverbs—an enactment of precipitation, not a description of it.

Stein was never given to adjectival mimesis. She achieved sensual specificity with her vocabularies rather than with images. But the deprivation so many readers have felt in their encounters with *Stanzas* has not only to do with the absence of descriptors, but with a dearth of the kinds of evocative and colorful words one finds in so many of Stein's otherwise difficult works. In *Stanzas* the most disturbing aspect is the predominance of unattributed pronouns. Of those, the personal pronouns minus referents are particularly bothersome. This poem has in it a vast horizon of Theys that describes both the limit of one's depth of field as reader and the potential of gazing beyond. That "beyond" won't, however, be a list of identities. "They," already plural, is multiplied to such an extent that it becomes in its steadfast opacity a force that powerfully affects the mood of the poem. The I seems not infrequently oppressed by the presence of all those inscrutable (even hostile?) Theys.

I've had many questions about the Theys perched on line after line. What collective noun best suits them? Something like a murder of crows? A pride of lions? A school, a drift, a host . . . ? Or, is their presence more like that of a Greek chorus sporting megaphone masks in refusal of identity, perversely projecting their silence? The Theys at times behave linguistically like feared parental figures, fathers in particular. The patriarchal They abounds in "Patriarchal Poetry" of course, and in *History or Messages from History,* where one finds, "They were outstanding in coining words without women."[20] Other possibilities: the They of angry siblings, estranged or judgmental family members, stern teachers, scornful peers, a public that ignores one's work—but most of all the unknown in others. The alterity of the They or Them is often theorized as rendered other by the subject in the foreground. Here the I—and any of the rest of the first-person pronouns—can be instantly rendered other by the They. A good deal of the meditative work in *Stanzas* seems to be about situating the reflective subjectivity of an I between the I of self-love, self-confidence, certainty . . . and the I of self-doubt; both must negotiate an ominously indeterminate zone of "I and They." The "I-They" (with attendant "Theirs") can be at least as fraught as the "I-Thou."

Stein ended *How To Write,* her collection of pieces on grammar and vocabulary, with a section called "Forensics." This brings to mind the crime lab, the court—places where identity and culpability may be determined. *How To Write* was written from roughly 1927 to 1931. It was published in 1931, the year before Stein wrote *Stanzas.* Here are the final phrases of the concluding paragraph:

In theirs. In unison. An advantage to forsake. Which they will. As they may glean. More facts. For which. By their ordinary values. They will be practically. As far apart. Forensics may be athirst for gold. It may with them battle and die. It can as much bequeath and condole. For them. To merit. That they. Should console. Them.[21]

In all three sections of *Tender Buttons* (the poem written in 1913 in exaltation of loving domesticity with a new wife) there are only six, perhaps seven, unattributed Theys. In *Stanzas in Meditation,* there are forty-seven (not counting "their"s and "them"s) in the first two stanzas of Part I alone. When the crowd of Theys suddenly clears, the I achieves meditative clarity, is confident again:

I wish now to wish now that it is now
That I will tell very well
What I think not now but now
Oh yes oh yes now.
What do I think now
I think very well of what now
What is it now it is this now
How do you do how do you do
And now how do you do now.
This which I think now is this. (V.VIII.1–10)

Stanzas ends with what sounds a bit like self-administered bucking up, but given what we know came next, the success of *The Autobiography of Alice B. Toklas* and all that followed, it seems well placed:

I will be well welcome when I come.
Because I am coming.
Certainly I come having come.
These stanzas are done. (V.LXXXIII.11–14)

Notes

1. Stein, "Finally George A Vocabulary of Thinking," in *How To Write,* 293.

2. "Abstract" is the adjectival winner of the formalist characterization contest with respect to *Stanzas in Meditation.* To be abstract is to exist as thought or idea without a physical or concrete presence, hardly possible for a poem made of words.

3. I'm referring here to Wittgenstein's "language games" as forms of life conducted through words entirely embedded in everyday life.

4. See Turner, *Baby Precious Always Shines.*

5. I'm not talking about quantum physics, but something more like the pattern-bounded indeterminacy of complexity theory. Hence "particulate" rather than "particle."

6. See Dydo, *Gertrude Stein: The Language That Rises,* 5–6. "Context" rather than "biography" does, however, leave the coast clear for a denial of personally expressive aspects of the work.

7. For a full account of this textual drama—as well as much more about *Stanzas in Meditation* from Dydo's perspective, see her *Gertrude Stein: The Language That Rises.*

8. She and Alice had been having troubles; her persistent rejections by publishers and her tepid reception by readers were growing more and more intolerable.

9. Stein to Lindley Hubbell, August 25, 1931, quoted in Dydo, *Gertrude Stein: The Language That Rises,* 506.

10. Stein to Louis Bromfield, summer 1932, quoted in Dydo, *Gertrude Stein: The Language That Rises,* 507. According to Dydo, "These are Stein's only comments on the work in progress." There are of course comments in *Stanzas* itself calling the work autobiographical.

11. See also Dydo's discussion of Shakespeare's *As You Like It* as determining influence on Stein's composition of *Stanzas.* Dydo, *Gertrude Stein: The Language That Rises,* 508ff.

12. Changed from "word" in manuscript to "world" in typescript. See textual notes by editors of this volume.

13. Last line of "A Carafe, That Is A Blind Glass" in *Tender Buttons,* in Stein, *Gertrude Stein: Selections,* 126.

14. Dydo, *Gertrude Stein: The Language That Rises,* 489.

15. Stein, "Poetry and Grammar," in *Lectures in America,* 213.

16. Stein, "Poetry and Grammar," 231.

17. Scalapino, *Objects in the Terrifying Tense / Longing from Taking Place,* 74.
18. Dydo, *Gertrude Stein: The Language That Rises,* 510ff.
19. Dydo, *Gertrude Stein: The Language That Rises,* 515.
20. Stein, *Gertrude Stein: Selections,* 264.
21. Stein, *How To Write,* 395.

Works Cited

Dydo, Ulla E. *Gertrude Stein: The Language That Rises, 1923–1934.* Evanston, IL: Northwestern University Press, 2003.

Fifer, Elizabeth. *Rescued Readings: A Reconstruction of Gertrude Stein's Difficult Texts.* Detroit: Wayne State University Press, 1992.

Scalapino, Leslie. *Objects in the Terrifying Tense / Longing from Taking Place.* New York: Roof Books, 1993.

Stein, Gertrude. *Fernhurst, Q.E.D., and Other Early Writings.* New York: Liveright, 1971.

——. *Gertrude Stein: Selections.* Ed. and Intro., Joan Retallack. Berkeley: University of California Press, 2008.

——. *How To Write.* Ed. Patricia Meyerowitz. New York: Dover, 1975.

——. *Lectures in America.* New York: Random House, 1935.

Turner, Kay, ed. *Baby Precious Always Shines: Selected Love Notes Between Gertrude Stein and Alice B. Toklas.* New York: St. Martin's Press, 1999.

Wordsworth, William. *The Prelude 1799, 1805, 1850.* Ed. Jonathan Wordsworth, M. H. Abrams, and Stephen Gill. New York: Norton, 1979.

The Turning Point:

Preface to the 1956 *Stanzas in Meditation*

DONALD SUTHERLAND

The works in the present volume were written between 1929 and 1933, one of the most dramatic periods in Gertrude Stein's long life with literary form.[1] The period was in a way the climax of her heroic experimentation with the essentials of writing; it tired her, and after it came her popular, broader and easier, more charming and personal works, but while the period lasted she carried writing as high and as far in her direction as she could, to a point that is still, over twenty years later, a crucial one for writing in general. Her summit of innovation, this last reach of her dialectic, is not easy of approach, the atmosphere is rare, but even the approaches

---

1. The 1956 Yale edition, *Stanzas in Meditation and Other Poems [1929–1933]*, collected a complete text of *Stanzas* with the long poem "Winning His Way: A Narrative Poem of Poetry" and twelve short poems. Three pages of Sutherland's preface omitted here treat those other poems.

are exhilarating and it is not difficult at least to map out the region and the way she came, much of it being our own ground at present.

In the preceding period, from 1911 to 1928, she had written about things and people in space—on the analogy of painting or the theatre. She had done so naturally, as that period was great in painting and lively in the theatre, and nearly everybody's writing was controlled by imagery. The spatial existence of anything made it real enough to write about and indeed to sustain the existence of the writing, but then something happened—even before the crash of 1929 and the small and large world events after it—something happened that took the sufficiency out of spatial existence. Painting went literary, even the movies began to talk, and writing abandoned imagery gradually for other kinds of reality, especially discourse. Why this all happened I don't know, but it did, and set up a situation I believe still remains to be resolved, both in theory and in practice. It goes something like this:

The mind—that is, the active, live, and most actual meaning—of a written work manifests itself in the ways it treats three materials: sight, sound, and sense, as Gertrude Stein counted them. They can as well be called the pictorial, musical, and ideal elements, or again, the spatial, temporal, and conceptual, but however roughly they may be distinguished a writer usually feels only one of them to represent the foremost face of natural reality and make the sharpest challenge to the mind, which means to make what it does at least as real to itself as the natural or given world. This one leading material or dimension assures the adequate reality of the work, while the other two may serve to reinforce, or refresh, or accompany, or arm, the mind in its major action upon the primary element. For some plain examples: In Pope the sense is primary or the authenticating element, while the sight and sound are there for emphasis and ornament, to help what oft was thought be well expressed or dressed; in Swinburne the sound—the whole musicality of rhythm and rhyme—is primary, while the sense and sight are embellishments; and in say Amy Lowell the sight is everything while the sound and sense are as may be. A similar prevalence of one element over others happens within the art of painting, where the validating element will be now line, now color, now volume, etc.; and within music, where it will be now melody, now harmony, now rhythm.

One might, with a preference for stability over excitement, like to place the excellence of a written work in an equal force or balance of sight, sound, and sense at once, but the trouble (or the mercy, if you prefer) is that rarely if ever in any historical period is experience lived equally in terms of space, time, and ideas, though of course they are always together in experience in some proportion or other. If the period is tranquil the sense of time is likely to be less vivid than the sense of objects in space; if the period is violent and changeable the sense of time will dominate. Sometimes the rationality of the universe is convincing enough and sometimes the irrationality of it is more so, so thought as the validating element in writing comes and goes.

Actual periods are of course more complex than that, as many writers work counter to their period in some way or degree, and the spatiality of writing in the period 1911 to 1928 was in part a counter to what was left of the late 19th century sense of time as history or even biology moving vastly on through a universe which was, if not rational, at least scientifically minded. So time and ideas were still interesting, but they had become problematical, indeed an annoyance to not a few, and all sorts of games could be played with them, while space was a given and saving reality, even to Proust and Joyce, as well as to Gertrude Stein.

But in about 1928 the general sense of the authenticity of space weakened. The pictorial element in writing, which had been highly evolved technically, continued of its own inertia, but it continued rather as decoration or illustration or symbol, because at this time writing began to base its reality on thought.

Most of the thought was political or religious or philosophical. T. S. Eliot went that way; so did Pound; Auden and that generation arrived, all bristling with ideas. Some absconse erudition and some Freudian apparatus did still hang on, passing for thought and even sounding like it, but I believe most of the thought was direct, fresh, and contemporary, really rousing at the time. Only, an idea that is exciting to live with rarely stays exciting long when written, supposing it even begins to be exciting enough for writing of such high intensity as poetry: it is awful what quantities of that poetry, written with a content of the most urgent ideas, are now no longer so much as curious, because the ideas were incompletely converted into the subjective continuum of poetry, and the pressing objective context which kept them alive for a time has withdrawn into history and left them stranded. So much of that poetry, being *about* ideas and not instinct with the poetry *of* ideas, has turned out parochial or didactic in the deplorable sense.

Gertrude Stein once said there were no ideas in masterpieces and next to no masterpieces in philosophy, yet at this time she felt, like everybody else, the need of ideas in writing, as experience was composing itself predominantly into issues, not states or events as before. But she knew very well that ideas had to be made intrinsic to poetry, made to exist as poetry, not used as external props, as occasions or justifications of poetry as if philosophy or religion or politics could delegate some of their authority and interest to poetry while remaining themselves and outside it.

Sight and sound are more readily assimilable than sense from the reality of experience into the reality of poetry: being sensory and particular they need bring little or no reference or association with them and can belong more closely than ideas to the actuality and specific form of the poem. Sound indeed, as rhyme and rhythm, can belong to the poem alone, and anyone prefers the auditory effects to stay inside the poem. One is ultimately annoyed or amused by onomatopoeia for example or say the use of spondees for something big or heavily moving in the subject matter; one likes the sound to be so far as possible self-contained, like "pure" music, a continuity of character or expression by itself, at most to follow the general emotion of the poem over the subject matter, and never but in passing or as an amiable concession to illustrate the objective behavior of the subject matter.

The same is almost as true of sight. In a thorough poem the actual look of the words on the page does count, but hardly as rhythm and rhyme do (except when, as with E. E. Cummings, it is deliberately made to), and sight is mainly a slightly less actual matter: imagery. Though the word is directly seen and the image is imagined, still the image is more actual than the idea. An image, like a concrete natural phenomenon, is "realized" by the intuition, whereas ideas are realized by reference, either to phenomena or to other ideas. An image, unless it is used as a symbol, is entirely there to the imagination, as an object is to the eye. Its primary relations can be not to the rest of natural reality from which it is drawn but to other images within the poem, making a kind of pictorial composition, or to the central emotion or key quality of the whole poem or passage. When Tennyson calls a falling stream a "downward smoke" or Hopkins speaks of "rose moles all in stipple upon trout that swim" the imagery is, on reflection, true enough to waterfalls and trout, but truer to the quality of the poems—to the languor of "The Lotus Eaters" in one case and to the exhaustive and bursting splendor of "Pied Beauty" in the other. So imagery can actualize and realize itself within the continuity of the poem, more or less completely, but it is hard to keep an idea, which is essentially a reference, from sticking out of the continuity, less like a sore thumb than like an index finger, directing the reader elsewhere. It is quite reasonable to despair of ideas for poetry; Cocteau could say poetry stops at the idea; and if poetry is essentially something and ideas are essentially about something not themselves, that seems to be that.

All the same, at the time, ideas were needed, and it came to Gertrude Stein, more clearly, I think, than to others, that after all grammar and rhetoric are in themselves actualizations of ideas and the beginning, perhaps, of a conversion of ideas into poetry, since they are in their way shapes or schemes, aesthetic configurations, even if not commonly felt to be so. The epigrammatic style of the 18th century, with its closed couplets, its balances, points, and antitheses, is not officially well thought of, but it was a partial solution to this problem. Other solutions had come long ago, when the articulation of general ideas was still a new game, after Homer, and even Sappho and Pindar felt the junctures of discourse as aesthetic schemes—not to mention the poets called or miscalled didactic, and of course Plato. But grammar and rhetoric degenerate into techniques of exposition and persuasion, into utensility and functionalism, ceasing to be the marvelous shapes or intellectual dance steps they were earlier.

The ancient distinction between the literary effects Persuasion and Ecstasy is good for distinguishing the effects of ideas in writing. In most of our writing ideas are meant to persuade, an inferior effect, and it is very hard to make them rise into ecstasy, even with elegance and grace and tensility and musicality in the rhetorical and syntactical figures. But that was what Gertrude Stein was trying to do in such works as "Stanzas in Meditation," and though I think she frequently succeeded, only time will tell with any sort of persuasion.

Time has persuaded us that something of this kind can be done in poetry, the plainest tradition being perhaps the Pindaric, from Pindar through Horace and Ronsard, the English Metaphysicals, even Wordsworth, and certainly Hopkins in "The Wreck of the Deutschland." This is not to say that the ideas of Milton, Dryden, and Pope, or of Wordsworth outside his one great ode, of Byron, and Shelley, or of many others—of Dante in particular whose excellence in using "the operations of the human mind" as poetical figures Shelley pointed out—never rise out of persuasion; but the fully lyricity of ideas* is, I think, more markedly and deliberately sustained in the Pindaric tradition, usually in the special form of the *ode*. The ode is usually full of ideas, but not composed in their logical or persuasive connections, rather disengaged from these deliberately, in order to have the quality of a vivid sudden willful happening, not that of a docile or mechanical consequence. This "beau désordre," as Boileau called it, is native to the ode, making it the natural vehicle for the lyricity of ideas.

In the ode and in poetry of the kind the delight is mainly in the

---

*I mean *liricità* as in Croce, who moreover describes the process of lyricizing ideas in Dante.

movement and accent of phrasing as the syntactical and rhetorical figures are played on or against or over the lines and metric, and, in case of rhyme, the rhymes. In Pindar the subject matter—the winners at the games and so on—is there but perfunctory, and occasional, rather a point of departure than a topic, and this bold preference in such writers for the movement and life of ideas as they actually eventuate in writing, over the claims of the exterior subjects, leads, typically, to such phenomena as the conceits of the Metaphysicals, where the acrobatic performance of the ideas is most of their meaning, or to the splendid commonplaces of classical poetry, whose "truth" as often as not is strictly confined to the mind of the poem (e.g. "Whatever is is right" or "Nessun maggior dolore," etc.) or to the Romantic exclamation of abstractions (e.g. "O World! O Life! O Time!"). For practical purposes these phenomena may be irrelevant or confusing or worse, but not for the most serious artistic purpose, which takes thought as an art form when not merely as raw material, much as mathematics can be so taken, whether the systems correspond to a reality outside themselves or not—the ecstasy of their intrinsic beauty being their "cash value." Plato, a poet and mathematician as well as a philosopher, could feel that way about ideas, calling philosophy a kind of music, dedicating his Academy to the Muses, and, once out of patience with another philosopher who was very earnest about ideas but less an artist in them than himself, telling him to sacrifice to the Graces.

But the essential motive for absorbing ideas into an art form (whether poems or fables or parables or plays or prose romances) is to repossess and revive in the subjective and living time of the human mind those concluded, inert, objective utensils which ideas become, once the mind has constructed them, for practical purposes, as accounts or maps of objective reality—or as tools or "weapons" for dealing with it. An idea is not ours and not alive unless it is essentially an event or part of an episode in human thinking, unless it occurs in a subjectivity. An idea that is alive and absorbing one year, say, because it relates to the main and active interests of the subjectivity at that time, is, the next year, only a fact or an object, sound asleep if not permanently dead, unless it is, by art, made to be a fresh event in a continuum of subjectivity, that is, the poem, the mime, the romance, or whatever. Outside of art the past idea has only an historical or academic interest, until it strikes the peculiar sympathies of a later period as all but contemporary with it and alive, but even then it has a zombie or somnambulant quality. The merely exposed and objectively articulated ideas of Aristotle and Saint Thomas, for example, whether true or not, exude that horror, and it takes all of Dante to make them sweet. While the dramatized ideas of Plato, even if less true for us, are still as fresh as daisies—so long, at least, as they are left in the dialogues.

In her way Gertrude Stein solved the problem of keeping ideas in their primary life, that is, of making them events in a subjective continuum of writing, of making them completely actual. For one thing, the ideas she uses, in "Stanzas," are about the actual writing before one, sometimes about her previous writing, other people's writing, or the ordinary events of her life at the time of writing. So the writing is, insofar as it is about anything, about ideas about writing, and this reflexive or so to say circular reference of the ideas is one way of making them self-contained and, while moving certainly, absolute. She was interested at this time in composition as something folded upon itself or contained in itself, and here the movement and reference of the ideas make such a thing. By taking as her center of reference the actual writing rather than writing in general, she gains a greater immediacy and completeness than other works on much the same scheme—the *Ars Poetica* of Horace, that of Boileau, that of Verlaine, and so on.

While one can, with the requisite attention, follow the movements of the ideas among or against each other and in relation to the verse, the very tense and elegant behavior of the syntax, she has so thoroughly suppressed the connections between these formal or verbal configurations of the ideas and any practical, theoretical, or historical context from which they have been abstracted that the work is at first bewildering. Often, yes, one can tell what the specific subject or occasion of a passage or stanza was, or make a sufficiently shrewd guess at the subject for the whole body of references to fall into place in history or philosophy, and take on an objective or extrinsic meaning, but this kind of clarity is, if a relief sometimes when it comes, really a temptation and a distraction from the actual aesthetic object. Gertrude Stein meant these lines of verse to be as attenuated and disembodied as the drawing of Francis Picabia—with whom a few of the stanzas are concerned (as pp. 241–42)—and who, she observed in *The Autobiography of Alice B. Toklas*, was in pursuit of "the vibrant line." Whether Picabia often captured it is a question, but a very good example of its capture would be the draughtsmanship of the Greek vase painter Exekias, if he were more familiar. At any rate, in a stanza concerning Picabia she says she told him to forget men and women—meaning that the line should become so intensely its own entity and sustained by an energy or "vibration" now intrinsic to it, that it could disengage itself from the character of the figures it began by bounding or delineating or expressing. Just so, she wanted her own writing—the grammatical sequence, the rhetorical figures, the line of discourse—to disengage itself by virtue of its own intensity of assertion from the concrete or specific situation whose articulation or definition or "bounding" was precisely the genesis of the idea in the form of a statement, a proposition, a sentence, a word, or whatever.

But can the "lyricity" of ideas really be made to fly, to transcend its origins and their references to any such degree, even if drawing sometimes can? Perhaps not, but I think anyone can see that a writer could passionately want it to be done—to go on, so to say, where Pindar and Plato left off, and create a continuum of absolute writing or absolute thought in words as it can be created in numbers. The audacity of the attempt in itself is staggering, and the difficulty was exhausting. Gertrude Stein finally gave it up and turned to writing about historical relations, and even the easier way out that symbolism is, though she indulged in it not very often.

(In "Stanzas" she does, if infrequently, use symbolism or a degree of it, metaphor: the first line of the first stanza is "I caught a bird which made a ball"—meaning "I captured a 'lyricity' that constituted a complete and self-contained entity." Such figures are not typical of what the work generally is or does. Her express attitude toward symbolism was to refuse it as such but to allow in theory and sometimes to practice what she called "symbolical literature"— apparently a literature containing symbolical imagery as above, but an imagery created for the sake of its character in the immediate composition, not for the sake of such a meaning as I have deciphered above. Symbolization would then be a method, like abstraction, of transmuting raw material into art, and not meant to "signify" the raw material—which is, like Picabia's "men and women," to be forgotten. This is theoretically all very well, and I admit that symbols provide a richness, a substantive weight, and some color in a perhaps too purely linear style, if they are taken literally as images and not interpreted, but they inevitably tempt one into interpretation, or me they do, and I mistrust them both in theory and in practice. I find them too interesting and not exciting enough. But a reader who can take them as they are meant— literally, as images and nouns—may well find they help to brace and sustain the "vibration" instead of interrupting it. However one feels about symbols, they are not, in this work, many.)

One of her difficulties was the fluidity of English, the invertebrate sequence and blur of overtones it has in normal use. Its Latin element is no longer a structural or linear resource, but mainly color or pedal, and at one point in the stanzas she longs for Italian, wishing "Italian had been wiser," that is, no doubt, that the superb rhetorical buoyancy and sharpness of Italian had not gone flaccid and indiscriminate as it did after Dante—or Tasso at the latest. Shelley could still use the "clear and complete language of Italy" as spoken or sung, for a foil or scale against which to make English even more fluid than it is, but current Italian is not the help it might have been in forcing English, saturated as it is with the indeterminate concreteness of the English mind, to the expression of what Gertrude Stein called with abundant reason the abstractness of the American mind. The clarity and completeness of Italian might help, but its lusciousness, which afflicted even Dante who invented the language, spoils when brought into American severity, rawness, edginess, what you will. Spanish is more promising, and Hemingway tried it, but something goes wrong there too. The only consolation is that translations of Gertrude Stein and imitations of Hemingway make excellent Italian literature. The real problem, of how to get a foreign language like English to express the exact tone and accent and movement of the American mind, still remains, and one may attach considerable importance to this most heroic attempt to solve it.

The above makes it sound like a laboratory and rather a grim go, which it is not. Gertrude Stein sacrificed to the Graces, and in the course of the "Stanzas" we have a good deal of comedy, general gayety, and such companionable remarks to the reader as "Thank you for hurrying through" or "I could go on with this." I have not, myself, seen all there is in the "Stanzas," far from it, nor all of what they are, but there is a luxuriance of pleasures waiting for almost any reader who is willing to enter into the "Stanzas" and stay a while. They are far more hospitable than they may at first appear.

The frugality of imagery will seem less forbidding if the reader sees that imagery was just what had to be reduced or liquidated at the time, in order to clarify the draughtsmanship of ideas, or if he recalls Dryden and the Metaphysicals when they are operating on the bare articulation of the language and the verse, with a minimum of coloristic or affective flourish. I think we now have to make some such effort, some deliberate tuning or focusing of the attention, since more recent poetry has disinterred if not revived imagery, in the lurider colors of its disintegration.

It may also require effort now to face a long philosophical poem, but the form was, oddly, of the period, as Bridges' *The Testament of Beauty* appeared then, Pound's *Cantos* were being written, and, on a smaller scale, T. S. Eliot's *Four Quartets*. Gertrude Stein's style and purpose have little enough in common with these poems, or with *The Excursion* or with *In Memoriam*, but the "Stanzas" do, by their general form, belong both to a fashion and to the tradition of the long, rambling, discursive poem whose interest and energy are primarily in the movement of the poet's mind writing.

A continuum of discourse, or of *sense* on its own, has a *sound*, an intrinsic musicality of its own, not only as Plato called philosophy a kind of music but as the ideas eventuate or evolve and move in the articulated time of the poem, so such poems are naturally called *The Prelude* or *Cantos* or *Four Quartets*; and the continuum has a space of its own, not only the marked "space of time" that a canto or stanza is, or by imagery when there is any, but by the extensions of thought which sentences are. Gertrude Stein kept, from grade school, a passion for the diagramming of sentences, and in most of her styles she wrote sentences as a kind of diagram of thought. Her superb sense of syntax led her to use it as a kind of draughts-manship, sometimes as the basis of a more flowing calligraphy, but in these Meditations rather as a "vibrant line" on the order of Picabia's or Exekias' or of that in much Byzantine painting. The intellectual space, rarely so reinforced by imagery and symbol as in Pound or Eliot, or by landscape as in Wordsworth, is both a matter of the stanza—as literally a "room"—and of the extent of the sentence, doubled or further articulated by the extent of the line of verse. To be a little clearer about it: She had said that sentences are not emotional, paragraphs are—that is, that a sentence lives by the balance or tension of its internal syntactical structure (not by its words as successive events), but the paragraph lives by the succession and culmination of the sentences in it—and much the same quality and kind of organization hold for the relation of line to stanza. The line, like the sentence, is conceived as primarily structural, or diagrammatic, as it were spatial and all but static, while the succession of the lines making up the stanza is conceived as temporal. Her lines have, usually, the extremely dry and tense syntactical posture of the 18th century line, or, better, of the closed 18th century couplet, but the stanzas have the mounting and sumptuous progress to a fullness of say the Spenserian stanza or the Tasso octave. I think she would have said this is an American kind of composition, not unlike the sequence of units in a comic strip—in any case very unlike the Miltonic or Romantic permeation of lines by the syntax, where the periods are "variously drawn out from one verse into another."

The metric itself, usually a very plain iambic affair with reversed feet ad libitum as is normal in discursive English poetry, does not really move much through the lines but is rather a matter of immediate emphasis, a rhetorical accent rather than a properly temporal element, or musical. It is what one could call an intensive, as against a progressive, metric, and surely the commonest kind in modern poetry. And the words themselves, being preponderantly monosyllables, tend to stay put and not to progress, to stand or arrive intensively—to vibrate—but to contain no succession.

Still, if one likes, there is a syntactical *phrasing* as well as structure, and one could call that a musicality, like the succession of the sentences and lines, but even the phrasing is staccato and in any case both the temporality and the spatiality of the "Stanzas" are "ideal"—functions of the sense, of the articulate "thoughts" succeeding each other in a meditation. Though there are exceptions enough, I think this is true, that as a rule the "Stanzas" re-create a temporality and a spatiality out of the single ideal element, rather than taking them as separate and extrinsic elements brought in for the embellishment or reinforcement of the first. Thus they have little to do with real time and space, but are as it were native to the poem, functions of the moving and extending sense, as that sense moves upon or around itself.

It is high time for an example. Here is a relatively simple one, "Stanza VIII" in Part V:

I wish now to wish now that it is now
That I will tell very well
What I think not now but now
Oh yes oh yes now.
What do I think now
I think very well of what now
What is it now it is this now
How do you do how do you do
And now how do you do now.
This which I think now is this.

This stanza is more readily glossed than most, and so not a fair example of disembodied sense, but the form is easier to appreciate perhaps against so plain and immediate a meaning. The poem expresses the action of the mind willing and realizing its own presence, in the present, to its own thought. It begins by recognizing that the actual present is the time to tell one's thought, in the very instant of thinking (not, for example, that the present is to be used for preliminaries and plans for expressing the results of one's present or past thinking later on, as is most common with methodical thought). Then there come various exclamations, questions, and greetings to the present, and the resolution of the question and effort in a recognition that what the mind is present to in its act of presence is simply the *thisness* of any object.

The meaning, or so much of it, can be further discoursed and commented upon by the reader, to the effect that, yes, the nowness and thisness of a thought, not its connections with past or future thoughts or with an objective context of thoughts, are the conditions of its life, and of thought generally at its most vibrant. Plato's dialogues, when the thoughts are instantaneous in the conversation (and not, as, alas, they often are, simply exposition disguised as interrupted monologue), and Montaigne's essays, where the thoughts are explicitly just passing events in his Grand Central of a mind or only valid for the passing moment and not even for the next essay, would seem to agree. Contrariwise one can meditate upon the thatness of objective thought, the beyondness of universalizing thought, or the thenness of historical and anthropological thought, as limitations to their interest. Such excursions into the factual and philosophical context from which the "Stanzas" were drawn, abstracted and constructed, are a pleasure, and one can be sure that most if not all the ground one is likely to cover came within Gertrude Stein's immense knowledge of such matters; but excursions into the original context, however rich, do desert the intensiveness and immediacy of the abstracted thought as expressed. One should stay with the text, and yet the excursions do make one realize the amount of accepted material and value that Gertrude Stein sacrificed for the sake of an uncertain result, with an audacity of decision that marks the major poets, philosophers, saints, generals, and financiers.

The resultant and *intensive* meaning of these poems is the movement of the mind within the poem itself, and in this case the movement of thought, which is positive and active at every syllable, and so has a very high frequency and continuous immediacy, is further intensified by the extreme compression of phrase and the irreducible simplicity of vocabulary. This last, which is not unlike that of Plato, or Aristotle, or Seneca—or, better, that of Voltaire or Diderot or Hume—not only provides an elegant singleness of meaning word by word, thus adding to the tenseness and intensity, but also forces the expression to be a matter of syntax and rhetorical figure of a most linear kind, like a drawing done with a very fine stiff pen. With next to no sonority or harmonics the poems operate on sheer melodic shape, phrasing, and rhythm, other supports being only the bracing or balancing of the syntactical units on or over the line, the repetition of words and phrases, and a very spare use of internal rhyme—that much harmonics if you will. But it is all in a quite pure harpsichord manner.

The single lines are sometimes divided: by rhyme (as in "That I will tell very well"), by repetition (as in "How do you do how do you do"), and by question and answer (as in "What is it now it is this now"). Then there is a balancing or drawing taut of the line by repetition with differing emphases—as in "I wish now to wish now that it is now," where each *now* has a different syntactical use as well as emphasis—and by a kind of binding symmetry as in "And now how do you do now" and in "This which I think now is this." The rhetorical emphasis is sometimes thrown to the end of the line as a climax—as in "not now but now" and in "oh yes oh yes now"— or suspended as in the almost parenthetical "now that it is now"— or recovered for a fresh sequence and line by subordination—as in "that I will tell very well / What I think . . ."—or by question and answer, as in "What do I think now / I think . . ." Such variations of emphasis and balance, the changes of speed, the changes from statement to exclamation to question to answer to a question that is not a question but a greeting (how do you do)—all this does, once you have your eye on it, make an extremely eventful and vibrant stanza, culminating in the symmetrical, balanced, triumphant statement and conclusion "This which I think now is this."

I have made this rather minute analysis, which suspends the live continuity of the poem and so is false to the essential, in order to show that the poem, which looks at first childishly simple and unorganized, is in fact a very varied and complex and highly organized expression, out of the simplest elements of language and thought. The "beautiful disorder" *is*, rigorously, "an effect of art." But her staying with such rudiments of thought, word, and figure, making everything of them, living in their sacredness and preciousness, when these are so often profane and despised, is a natural result of that purity and tenderness and all but religiosity of intention toward language which Sherwood Anderson remarked in her long ago—especially toward "the little housekeeping words, the swaggering bullying street-corner words, the honest working, money saving words, and all the other forgotten and neglected citizens of the sacred and half forgotten city [*of words*]." So that when, as she said, she "completely caressed and addressed a noun" in writing "A rose is a rose is a rose is a rose," it was not a passing fancy but from the center of her intention.

With the best will in the world, our sense of language is debauched, as politics, advertising, the newspapers, and even conversation rarely spare it, so it may be difficult to focus on the small essentials of the language or to see a full beauty in them; and yet a reader who is really accustomed to modern poetry or to say Gerard Manley Hopkins may have less trouble. Hopkins deals in a richer musicality and a sumptuous imagery, but as a rhetorician and, intellectually, as an *actualist* to the verge of heresy, he is germane to the manner. His sense of the syllable, the monosyllable and its placing, with its fullest meaning, and his sense of the simplest and minutest grammatical and rhetorical figures, if familiar to the reader at all, may help him with these "Stanzas," if the "Stanzas" are unfamiliar.

Few of the "Stanzas" are as easy as the one I quoted, and only the most intrepid reader should try to begin them at the beginning and read through consecutively. If read at random, as one may read the Old Testament or *In Memoriam*, they yield more more readily, or so they have to me. Another way of warming to the work or of getting one's attention in focus, is to pick out the one-line stanzas scattered through the work and get the hang of them before trying the longer ones. For the sake of a little more order and method in case of need, I offer this list of relatively simple stanzas, though it should be strayed from:

Part II, 14, 18; Part III, 2, 10, 12; Part IV, 9, 24; Part V, 5, 13, 25, 29, 33, 41, 48, 51, 59, 60, 61, 63, 75.[2]

No, they are better read at random, because one of the delights of rambling about in them is encountering very fine aphorisms. Here are a few I liked:

"In changing it inside out nobody is stout"—meaning nobody thrives by making the subjective objective. This could lead directly to a dispute about the "objective correlative" as against a subjective correlative, but it is meant to stand and not lead, not even to the thought which succeeds it in the meditation.

"That which they like they knew"—meaning that what people like is what is already familiar. Here, explanation is otiose to the point of fatuity, except that by contrast a paraphrase does point up the solid elegance of Gertrude Stein's expression, the fine ring of her new coinage of an old commonplace.

---

2. Sutherland's list reflects an incorrect numbering of stanzas in Part III, present in the manuscript, both typescripts, and the 1956 Yale text. The Part III stanzas he refers to here are actually 2, 11, and 13. Additionally, it appears likely that he followed the partially incorrect numbering of Parts IV and V found in typescript 2. Part IV, 17 (instead of 24) and Part V, 76 (instead of 75) better fit his description of "relatively simple stanzas." For a complete account of variations in stanza numbering in the manuscript, typescripts, and Yale text, see Appendix C.

"There is no hope or use in all." This axiom is as pretty in itself as Euclid's on the straight line, and its applications are many, but in the "Stanzas" the natural application is to writing, and there it is true enough, that a complete work or a complete thought is an absolute in itself and contains no future, neither hope nor use, and this may exalt you or horrify you, depending on what you feel a piece of writing should be or do, on whether you like thought as an end or as a means.

"What is strange is this." Or, it is immediate experience, not the remote and imagined, which contains novelty and romance. The sentence could stand as a motto for nearly all of Gertrude Stein's work, or of Hopkins', indeed for all philosophies of immanence or presence. One may disagree with such an aphorism, as one may not agree that all things flow or that to be is to be perceived, but one cannot resist the shapeliness of its utterance, nor even deny that it covers its immense ground, indeed holds it.[3]

In 1932, after reaching the terrible attenuation of the "Stanzas" at their purest, she suddenly changed and, partly for distraction, wrote *The Autobiography of Alice B. Toklas*, concrete to the point of gossip, and as simple a narrative as anyone could ask, though in some of the purest prose of our time. Though many works were still to come, and many handsome exploits both in her popular style and in more difficult styles, she never, I think, returned to the problem of the "Stanzas." The forms she used for philosophical discourse were in many ways richer, with plays and images and parables, with a great variety of intellectual games, but none of

---

3. The pages that treat other poems begin here and extend from pages XX–XXIII in the 1956 Yale edition.

them is quite the monumental attempt at absolute thought the "Stanzas" are. She left off abruptly but at the same time deliberately and with a curious acquisition of calm, a sort of rocklike wisdom. The poems called rightly enough "Afterwards" and "First Page," written in 1933, mark her departure and a new beginning. They are less intense, less vibrant, than the "Stanzas," but they have a very moving tranquillity. In "First Page" comes the passage:

> This which I say is this. One way of being here to-day.
>
> I simply wish to tell a story, I have said a great many things but the emotion is deeper when I saw them [*that is, when her writing was largely sight or "painting"*]. And soon there was no emotion at all and now I will always do what I do without any emotion which is just as well as there is not at all anything at all that is better.

Not that she did not return to emotion, for World War II brought out some of her most passionate and eloquent writing, but this lucid tranquillity remained at the heart of it, and gave her courage to face the dangers of the war, and afterwards to die as she chose. But all that belongs to her life, her legend, her writing. It is, as she would say, all there. And I think the "Stanzas" and "Winning His Way" are, rather, *here*, that it is at the point at which she left them that we come in.

The Impossible: Gertrude Stein

JOHN ASHBERY

Stanzas in Meditation (1956) is the latest volume in the series of Gertrude Stein's unpublished writings which Yale University Press has been bringing out regularly for the last decade. It will probably please readers who are satisfied only by literary extremes, but who have not previously taken to Miss Stein because of a kind of lack of seriousness in her work, characterized by lapses into dull, facile rhyme; by the over-employment of rhythms suggesting a child's incantation against grownups; and by monotony. There is certainly plenty of monotony in the 150-page title poem which forms the first half of this volume, but it is the fertile kind, which generates excitement as water monotonously flowing over a dam generates electrical power. These austere "stanzas" are made up almost entirely of colorless connecting words such as "where," "which," "these," "of," "not," "have," "about," and so on, though now and then Miss Stein throws in an orange, a lilac, or an Albert to remind us that it really is the world, our world, that she has been talking about. The result is like certain monochrome de Kooning paintings in which isolated strokes of color take on a deliciousness they never could have had out of context, or a piece of music by Webern in which a single note on the celesta suddenly irrigates a whole desert of dry, scratchy sounds in the strings.

Perhaps the word that occurs oftenest in the *Stanzas* is the word "they," for this is a poem about the world, about "them." (What a pleasant change from the eternal "we" with which so many modern poets automatically begin each sentence, and which gives the impression that the author is sharing his every sensation with some invisible Kim Novak.) Less frequently, "I" enters to assess the activities of "them," to pick up after them, to assert her own altered importance. As we get deeper into the poem, it seems not so much as if we were reading as living a rather long period of our lives with a houseful of people. Like people, Miss Stein's lines are comforting or annoying or brilliant or tedious. Like people, they sometimes make no sense and sometimes make perfect sense or they stop short in the middle of a sentence and wander away, leaving us alone for a while in the physical world, that collection of thoughts, flowers, weather, and proper names. And, just as with people, there is no real escape from them: one feels that if one were to close the book one would shortly re-encounter the *Stanzas* in life, under another guise. As the author says, "It is easily eaten hot and lukewarm and cold / But not without it." (Part, stanza, and line numbers consistent with this edition have been added to identify quoted passages.)

Stanzas in Meditation gives one the feeling of time passing, of things happening, of a "plot," though it would be difficult to

say precisely what is going on. Sometimes the story has the logic of
a dream:

> She asked could I be taught to be allowed
> And I said yes oh yes I had forgotten him
> And she said does any or do any change
> And if not I said when could they count. [IV.XVIII.1–4]

while at other times it becomes startlingly clear for a moment, as
though a change in the wind had suddenly enabled us to hear a
conversation that was taking place some distance away:

> He came early in the morning.
> He thought they needed comfort
> Which they did
> And he gave them an assurance
> That it would be all as well
> As indeed were it
> Not to have it needed at any time [I.II.13–19]

But it is usually not events which interest Miss Stein, rather it is
their "way of happening," and the story of *Stanzas in Meditation* is
a general, all-purpose model which each reader can adapt to fit his
own set of particulars. The poem is a hymn to possibility; a cele-
bration of the fact that the world exists, that things can happen.

In its profound originality, its original profundity, this poem
that is always threatening to become a novel reminds us of the late
novels of James, especially *The Golden Bowl* and *The Awkward Age*,
which seem to strain with a superhuman force toward "the condi-
tion of music," of poetry. In such a passage as the following, for
instance:

Be not only without in any of their sense
Careful
Or should they grow careless with remonstrance
Or be careful just as easily not at all
As when they felt.
They could or would would they grow always
By which not only as more as they like.
They cannot please conceal
Nor need they find they need a wish [III.XVIII.17–25]

we are not far from Charlotte's and the Prince's rationalizations. Both *Stanzas in Meditation* and *The Golden Bowl* are ambitious attempts to transmit a completely new picture of reality, of that *real* reality of the poet which Antonin Artaud called "une réalité dangereuse et typique." If these works are highly complex and, for some, unreadable, it is not only because of the complicatedness of life, the subject, but also because they actually imitate its rhythm, its way of happening, in an attempt to draw our attention to another aspect of its true nature. Just as life seems to alter the whole of what has gone before, so the endless process of elaboration which gives the work of these two writers a texture of bewildering luxuriance—that of a tropical rain-forest of ideas—seems to obey some rhythmic impulse at the heart of all happening.

In addition, the almost physical pain with which we strive to accompany the evolving thought of one of James's or Gertrude Stein's characters is perhaps a counterpart of the painful continual projection of the individual into life. As in life, perseverance has its rewards—moments when we emerge suddenly on a high plateau with a view of the whole distance we have come. In Miss Stein's work the sudden inrush of clarity is likely to be an aesthetic experience, but (and this seems to be another of her "points") the description of that experience applies also to "real-life" situations, the aesthetic problem being a microcosm of all human problems.

> I should think it makes no difference
> That so few people are me.
> That is to say in each generation there are so few geniuses
> And why should I be one which I am
> This is one way of saying how do you do
> There is this difference
> I forgive you everything and there is nothing to forgive. [IV.I.37–43]

It is for moments like this that one perseveres in this difficult poem, moments which would be less beautiful and meaningful if the rest did not exist, for we have fought side by side with the author in her struggle to achieve them.

The poems in the second half of the book are almost all charming, though lacking the profundity of *Stanzas in Meditation*.[1] Perhaps the most successful is "Winning His Way," again a picture of a human community: "The friendship between Lolo and every one was very strong / And they were careful to do him no wrong." The bright, clean colors and large cast of characters in this poem suggest a comic strip. In fact one might say that Miss Stein discovered a means of communication as well-suited to express our age as, in their own way, the balloons (with their effect of concentration), light bulbs, asterisks, ringed planets, and exclamation marks which

---

1. Ashbery here describes "Winning His Way: A Narrative Poem of Poetry" and twelve short poems that were printed with *Stanzas in Meditation* in the 1956 Yale edition.

comic-strip characters use to communicate their ideas. In "Winning His Way," for example, she experiments with punctuation by placing periods in the middle of sentences. This results in a strange syncopation which affects the meaning as well as the rhythm of a line. In the couplet

Herman states.
That he is very well.

the reader at first imagines that she is talking about a group of states ruled over by a potentate named Herman; when he comes to the second line he is forced to change his ideas, but its ghost remains, giving a muted quality to the prose sense of the words.

Donald Sutherland, who has supplied the introduction for this book, has elsewhere quoted Miss Stein as saying, "If it can be done why do it?" *Stanzas in Meditation* is no doubt the most successful of her attempts to do what can't be done, to create a counterfeit of reality more real than reality. And if, on laying the book aside, we feel that it is still impossible to accomplish the impossible, we are also left with the conviction that it is the only thing worth trying to do.

Stanzas in Meditation

Part One

STANZA I

I caught a bird which made a ball
And they thought better of it.
But it is all of which they taught
That they were in a hurry yet
In a kind of a way they meant it best
That they should change in and on account
But they must not stare when they manage
Whatever they are occasionally liable to do
It is often easy to pursue them once in a while
And in a way there is no repose
They like it as well as they ever did
But it is very often just by the time
That they are able to separate
In which case in effect they could
Not only be very often present perfectly
In each way whichever they chose.
All of this never matters in authority
But this which they need as they are alike

Or in an especial case they will fulfill
Not only what they have at their instigation
Made for it as a decision in its entirety
Made that they minded as well as blinded
Lengthened for them welcome in repose
But which they open as a chance
But made it be perfectly their allowance
All which they antagonise as once for all
Kindly have it joined as they mind

STANZA II

It is not with them that they come
Or rather gather for it as not known
They could have pleasure as they change
Or leave it all for it as they can be
Not only left to them as restless
For which it is not only left and left alone
They will stop it as they like
Because they call it further mutinously
Coming as it did at one time only
For which they made it rather now
Coming as well as when they come and can
For which they like it always
Or rather best so when they can be alert
Not only needed in nodding
But not only not very nervous
As they will willingly pass when they are restless
Just as they like it called for them
All who have been left in their sense

All should boisterous make it an attachment
For which they will not like what there is
More than enough and they can be thought
Always alike and mind do they come
Or should they care which it would be strange.
Just as they thought away.
It is well known that they eat again
As much as any way which it can come
Liking it as they will
It is not only not an easy explanation
Once at a time they will
Nearly often after there is a pleasure
In liking it now
Who can be thought perilous in their account.
They have not known that they will be in thought
Just as rich now or not known
Coming through with this as their plan
Always in arises.
Liking it faintly and fairly well
Which meant they do
Mine often comes amiss
Or liking strife awhile
Often as evening is as light
As once for all
Think of how many open
And they like it here.

STANZA III

It is not now that they could answer
Yes and come how often
As often as it is the custom
To which they are accustom
Or whether accustomed like it
In their bought just as they all
Please then
What must they make as any difference
Not that it matters
That they have it to do
Not only for themselves but then as well
Coming for this.
He came early in the morning.
He thought they needed comfort
Which they did
And he gave them an assurance
That it would be all as well
As indeed were it
Not to have it needed at any time
Just as alike and like
It did make it a way
Of not only having more come
She refused to go
Not refused but really said
And do I have to go
Or do I go
Not any more than so
She is here when she is not better

When she is not better she is here
In their and on their account
All may remember three months longer
Or not at all or not in with it
Four leaf clovers make a Sunday
And that is gone

STANZA IV

Just when they ask their questions they will always go away
Or by this time with carefulness they must be meant to stay
For which they mind what they will need
Which is where none is left
They may do right for them in time but never with it lost
It is at most what they can mean by not at all for them
Or likeness in excellent ways of feeling that it is
Not only better than they miss for which they ask it more
Nearly what they can like at the best time
For which they need their devotion to be obtained
In liking what they can establish as their influence
All may be sold for which they have more seeds than theirs
All may be as completely added not only by themselves.
For which they do attack not only what they need
They must be always very ready to know.
That they have heard not only all but little.
In their account on their account may they
Why need they be so adequately known as much
For them to think it is in much accord
In no way do they cover that it can matter
That they will clear for them in their plight

Should they sustain outwardly no more than for their own
All like what all have told.
For him and to him to him for me.
It is as much for me that I met which
They can call it a regular following met before.
It will be never their own useless that they call
It is made that they change in once in a while.
While they can think did they all win or ever
Should it be made a pleasant arrangement yet
For them once in a while one two or gather well
For which they could like evening of it all.
Not at all tall not any one is tall
No not any one is tall and very likely
If it is that little less than medium sized is all
Like it or not they win they won they win
It is not only not a misdemeanor
But it is I that put a cloak on him
A cloak is a little coat made grey with black and white
And she likes capes oh very well she does.
She said she knew we were the two who could
Did we who did and were and not a sound
We learned we met we saw we conquered most
After all who makes any other small or tall
They will wish that they must be seen to come.
After at most she needs be kind to some
Just to like that.
Once every day there is a coming where cows are

STANZA V

Why can pansies be their aid or paths.
He said paths she had said paths
All like to do their best with half of the time
A sweeter sweetener came and came in time
Tell him what happened then only to go
Be nervous as you add only not only as they angry were
Be kind to half the time that they shall say
It is undoubtedly of them for them for every one any one
They thought quietly that Sunday any day she might not come
In half a way of coining that they wish it
Let it be only known as please which they can underate
They try once to destroy once to destroy as often
Better have it changed to progress now if the room smokes
Not only if it does but happens to happens to have the room
    smoke all the time
In their way not in their way it can be all arranged
Not now we are waiting.
I have read that they wish if land is there
Land is there if they wish land is there
Yes hardly if they wish land is there
It is no thought of enterprise there trying
Might they claim as well as reclaim.
Did she mean that she had nothing.
We say he and I that we do not cry
Because we have just seen him and called him back
He meant to go away
Once now I will tell all which they tell lightly.
How were we when we met.

All of which nobody not we know
But it is so. They cannot be allied
They can be close and chosen.
Once in a while they wait.
He likes it that there is no chance to misunderstand pansies.

STANZA VI

I have not heard from him but they ask more
If with all which they merit with as well
If it is not an ounce of which they measure
He has increased in weight by losing two
Namely they name as much.
Often they are obliged as it is by their way
Left more than they can add acknowledge
Come with the person that they do attach
They like neither best by them altogether
For which it is no virtue fortune all
Ours on account theirs with the best of all
Made it be in no sense other than exchange
By which they cause me to think the same
In finally alighting where they may have at one time
Made it best for themselves in their behalf.
Let me think well of a great many
But not express two so.
It is just neither why they like it
Because it is by them in as they like
They do not see for which they refuse names
Articles which they like and once they hope
Hope and hop can be as neatly known

Theirs in delight or rather may they not
Ever it shone guessing in which they have
All may be glory may be may be glory
For not as ladling marguerites out.
It is best to know their share.
Just why they joined for which they knelt
They can call that they were fortunate.
They may be after it is all given away.
They may. Have it in mine.
And so it is a better chance to come
With which they know theirs to undo
Getting it better more than once alike
For which fortune favors me.
It is the day when we remember two.
We two remember two two who are thin
Who are fat with glory too with two
With it with which I have thought twenty fair
If I name names if I name names with them.
I have not hesitated to ask a likely block
Of which they are attributed in all security
As not only why but also where they may
Not be unclouded just as yes to-day
They call peas beans and raspberries strawberries or two
They forget well and change it as a last
That they could like all that they ever get
As many fancies for which they have asked no one.
Might any one be what they liked before
Just may they come to be not only fastened
It should be should be just what they like
This May in unison

All out of cloud. Come hither. Neither
Aimless and with a pointedly rested displeasure
She may be glad to be either in their resigning
That they have this plan I remember.
Well welcome in fancy
Or just need to better that they call
All have been known in name as call
They will call this day one for all
I know it may be shared by Tuesday
Gathered and gathered yes.
All who come will will come or come to be
Come to be coming that is in and see
See elegantly not without enjoin
See there there where there is no share
Shall we be three I wonder now

STANZA VII

Make a place made where they need land
It is a curious spot that they are alike
For them to have hold of which in need of plainly
Can be suddenly hot with and without these or either
For themselves they can change no one in any way
They may be often placid as they mean they can force it
Or wilder than without having thought Frank Wilder was a
    name
They knew without a thought that they could tell not then
Not known they were known then that is to say all though
They were just as famous as in when in eloquence shortly
Every one knowing this could know then of this pleased

She may be thought in when in which it is in mine a pleasure.
Now let me think when.
There should not be this use in uselessness.
It is easier to know better when they are quite young
Over five and under fourteen that they will be famous.
Famous for this and then in a little while which it is lost.
It is lost.
By the time that they can think to sing in mountains.
Or much of which or meadows or a sunset hush or rather
By this time they could which they could think as selfish.
No one can know one can now or able.
They may be thought to be with or to be without now.
And so it happens that at that time they knew
Or it happens that as at that time they knew
Which made pages no delight they will be felt not well
Not as ours hours are polite.
Or they think well or violent or weeding
Or may be they shall be spared or if they can be wanted
    finishing
Or better not prepared.
It is not ordinary standing or standard or which.
Might they be mostly not be called renown.
Should they finish better with batches.
Or why are theirs alright.

STANZA VIII

I ought not to have known that they came well
Came here to want it to be given to them
As if as much as they were ever anxious to be not

Only having seen me they could be nearly all polite.
It was difficult to know how they felt then.
Now I know everything of which it is that there is no difference
Between then and now but very much the same
As of course then it was not only here.
There they came well
Here they come well
Often make it be believed that they marry
It is not only that there was no doubt.
Indicated why they left in fear
Just as the same just is the same
They will be ought and autocratic
Come when they call.
They are called that they see this
They which is made in any violence
That they mean please forgive a mess
They can be often polite in languages.
Nobody thinks a thing.
They will welcome all shawled
I like a noon which has been well prepared
Well prepared never the less.
Hours of a tree growing. He said it injured walls.
We said the owner and the one then here preferred it.
Imagine what to say he changed his mind.
He said it would not matter until ten years or five.
She may be not unusual.
Or she may be taught most in exaggeration.
Or she may be moved once to balance all
Or she may be just unkind.
It is hoped that they feel as well

Oh yes it is hoped that they feel as well.
Argued with what they like or where they went.
Which they must have in any case
For accidentally they do not mean this.
Will there be any difference with how much they know
Or better than on account of which they wish and wish
  arranged
Can we call ours a whole.
Out from the whole wide word I chose thee
They may be as useful as necessity
More than they called which they could ask combined
Or made of welsh a treasure.
They mean me when they mean me

STANZA IX

With which they may be only made to brush
Brush it without a favor because they had called for it
She may be never playing to be settled
Or praying to be settled once and for all
To come again and to commence again or which
They will be frequently enjoyed
Which they never do as much as they know
That they like where they happen to have learnt
That seeds are tall and better rather than they will
It is much chosen.
Every year dahlias double or they froze

STANZA X

Might they remember that he did not dislike
Even if there was a reason that he did not choose
Nor rather as it happened which when he did not go away
They might which they not alone as nearly selfish
They will have placed in their own winning.
I know how much I would not have liked that.
They may be taken which is not the same as told
Made in which time they will frankly share
Might it be often not as well that they will change
Or in a way or principally in place
Made which they may which they made made unkind
It is not why they asked them would they like it
It is managed when they are able to agree
I come back to think well at once of most
Not only that I like it that they like it
But which in which way
That they chose
It is for instance not at all a necessity.
That once or twice or agreeable
Might they be very often very welcome
By which they mean will they come.
I have thought that the bird makes the same noise differently
Just as I said how will you do it if you like it
And they will not stretch well from here to there
If they know that in the full moon they should not plant it
Just before.
All might all mean that is the way to do
Not better than they have lost

But which they manage in their requital
I have known that sound and this as known
Which they will interlace with not only there
But the pale sky with the pale green leaves
Or which they will as they belong to trees
In this in their amount.
I come back to remember they will pay
Which they may do which they may say
Or which they may do whatever they do say
Always as often as they mention this
Which might annoy them does annoy them
As they call a pail a pail and make a mountain cover
Not only their clouds but their own authority
For having been here then as it is better to be
Which is an arrangement better made for them
Than not alone for them for which they will be willing.
It came very closely but no one was just yet
Not to be frightened as they meant at all
I do not care that he should make threads so
Threads are tenderly heads are tenderly so and so
Very well merited
I should judge just inclined
Neither as disturbance or better yet
Might it be changed but once before
Left them to gather it wherever they can and will
Just the same.
It might be very well that lilies of the valley have a fragrance
And that they ripen soon
And that they are gathered in great abundance
And that they will not be refreshing but only

Very lovely with green leaves
Or managed just the same when payed or offered
Even if they do.
They will never be careless with their having stayed away.
I know just how they feel with hope
And their wishes after all will we come
No we will not come.
In any absent way we will not only not be there
But when will we be here in one way
Any mixing of which it is in their presence
They or renowned or will they be made there
Will they be made there could be a question
Any answer could not be a question to their arrangement.
After all if it came out it meant it came again
Of course any one always is an answer.
Once in a while one or two
They could count now with any obstruction
As much as they advance.
Will or well a price.
In looking up I have managed to see four things.

STANZA XI

But which it is not by that they are rich
But only for it not only when they may count
Or by the opening that they will go round
As having value for which they may plan more
In which they can attract a celebration
Of their own cause not only just as well as all absurd
Can they be well awakened because they have not heard

Or may they come to account as much as not abandon
By the time that they caused them not to blame
Just as much as they could as they fasten
Linking it not only as absurd but fairly often
Be they as well aware as not only not only fasten
But which they may wish as not only opening
Or very carelessly arrange by the time they will go
Finally not only why they try but which they try
In case of joining.
Why should nobody wait when they come there
They have met one who likes it by and by
He will learn more than it is often read
That they could always please
More than just by their count
After all why may they liken it to this
Or not only add very much more
Or not be any one known as politeness
It is not at all like or alike
An invitation suffices for the present
In the middle of their exchange
They may cease moderation
Or embellish no one at a time
But then to wonder if they will be more
Or if there will be more which follows by
They will be not at all leaving it
Any way do they differ as to excitement
Or stopping hastily with while in ambush.
They do delight that it was any bird
Made to be near than they could like to plan
Should be thought successor to their own

Without in pleasure may they like may now.
Just as soon as ever if they come
By that in trial that they manage
It is for this for which for them for her
Coming to think it only as they knew
Known makes it plain I shall
Think birds and ways and frogs and grass and now
That they call meadows more
I have seen what they knew.

STANZA XII

She was disappointed not alone or only
Not by what they wish but even by not which
Or should they silence in convincing
Made more than they stand for them with which
But they may be more alike than they find finely
In not only ordinary care but while they care
It is by no means why they arrange
All of which which they frustrate
Not only gleaning but if they lie down
One watching it not be left aloud to happen
Or in their often just the same as occasionally
They do not usually use that they might have mention
That often they are often there to happen.
Could call meditation often in their willing
Just why they may count how may one mistaken.
In not quite correctly not asking will they come.
It is now here that I have forgotten three.

STANZA XIII

She may count three little daisies very well
By multiplying to either six nine or fourteen
Or she may be well mentioned as twelve
Which they make like which they may like soon
Or more than ever which they wish as a button
Just as much as they arrange which they wish
Or they may attire where they need as which say
May they call a hat or a hat a day
Made merry because it is so.

STANZA XIV

She need not be selfish but he may add
They like my way it is partly mine
In which case for them to foil or not please
Come which they may they may in June.
Not having all made plenty by their wish
In their array all which they plan
Should they be called covered by which
It is fortunately their stay that they may
In which and because it suits them to fan
Not only not with clover but with may it matter
That not only at a distance and with nearly
That they ran for which they will not only plan
But may be rain can be caught by the hills
Just as well as they can with what they have
And they may have it not only because of this
But because they may be here.
Or is it at all likely that they arrange what they like.

Nobody knows just why they are or are not anxious
While they sit and watch the horse which rests
Not because he is tired but because they are waiting
To say will they wait with them in their way
Only to say it relieves them that they go away
This is what they feel when they like it
Most of them do or which
It is very often their need not to be either
Just why they are after all made quickly faster
Just as they might do.
It is what they did say when they mentioned it
Or this.
It is very well to go up and down and look more
Than they could please that they see where
It is better that they are there

STANZA XV

Should they may be they might if they delight
In why they must see it be there not only necessarily
But which they might in which they might
For which they might delight if they look there
And they see there that they look there
To see it be there which it is if it is
Which may be where where it is
If they do not occasion it to be different
From what it is.
In one direction there is the sun and the moon
In the other direction there are cumulus clouds and the sky
In the other direction there is why

They look at what they see
They look very long while they talk along
And they may be said to see that at which they look
Whenever there is no chance of its not being warmer
Than if they wish which they were.
They see that they have what is there may there
Be there also what is to be there if they may care
They care for it of course they care for it.
Now only think three times roses green and blue
And vegetables and pumpkins and pansies too
She knew she grew all these through to you
And she may be there did he mind learning how now
All this cannot be mixed.
Once again I think I am reflecting
And they may be patient in not why now
And more than if which they are reflecting
That if they with which they will be near now
Or not at all in the same better
Not for which they will be all called
By which they will may be as much as if wishing
But which each one has seen each one
Not at all now
Nor if they like as if with them well or ordinarily
Should they be more enjoined of which they like
It is very well to have seen what they have seen
But which they will not only be alike.
They are very evenly tired with more of this
For they will happen to be in which resolve
Always made by which they prepare that no one
Is more able to be sure of which

They will not will they compel
Not only where they see which they see
But will they be willing for needing
Only which they could call not by it
If they have come again to do it not at all
As very much made in once by their own saying
Yes of course which they will not be at all
Not only not for them in which they like
I lead all may be caught by fattening
Or not either sent all which may positively say so
In their own pleasure neither which they like
It is mine when they need to accept add me
For which they mind one at a time
It is at one time no different between how many hills
And they look like that caught in I mean
For which they will add not when I look
Or they make it plain by their own time.
This which they see by
They turn not their back to the scenery
What does it amount to.
Not only with or better most and best
For I think well of meaning.
It is not only why they might stare to change
Or feel crops well as he has promised, he said.
That there would be several days not of rain
And there would then be plenty of good weather
Probably the crops would be good.
Alright they think in wishes
And some superstitions and some
Beginning and fortunately with places of ditches

And also formidably of which when
When they find the clouds white and the sky blue
The hills green and different in shape too
And the next to what followed when the other bird flew
And what he did when he dug out what he was told to
And which way they will differ if they tell them too
And what they do if they do not cover the vine too
They do it by hand and they carry it all too
Up the way they did still have it to do
And so they think well of well wishers.
I have my well-wishers thank you

Part Two

STANZA I

Full well I know that she is there
Much as she will she can be there
But which I know which I know when
Which is my way to be there then
Which she will know as I know here
That it is now that it is there
That rain is there and it is here
That it is here that they are there
They have been here to leave it now
But how foolish to ask them if they like it
Most certainly they like it because they like what they have
But they might easily like something else
And very probably just as well they will have it
Which they like as they are very likely not to be
Reminded that it is more than ever necessary
That they should never be surprised at any one time
At just what they have been given by taking what they have
Which they are very careful not to add with
As they may easily indulge in the fragrance
Not only of which but by which they know
That they tell them so.

STANZA II

It is very often that they like to care
That they have it there that the window is open
If the fire which is lit and burning well
Is not open to the air.
Think well of that is open to the air
Not only which but also nearly patiently there
It is very often why they are nearly
Not only with but also with the natural wine
Of the country which does not impoverish
Not only that but healthily with which they mean
That they may be often with them long.
Think of anything that is said
How many times have they been in it
How will they like what they have
And will they invite you to partake of it
And if they offer you something and you accept
Will they give it to you and will it give you pleasure
And if after a while they give you more
Will you be pleased to have more
Which in a way is not even a question
Because after all they like it very much.
It is very often very strange
How hands smell of woods
And hair smells of tobacco
And leaves smell of tea and flowers
Also very strange that we are satisfied
Which may not be really more than generous
Or more than careful or more than most.

This always reminds me of will they win
Or must they go or must they be there
They may be often led to change.
He came and when he went he said he was coming
And they may not be more in agreement
Than cakes are virtuous and theirs is a pleasure
And so they either or a splendid as a chance
Not to be seen to be not impervious
Or which they were not often as a chance
To be plainly met not only as anxious.
Will they come here I wonder why
If not will they try if they wonder why
Or not at all favorably
Just as may as in a way
A cow is and little cows are
He said it so and they meant more
Which it is for this an occasion or not
Just as they please
May they be just as careful as if they have a chance
To be not only without any trouble
Or may be they came

STANZA III

They may lightly send it away to say
That they will not change it if they may
Nor indeed by the time that it is made
They may indeed not be careful that they were thankful
That they should distinguish which and whenever
They were not unlikely to mean it more

Than enough not to decide that they would not
Or well indeed if it is not better
That they are not cautious if she is sleepy
And well prepared to be close to the fire
Where it is as if outside it did resemble
Or may be they will relinquish.
I think I know that they will send an answer.
It may be sensibly more than they could
That one sheep has one lamb and one sheep has two lambs
Or they may be caught as if when they had been
Not only as they like but she can say
He can say too two may be more that is to say
Three may be more than one more.
And only after they have five nobody
Has quarreled not only for them but after a while
She knows that they know that they
Are not remarkable.
It is often more which they use that they
Knowing that there is a month of May
In which often they use or may they use
Which they knew it could be in no venture
That they will use he will carefully await
And leave it like that to be carefully watching
Will we come and will we come then
They may to which may they be to which they use
Or not at all as in a fashion
More than kind.
It is often so that they will call them
Or may be there for which they will not see them
Nor may they as what they will like

In for instance will they change this for them.
Coming by themselves for them in no matter
Could one ask it is not usual
That if they are polite they are politer
Or either of them not to be one for them
Which they may call on their account for them.
It is all all of which they could be generous
If no one gave more to them
They could be with them all who are with them
For them may they be more than many
Not only but righteous and she would be
Not angry now not often for them
With not as told not by them
It is very well to have no thorough wishes
Wish well and they will call
That they were remarkable
And it is well to state that rain makes hills green
And the sky blue and the clouds dark
And the water water by them
As they will not like what they do not have
As nobody has been indifferent
Not only will she regret
But they will say one two three
Much as they use.
It is very well to know.
More than to know
What they make us of
Although it is cold in the evening
Even if a fire is burning and
Summer is of use to them

STANZA IV

All who have hoped to think of them or wonder
Or maybe they will like what they have had
More than they should if they went away freshly
And were very modest about not knowing why it was
That they were not denied their pleasure then
For which they may be more than not inclined
Which makes it plainly that in one way it made no difference
That they were always said to be just when they came
There where they liked and they were not allowed
Not only ordinarily but just now
They were agreeable which is why they are they
They hesitate they move they come where they are standing
They will take courage which they will not want
Nor will they worry very much as why they wait
They will not be often there
Think well of how very agreeable it is to meet them
To say yes we will go we know where we have been
We will say yes it is not without trouble that we came
Nor do we manage definitely to share.
But we must with one and all go there.
It will be often fortunately that strawberries need straw
Or may they yes indeed have marsh grass ready
It will support all who will have support
And she will kindly share hers with them
His with them
More than that they will stop this for them
Not only certainly but very surely
No one needs kindly any disappointment

Will they step in and out and may easily
One heel be well and one heel one be well
Or as an over ready change for once in a while
There may be reasons too why there are reasons why
If they may be said as much
That they will stay behind not only here but there
For them in a way they stay

STANZA V

Be careful that it is not their way not to like that
Not only not to be careful but to be very much obliged
Also moreover not to be the cause of their going
But which they will endeavor not to change
Not only for this but by the time
That which they knew there they must remain
If for them not at all it is not only why they like
But which they may wish from foolishness
Once at a glance.
It is not only why they are careful to replace
Not only which they may as they disturb
Or any weakness of wishing they would come there
More often than they do or carefully not at all
As it is their care to bestow it at one time
Should they because or in or influence
Not only called but very likely called a sneeze
From first to last by them in this way introduces
Them one at one time.
It is at once after that they will be better than theirs
All alike or all alike as well or rather better not

It can only not do not do all of which
They prefer elaborate to why they while away
Their time as they may accidentally manage
As a chance in which provocation is what they can call
Or while they went they gathered more
In made in gain
And more than all of it called cold
Or why they should arrange carefulness
Not only is our neat but as our plan
Named called useful as it is understood
Just why they could they interpose
Just fortunately in around about
At all managed getting ready there
To be determined but not by themselves alone
As often as they are more there
Which interested them.
They could be bought necessarily two or taken
In place of when they were attached to whatever
It is left to be planned that they can call
For it in all the hope that they can go
Or stay away whichever it is made to like
As they may mean or mean to do
It is fortunately by all of them
Made not only with this but for this.
A change from rest or a change from the rest
Well and welcome as the day which when the sun shines
Makes water grow or covers others more
Than when they looked there where they saw
All of which when they had not wondered

Would they like it there best
Might I ask were they disappointed.

STANZA VI

When they were helped as every one can
Once when they do and once when it is
Not only their feeling but also their way
Not to suppose that they will wish
That they may receive nor more than suggest
From which they look as much as if ever they can
That they will oblige which will be for them
Not only theirs but nearly as much
As theirs not alone but which they may
Not only join but nearly so
Make their arrangement believe their own way
Come whichever they can in what ever way
That they conclude that they must use
It not only for them but without any doubt
As they will hear better or not so well
In which and on which occasion
They will not only call but let them know
Not only what they allow but whatever they wish
As not only theirs.
It is a chance that they will be left
Or be consoled by each with one as no mistake
But they attach themselves they do trouble
They come when they will
They allow They can establish.
They can even agree not only to what they have

But should they be more than bereft
If they not only see but not only see
All or more than all because and because
Of which they are obliged
Being as they are to go there.
It is very kind of them to come.
As well as they may because and moreover
When they think well they think without that
Which moreover makes it yield
Because it is an instance of often now
Not only with it but without it
As even when and once in a while
As much as they change theirs in their own
As once allowed because they undertake may
As they can positively learn
Which it is mine to have then.
All that they can do is theirs not only then
They may often be thought all as at once
More often they will relish
At once they may change it
It is not only if at once that they are all
Or do they like it too
Or may they see it all
Or even might they not like it
If it is at once whatever they claim.
It is not only not a misfortune
It is wholly theirs to be believe me

STANZA VII

What do I care or how do I know
Which they prepare for them
Or more than they like which they continue
Or they may go there but which they mind
Because of often without care that they increase aloud
Or for them fortunately they manage this
But not only what they like but who they like.
There may be said to be all history in this.
They may be often opposite to not knowing him
Or they may be open to any impression
Or even if they are not often worried
They may be just bothered
By wondering do they often make it be alike afterward
Or to continue afterward as if they came
It is useless to introduce two words between one
And so they must conceal where they run
For they can claim nothing
Nor are they willing to change which they have
Oh yes I organise this. But not a victory
They will spend or spell space
For which they have no share
And so to succeed following.
This is what there is to say.
Once upon a time they meant to go together
They were foolish not to think well of themselves
Which they did not were they willing
As they often were to go around
When they were asked as they were well aware

That they could think well of them
Remember this once they knew that they way to give
Was to go more than they went
For which they meant immediately faster
It is always what they will out loud
May they like me oh may they like me.
No one can know who can like me.
This is their hope in wishing however
When they were not only laden with best wishes
But indeed not inclined for them to be careless
Might they be often more than ever especially
Made to be thought carelessly a vacation
That they will like this less.
Let me listen to me and not to them
May I be very well and happy
May I be whichever they can thrive
Or just may they not.
They do not think not only only
But always with prefer
And therefor I like what is mine
For which not only willing but willingly
Because which it matters.
They find it one in union.
In union there is strength

STANZA VIII

She may be thought to be accurate with acacia
Or by and by accustomed to be fairly
Just why they should in often as in or often

Could they call a partly necessary for them
Or why should anxiousness be anxiousness
Or their like that because more than they could
They will be named what do they do if they like
Or could they be troubled by it as a thought
Should they consider that they will gain
By not having it made for them to join
They will plainly state that only then only only there
More than if they will show all of it
Because please be plain for this time
And do not couple that they abandoned
Or which they abandoned because not only they were not used
In better than whenever or wherever they will go
I think I do not sympathise with him.
It is often known how they are just how they are
And if they are often just as well as being here
It is not at all unlikely they will change
And this you know all of it which you know
Be only thought not to please.
I think that if I were faithful or as bought
Or should be checked or as thought
Or finally they can claim for it more
Or just why they are identified
Or pleading they will call it all they know
Or have it that they make it do
Not only as they have not only as they have
It is other than theirs that they think is worth while
But which they come frequently to separate
In advantageous or advantage by their time
That they will come at once or not

For which they will come way of nine
She may be thought better have it spared them
That they will cover other than allowance.
He will come to show well enough all there
Or better have it strange or come again
Night like or night like do.
It is very foolish to hesitate between do and dew.
Or not at all broadly on which account
They can favor or fulfill or never marry
It is while while they smell that all it came
It came to be very heavy with perfume
Just like it may only it was not more than just
Why they went back.
Back and forth.
I have often thought it to be just as well
Not to go only why not if they are going
But they will like why they look
They look for them and they are reminded.
That often any day all day
They will not go alike but keep it.
However much they say.
How many did you know
Or not say no.
Or no
Come to couple spelling with telling.

STANZA IX

Just why they could not ask them to come here
Or may they press them to relieve delight

Should they be planned or may they cause them then
To have it only lost they do not care to leave
Should they come when and will they forward it back
Or neither when they care just when they change
May they not leave or will they not allow
More than they wish it is often that it is a disappointment
To find white turkeys white and little ones the same
Should they be pleased or should they rather not be pleased
Or more than they do should they rather keep it for them
Or more than this should they not infrequently
Or now when they see the difference between round and about
Or not only why they change but what they change
One for one another.
It is often a very best need that they have
To come to see that after all
It was after all when they came back
Or need they not be provoked
By thinking that they will manage to please them.
How often very often do they go
Not which they wish or not which they wish
However it is better not to like it at all
I find it suddenly very warm and this may easily be
Because after all may be it is
In which case do they need any more explanation
Or indeed will they bother
Or after all can there be any difference
Between once in a while and very often
And not at all and why not and will they
Should they be pleased with everything just the same
So that they will think how well they like

What they will do which they do
For them at all.
It is often no matter and a difference
That they see this when they look here
And they may very well be ready
To see this when they look where they do
Nor or may they be there where they are
But not there where they are when
They are at once pleased with what they have
As they do not wish not only but also
To have it better where they like.
It is often no purpose not to have disgrace
Said that they will wait.
All often change all of it so.
It may be decided or not at all
That it is meant should they use
Or would they care to think well long
Of what they think well.
And thank you
It is why they ask everything of them.
Should it be equally well planned
Made to carry or please it for them too
As they may often care or the difference
Between care and carry and recall
Should they find it theirs may they
Will they not be thought well of them.
Or not at all differently at once.
She may have no illusions
Nor be prepared not to be baffled
Or think well of then for which awhile

They chose.
It is for this that they come there and stay.
Should it be well done or should it be well done
Or may they be very likely or not at all
Not only known but well known.
I often think I would like this for that
Or not as likely
Not only this they do
But for which not for which for which
This they do.
Should it be mine as pause it is mine
That should be satisfying

STANZA X

It is not which they knew when they could tell
Not all of it of which they would know more
Not where they could be left to have it do
Just what they liked as they might say
The one that comes and says
Who will have which she knew
They could think all of which they knew as full
Not only of which they could they had as a delight
Or could it be occasionally just when they liked
It was not only theirs that they used as this
Not which they had with them not with them told
All have it not in any way in any anger
But they have it placed just when not there
For which they will allow could it or would it be told
That they shall not waste it to say to them

All of which after a while it is
As an arrangement
Not only theirs and only not at all.
They must be always careful to just be with them
Or they will not only not be but could be thought
To change which they will never know
Not only only all alike
But they will will be careful
It is not only this that antagonises that
Or they may be just as well in their refreshment
They will do always they will always do this
They could not relieve often which they do
They could be thought will it do
Once more come to gather does it matter
That it could be that they showed them this
But not this that they showed them that they showed them that
Or only once or not with not as only not once
Could they come where they were
Not only so much but also this much
Just whenever they liked this much
Which they were to declare
That no one had had corroboration
For which they will not only like
Letting once make it spell which they do
They can call it not be it as careless
Not only to ask but neither rested for
Which they will better can it have it
Not only there around but this
It is pleasantly felt for all
Not only why they liked with which

They came for it with their undertaking
Made that they will or use or will they use
By which they will know more than they incline
Coming as it does coming as it does
Are they allowed
After all if it is so

STANZA XI

I thought how could I very well think that
But which they were a choice that now they knew
For which they could be always there and asking
But made not more than which than they can like
Not only why they came but which they knew
For their own sake by the time that it is there
They should be always rather liking it
To have not any one exclaim at last
It must be always just what they have done
By which they know they can feel more than so
As theirs they can recognise for which they place
And more and moreover which they do
It is not only to have all of it as more
Which they can piece and better more than which
They may remain all or in part
Some can think once and find it once
Others for which for which they will
It is at no time that they joined
For which they joined as only
Not for which it is in partly measure
Having alike be once more obtained

They make no trouble as they come again
All which they could
But they will care
All for which it is at once thought
Just when they can surprise
No one in what they could there
Make without any pause a rest.
They will think why they
And they will come
In response.
Should they be well enough.
Otherwise they can consider that
Whatever they have missed.
I think I know I like I mean to do
For which they could they will place
He will place there where
It is finally thought out best
No means no means in inquietude
Just when they give and claim a reward
Not for which they go and get this
They have been with the place their place
Why is there not why is there not with doubt.
Not able to be with mine.

STANZA XII

One fortunate with roses is fortunate with two
And she will be so nearly right
That they think it is right
That she is now well aware

That they would have been named
Had not their labels been taken away
To make room for placing there
The more it needs if not only it needs more so
Than which they came

STANZA XIII

But it was only which was all the same

STANZA XIV

It is not only early that they make no mistake
A nightingale and a robin.
Or rather that which may which
May which he which they may choose which
They knew or not like that
They make this be once or not alike
Not by this time only when they like
To have been very much absorbed.
And so they find it so
And so they are
There
There which is not only here but here as well as there.
They like whatever I like.

STANZA XV

It is very much like it.

STANZA XVI

Could I think will they think that they will
Or may they be standing as seated still
For which they will leave it make it be still
That they will reach it for which they will until
They should be said to be planned for which they will
Not which they need not plan not more than will
It is an estimate of ferocity which they would not know
Not with surprise nor from the wish
That they would come at all
May they be mentioned
For which they can not be only lost
For which they will may they may they come in
For which they will not but very likely
But they can not be there with which they will
For they may be with that kind that is what is
When they can like it as they do
But which they can not be for them
All made as they are not without it
Often left to them to come to arrange this
More than they can at most.
It was not only that they liked it
It is very kind of them to like it.

STANZA XVII

Come which they are alike
For which they do consider her
Make it that they will not belie
For which they will call it all

Make them be after not at least ready
Should they be settled strangely
Coming when they like an allowance
Naming it that they change more for them
With which which is certainly why they waited
They may be more regularly advised
In their case they will be able
Not only which they know but why they know
It is often that do their best
Not only as it is but which in change
They can be as readily which it is alike
Theirs as they better leave
All which they like at once
Which nearly often leave
This is the time in which to have it fasten
That they like all they like
More than which they may redeem.
It is often very well to if they prey
Should they could should they
They will not be imagined fairer
If they next from then on
Have it as not diminished
They can place aisle to exile
And not nearly there
Once in a while they stammer but stand still
In as well as exchange.
Once in a while very likely.
It is often their choice to feel it
As they could if they left it all
A ball fall.

Not two will give
Not one will give one two
Which they may add to change.
They will change what they like
Just what they do.
One two three or two

STANZA XVIII

She may be kind to all
If she wishes chickens to share
Her love and care
But they will think well of this
Which may not be amiss
If they like.
Two dogs for one or some one.
It is a happy wish
For some one.

STANZA XIX

She may think the thought that they will wish
And they will hold that they will spell anguish
And they will not be thought perverse
If they angle and the will for which they wish as verse
And so may be they may be asked
That they will answer this.
Let me see let me go let me be not only determined
But for which they will mind
That they are often as inclined
To have them add more than they could

She will be certainly seen if not as much
They will be left to be determined
As much as if they pleased they pleased
Not only theirs but only theirs
For them as much as known and not only
Not repeated because they will be seen
Partly and for less for which they are not very clearly
Made to be better than often as serviceable
Is it as much as why they like
For which they are often as much mistaken
Anything astonishes a mother or any other.
A stanza in between shows restlessly that any queen
Any not a stanza in between for which before which
Any stanza for which in between
They will be for which in between
Any stanza in between as like and they are likely
To have no use in cherishing.
They could be not alone consoled
They could be they may may they
Finally relieve.
It is often eight that they relinquish a stanza
Just when they feel that they are nearly
That they may could and do color
For which they will not only be inconvenient
For which they all for a forest
Come in as soon as our allowed
They prepare nor do they double
Or do they add prefer to before and call
She may be ours in allusion not only to
But why they will as much encourage

Readily for instance or may for instance
Come with not only as much as they tell
They tell it because if not why not
Such should be called their glory or their make
Of angling with and for around
May it be wading for which they wade
Theirs once again the same
All which they said it said it in and answered
May be they like
Might it be uncontained likely
That they should as much joined with ease
But not by this for once once is not only one
They presume once alike not by their own present.
They present well. It followed once more
Only theirs in case. For which.
They add conditionally to not previously adding
More than they gave to one.
One is not one for one but two
Two two three one and any one.
Why they out tired Byron

Part Three

STANZA I

For which may they it which
That they may then or there either
By means of it for which they could
Recognise it is more than in going
They can come will they come until
The exacting by which they in exact
For which they will in and
They need not be for which they go
Theirs is all but not which it is in a chance
That they could incline to be inclined
For them or not or more inclined
Now not at all deserting
Nor not at all deserting
For which they finish English
May they make cake or better
For which when did he like
Theirs or not at all theirs
They will not leave a well alone
Or not because now the water comes
Just as they could.

They are always just not even
He is at least tired by the heat
Or he will
Just not join not just join
All that they like to do.
It is why I see when I look out at it
That it is just like when I see it
And it is fortunately not a bit of it
By this for which they please come out
Of there.
May they call one forty might
Or it is not might it
If it is not only they did
But which will they if they do
Not only this or which but may or may
Should more not any more
Any day make raspberries ripe
As they may do make what they do there
In leaning having had which
Not only while they do not but while they do
In often not at all now I am sure
Not sure not only how
But can it be at once.
Now to suppose it was like that.
Every time he went he went
And so it was not that they went
Not not at all.
And when he came back not when he went
He came back not when he came back
When he went.

One not to come to go when not to be
Not only not from here not here from there
Just as they used as usual
For which it it is not that that it
Must not do go
They leave it there is no there they do do
They do not do one two
As all round any arranged is not in at best
Once they he did once he they did or not
At all at any time.
It is so much that there is no difference in so much.
One one and two two one.

STANZA II

I think very well of Susan but I do not know her name
I think very well of Ellen but which is not the same
I think very well of Paul I tell him not to do so
I think very well of Francis Charles but do I do so
I think very well of Thomas but I do not not do so
I think very well of not very well of William
I think very well of any very well of him
I think very well of him.
It is remarkable how quickly they learn
But if they learn and it is very remarkable how quickly they
    learn
It makes not only but by and by
And they may not only be not here
But not there
Which after all makes no difference

After all this does not make any does not make any difference
I add added it to it.
I could rather be rather be here.

STANZA III

It was not which they knew
But they think will it be though
The like of which they drew
Through.
It which may be that it is they did
For which they will be never be killed
By which they knew
And yet it is strange when they say
Who.
And so not only not here
May be they will be not in their place there
For which they will what will they may be there
For them for which not only very much
As is what they like there.
Now three things beside.
Add which not which to which
They wish which they divide.
If a fisherman fishes
Or else a well
Very well does an attack
Look back.
For that in use an extra make a moment
Further in use which they can be there when
In open use of which they like each one

Where they have been to have been come from.
It is often that they do regularly not having been
Before.
As much as and alike and because
Once before always before afraid in a dog fight
But not now.
Not at all now not when they not only wish to do
May they be ours and very pretty too
And you.
Once more I think about a lake for her
I do not think about a lake for them
And I can be not only there not in the rain
But when it is with them this it is soon seen
So much comes so many come.
Comfortably if they like what they come.
From.
Tables of tables and frames of frames.
For which they ask many permissions.
I do know that now I do know why they went
When they came
To be
And interested to be which name.
Who comes to easily not know
How many days they do know
Or whether better either and or
Before.
She may be eight in wishes
I said the difference is complicated
And she said yes is it it is
Or she said it is is it.

There seems so much to do
With one or two with six not seven
Either or.
Or believe.
That not only red at night can deceive.
Might they we hope better things of this.
Or of this.
Is.
When they are once or twice and deceive.
But leave
She may be called either or or before
Not only with but also with
With which they wish this
That they will like to give rain for rain
Or not.
It is just like it sounds.
I could not like it then nor now
Out now
Remained to how.
However they are careful.
Having forgotten it for them
Just how much they like
All potatoes are even when they have flowers
All adding is even
If they asked them
Would they ask them.
It would not be like alike for which
They did.
They had and did.
But which they had which they had which they is and did.

Gotten and gotten a row
Not to in did not and in said so
It is not only that I have not described
A lake in trees only there are no trees
Just not there where they do not like not having these
Trees.
It is a lake so and so or oh
Which if it is could it does it for it
Not make any do or do or it
By this it is a chance inclined.
They did not come from there to stay they were hired
They will originally will do
It is not only mine but also
They will three often do it.
Not now.
Do I mind
Went one.
I wish to remain to remember that stanzas go on

STANZA IV

Not while they do better than adjust it
It can feeling a door before and to let
Not to be with it now not for or
Should they ask it to be let
May they be sent as yet
For may they may they need met
Way and away in adding regret to set
And he looks at all for his ball.
I thought that I could think that they

Would either rather more which may
For this is and antedated a door may be
Which after all they change.
He would look in the way
Of looking.
Now added in again.
It is a way having asked in when
Should they come to be not only not adding some.
I think it is all very well to do without that
But it is why they could be with without that
For which they called a time
Not having finished to say that nearly there
They would be neither there as box wood grows
And so if it were they could be as easily found
As if they were bound.
Very nearly as much a there
That is one thing not to be made anything
For that but just for that they will add evening to anything

STANZA V

Not which they know for which they like
They must be last to be not at it only with
It can for which they could with and a
Many can not come in this for nor without them
Some of which will they for them awhile
For which it is not only at an attempt
They can find that they can retouch
Not only what should be cared for
So they make this seem theirs

And only integrally shared as much as fine
They will out and out confer
That they will always may be so
As what they like.
Be mine prepared
What may it be not for their add it to
Can and delight for which not why they neglect
Just when or just when
For which not more than
Or by nearly
It is not their coat.
They must care for their furniture
Not but as one
For could and forfeit too
Coming and one.
It is not only that they could be here
When they are often made just may
It is my own that no one adds for it
Not only is it added well
She can only cloud go around
By that in awoken
Could and clad
May they be eaten glad
Should not only should not under known
Say any way
A way
Equal to any stanzas are all three
They must be spared to share
Should it not only this and all around
They will have will appointed

Not only why they look not that
They call meadows may or all
For it is not only only their name
But which is a plain and a plain plaintive
Too or more.
I can not be indifferent to a little while
By which all tall at all
They could be not only any in any case
What does he mean by that
Not only not only not any interest not interested
But they will a valley.
Once every day they ate to a day
Not obliging not at not to obliging
But she will have meant
Or they will but they maintain
Ease by a minute.
It is not only their four in amount
Or while or a while
Or going
Or just as soon by which ought
Will they not have any as presence
They could be ought they be manage
Not only she thinks which
Just as never which many which
Made or manage they thrust.
It is often all they order or in order
But which they endanger
Do or not do.
However may be in account of whatever they do.

STANZA VI

It is not a range of a mountain
Of average of a range of a average mountain
Nor may they of which of which of arrange
To have been not which they which
May add a mountain to this.
Upper an add it then maintain
That if they were busy so to speak
Add it to and
It not only why they could not add ask
Or when just when more each other
There is no each other as they like
They add why then emerge an add in
It is of absolutely no importance how often they add it.

STANZA VII

By which are which add which a mounting
They need a leaf to leave a settling
They do not place a rein for resting
They do not all doubt may be a call
They can do which when ever they name
Their little hope of not knowing it.
Their little hope of not knowing it.

STANZA VIII

By it by which by it
As not which not which by it
For it it is in an accessible with it

But which will but which will not it
Come to be not made not made one of it
By that all can tell all call for in it
That they can better call add
Can in add none add it.
It is not why she asked that anger
In an anger may they be frightened
Because for it they will be which in not
Not now.
Who only is not now.
I can look at a landscape without describing it.

STANZA IX

That is why a like in it with it
Which they gay which they gay
But not only just the same.
Now who are now
Our who are now
It is not first not they are
But being touching all the same
Not and neither or the name.
It is very anxious not to know the name of them
But they know not theirs but mine.
Not theirs but mine.

STANZA X

Tell me darling tell me true
Am I all the world to you
And the world of what does it consist

May they be a chance to may they be desist
This came to a difference in confusion
Or do they measure this with resist with
Not more which.
Than a conclusion
May they come with may they in with
For which they may need needing
It is often by the time that not only
Which waiting as an considerable
And not only is it in importance
That they could for an instance
Of made not engaged in rebound
They could indeed care
For which they may not only
Be very often rested in as much
Would they count when they do
Is which which when they do
Making it do.
For this all made because of near
No name is nearly here
Gathering it.
Or gathering it.
Might it in no way be a ruse
For it which in it they an obligation
Fell nearly well

STANZA XI

Now Howard now.
Only righteous in a double may

It is ought frown
They could however collaborate
As only in the way
Of not only not renowned.
What is it often
Oh what is it often
Or should
Should as any little while.
Think more what they mean
Oh think more what they mean
Now I know why he said so
Oh no.
It is if it is.
What is the difference.
What is the difference both between for it and it
And also more also before not it.
It can be an absence better than not before.
It is just why they tried.

STANZA XII

I only know a daisy date for me
Which is in wishes can forget for it
Not which not that that is
And is that that not be that with
It is not any one can think
Why be without any one one can
Be favored flavored not which
It is not only not only neither without
But this is only so.

I cannot often be without my name.
Not at all
They will not wonder which at a time
And may it be alright.
They can lead any one away.
Now look not at that.
Having heard now hearing it
Should just engage those
Not always connected
Readily express
For them forget
It is very easy to be afraid to hear one come in.
All like all to go
There is often when they do not mention running
Or walking or not going
Or not why they do not find it in for him.
Just why they should or just why
Ate or bate or better or not sigh
He she can sigh and try why
They seize sigh or my.
If is often when it is not stated
That at it two or to
That it is better added stated
That they are to
I often like it not before
They do not or do not listen one to one another
Or by guess.
It is just as much as allowed
Why they carry or
All would or wood or wooden

Or all owed
Or not vestiges or very sight
Of water owned or own
Or not well velvet
Or not aligned
Or all or gone
Or capitally
Or do or comforting
Or not
Renown.
They will say pages of ages.
I like anything I do
Stanza two.

STANZA XIII

Stanza ten make a hen
Stanza third make a bird
Stanza white make a dog
Stanza first make it heard
That I will not not only go there
But here

STANZA XIV

In changing it inside out nobody is stout
In changing it for them nobody went
In not changing it then.
They will gradually lengthen
It.

STANZA XV

I could carry no one in between

STANZA XVI

Can thinking will or well or now a well.
Wells are not used any more now
It is not only just why this is much
That not one may add it to adding main
For never or to never.
Suppose I add I like to
I may should show choose go or not any more not so
This is how any one could be in no hope
Of which no hope they did or did not
There is no difference between having in or not only not this
Could it be thought did would
By it a name.
I think I could say what nobody thought
Nobody thought I went there
This is however that they add sufficiently
Because it is not better allowed
All will come too.
Just joined how to houses
But they will like an only name
They could be thought why they had a weakness
To be sure.
Now this is only how they thought.
Let no one leave leaves here.
Leaves are useful and to be sure
Who can or could be can be sure.

I could think add one add one advantage
That is how they like it.

STANZA XVII

She does not who does not it does not like it
Our our guess yes
But it does not it does not who does guess it
But they will place it or not place it yes
They could in insistence have nobody blamed
Which they do ours on account
May they or may they may they blame this
This that they will wail when not in resting
But which they for which they could date and wait
Will they do what they are careful to do too
Or like this will they like this where they go
When it is not only not certain where they went they were here
At all as likely as not up and down up and down to go
Not because before by which they attracted
They were with an on account which they knew
This not only not which they need blessing
Which or not which when they do not or which way
They do go
It is not inadvertent that they oblige
It is waiting they gather what do they like
Cherries not only not better not ripe
It was a mistake not to make not only a mistake with this
In not only in all noon after noon that they like
It is always arbitrary to come with bliss
For them to join it to come with it

They could manage just what they did
But did they not feel that
They could be not only not allowed but not clouded
It was very different again
Just when they join that they look.
They refer to a little that is a little trunk
A very little trunk once.
How very sorry they are for not for placing
Well place well
Just once to join and not too alike
That they go
Or will they not only in place of which to happen to be last not
    to save it to say so
Or go.
And so they went carefully together.
As they like it which
They mean that for when
It is not mine
Fine

STANZA XVIII

It is not which they will not like or leave it as a wish which they
    compare
All for most all for that did they if not as it is
Should they dare or compare
Could it have been found all round
Or would they take pleasure in this
Or may they not be often whichever
As they told theirs in any day.

Does it make any difference if they ask
Or indeed does it make any difference
If they ask.
Would they be different if nobody added it all
Or looking just alike do they mind any extra
May they or should they combine
Or should they not easily feel
That if they could they may or should
We ask.
Be not only without in any of their sense
Careful
Or should they grow careless with remonstrance
Or be careful just as easily not at all
As when they felt.
They could or would would they grow always
By which not only as more as they like.
They cannot please conceal
Nor need they find need they a wish
They could in either case they could in either case
Not by only for a considerable use.
Now let only it be once when they went
It is of no importance to please most
One of them as it is as it is now
It is not only for which they cause
That it is not only not why they like
Them.
They could often be a relish if it had not been thought
That they should unite.
They will be only not more a choice
For which alone they remain.

Proclaim.

I wondered why they mentioned what they like.

All of which only what they knew

Just why they yearn

Or not rest more.

A counter and not a counter pane

They could be relished.

Just why they called wait wait.

What is it when there is a chance

Why should they like whatever they do

Not only if they will but if they will

Not only

It is not more than this shame.

Shame should not be for fountains.

Nor even not yet

But just when the mountains are covered

And yet they will please of course they will please

You which it is.

Not any not on any account

May it not only be why they went.

It is always which they like.

It is a thought give a thought to Cuba

She could in cooking

And only not let owls frighten not birds

Not only not

Because in only ending birds

Who ends birds where.

Now I have said it.

It is of no use one year

A toad one year

A bird a little very little as little bird one year
And if one year
Not only not at all one year.
It came very difficultly.
Just not in not in not in not as in him.
And so on account on account of reproach.
Could they if not she would be startled.
But they cost neither here no there.
Just as I think.
Once when they should they if indifferently would
When to look again
Pinny pinny pop in show give me a pin and I'll let you know
If a pin is precious so is more.
And if a floor is precious so is not a door.
A door is not bought twice.
I do think so earnestly of what.
She had no chagrin in beauty
Nor in delight nor in settled sweetness
Nor in silliness alright.
But why often does she say yes as they may say
She finds that if one is careful one has to be very much
Awake to what they do all need.
Now often I think again of any english.
English is his name sir.
That much is not only not only not a disadvantage
Over them.
Once more I wish italian had been wiser.
But will they wish
They wish to help.
And their wish succeeded.

And added.
Once more I return to why I went.
I went often and I was not mistaken.
And why was I not mistaken
Because I went often.

STANZA XIX

Not only this one now

STANZA XX

How can no one be very nearly or just then
Obliged to manage that they need this now
She will commence in search not only of their account
But also on their account as arranged in this way
She will begin she will state
She will not elucidate but as late
She will employ she will place adding
Not with it without it with their account
Supposing they may say the land stretches
Or else may be they will say it is all told
Or perhaps also they will say
Or perhaps also they will say that they went from here to there
Or not only just then but when just then
Also perhaps not only might they not try
Maybe not only what they wish but will they wish
Perhaps after a while it is not why they went
Not only which it is but after it is
They might be thought to have it not known
Only which they are obliged

To feel it at all not which they can know
They could call colors all or not
Incomplete roses.
They find fish an ornament
And not at all jealously at any and all resemblance
They have been warned to try and be called all
For which they plan a favor
Should they be thought to be caught all around
By that time it is well to think it all
Not only may they be
It is a pleasure that twice is neglected
In which amount.
They anticipate in place.
Could no one try of fancies.
However how is it if it is right and left.
Or rather should it did it happen to be more
They can allowed or stranger
They have not then once cost
But which in theirs and on which occasion
May they be minded.
Now how can I think softly of safety
Which which they do
It is not only their only hindrance
But not well won not with it.
In intermittence may they remind sees.
She may fortunately not count
If she says but which if they say
But which they find.
Now only this when they all think.
How can she manage our places.

It is for this they could recall
Better than all do.
It was not often that I could not join them
Which they did.
Now how could you disguise joins
By which it is in ate and dishes
They could be only they could be only worried
By what they remain with what they will
Or not unkind.
This is what I think I think I often did the same
When they should be all there as known
After all I am known
Alone
And she calls it their pair.
They could be cut at noon
Even in the rain they cut the hay
Hay and straw are not synonymous
Or even useful with them
Or even useful with them
Or as a hope that they did
Which after all they did not.
In this way any one or did add not a precaution.
Think how well they differ caution and precaution
Or not.
Or should they allow ours in glass
For them they carry
Better not be strange in walking
They do or do not walk as they walk as they part.
Will they mean mine or not theirs
They will they will like what they entitle

Should they be theirs.
He asked did they that is it
That is did it mean it was with them
There with them
They could not be ought not be mine.
So then
All of which reminds no one
Having said.
Do which or they may be kind.
She says some or summer could be.
Not only not again for when.
I can think exactly how I found that out.
Just when they say or do
Once and before.
It is not only that they like
In the meantime.
If even stanzas do.

STANZA XXI

Not what they do with not
Not only will they wish what
What they do with what they like
But they will also very well state
Not only which they prefer by themselves
And now add it in aging ingenuity
But which they will as soon as ever they can
But which they tell indeed may they or may they not proudly
Not only theirs in eight but which they meant
They will all old declare

That believing it is a patent pleasure in their care
Nor when where will they go older than not
Nor will they furnish not only which they had but when they
    went
In reason.
It is often that they allow a cloud to be white
Or not only patently white but also just as green
Not only theirs in pleasure but theirs in case
Not only however but not only however
Or not at all in wishes that they had chickens
Which may be alternately well or ducks
Or will they spread for them alone
To be not only their care.
This which and whatever I think
I not only do but make it be my care
To endanger no one by hearing how often I place
Theirs not only why they are best not
Not by it as they like.
I have thought while I was awakening
That I might address them
And then I thought not at all
Not while I am feeling that I will give it to them
For them
Not at all only in collision not at all only in mistaken
But which will not at all.
I thought that I would welcome
And so I could be seen.
I then thought would I think one and welcome
Or would I not.
I then concluded that I might be deceived

And it was a white butterfly
Which flew not only not but also
The white dog which ran
And they they were accomplished
And once in a while I would rather gather
Mushrooms even than roses if they were edible
Or at least what not.
I do not wish to say what I think
I concluded I would not name those.
Very often I could feel that a change in cares
Is a change in chairs and not only can and cares
But places
I felt that I could welcome in anticipation wishes
Not only which they do but where they do
How are our changes.
When they could fix titles or affix titles.
When this you see hear clearly what you hear.
Now just like that not just like that
Or they will enjoin and endanger
Damage or delight but which they crow
They have threatened us with crowing
Oh yes not yet.
I cannot think with indifference
Nor will they not want me
Do will they add but which is not
Where they could add would or they would or not
For which they for which fortunately
Make it be mine.
I have often thought of make it be mine.
Now I ask any one to hear me.

This is what I say.
A poem is torn in two
And a broom grows as well
And which came first
Grows as well or a broom
Of course any one can know which of two
This makes it no accident to be taught
And either taught and either fight or fought
Or either not either which either
May they be either one not one only alone.
Should it be thought gracious to be a dish
Of little only as they might mean curiously
That we heard them too
And this I mean by this I mean.
When I thought this morning to keep them so they will not tell
How many which went well
Not as a conclusion to anxious
Anxious to please not only why but when
So then anxious to mean. I will not now

STANZA XXII

Now I recount how I felt when I dwelt upon it.
I meant all of it to be not rather yes I went
It is not that now they do not care that I do
But which one will
They can not be thought nervous if they are left alone
Now then I will think of which went swimming.
It does make a difference how often they go
Or will they prepare that I know

I know this I know that I shall say so
Or may they choose an anagram
This one said this one.
If one we hurried for this one
Just when they did wish that it should be settled then
They could think let us go
Just when they will they can
All my dear or but which they can
Having been long ago not knowing what I felt
And now
It does make a difference that well enough a cow
Can be recognised now so then
If not twenty as ten
Or one enough without it then.
This that I may
I repeat I do not know what I felt then
Which they do which they do
Nor will they track it if they follow then
How are it is to do
A kite is a delight this I can do then
But not with then for which they allow them
This is the way not to end but to see when the beginning.
I like a moth in love and months
But they will always say the same thing when
They sing singing
I wish I could repeat as new just what they do
Or alike as they hear when they do not listen to every one
So she said it they but which they
She said the nest was empty but not so
The nest was empty that is to say not there

It was as if she looked alike
By which no one mean startled
Like that
I think I will begin and say everything not something
But not again and only again alike
Thank you for the touch of which they leave
He easily destroys my interest in may be they do but I doubt it
But not at all with which by nearly which time
But just as well heard
Why should he not say he did say that
And it was amusing.
And by and by not which they do
I now I do not know what I feel
So in extra inclusion.
What do I think when I feel.
I feel I feel they feel they feel which they feel
And so borrowed or closed they will they will win
How can any one know the difference between worry and win.
This is not the only time they think which they know
Or better not alright.
How can they eager either or and mend
She can mend it not very well between.
Of course he knows at what he does not only hear
Oblige me. I also oblige him. And think then.
Do I repeat I do not know what I do not see to feel which they
    hear
Oh yes

STANZA XXIII

When she meant they sent or a grievance
Was she meant that he went or a need of it henceforward
Was it with it that they meant that he sent or he thought
That they should not plainly have not bought
Or which they went to be naturally there
It is a pause in mistaken.
They could know that they would call
Or they would prefer it to before
On their account.
I should look if I saw
But she would send if she would intend to prefer
That they might cause it best and most.
It is not only which they go but when they go
Or if not said to send or say so
Now think how palpably it is known
That all she knows which when she goes
They look for him in place of that
Of which they are used or to be used
In preference
And so they halt more to partly do
Do or due or only dew or did you do it.
I could not favor leaves of trees to in any case
Place me to mine.
This is not what they care or for poetry.

Part Four

STANZA I

Who should she would or would be he
Now think of the difference of not yet.
It was I could not know
That any day or either so that they were
Not more than if they could which they made be
It is like this
I never knew which they may date when they say
Hurry not hurry I could not only not do it
But they prepare.
Let me think how many times I wished it.
It flattered me it flattered me it flattered me
And I was all prepared which they sent
Not only not why but where if they did not enjoy
Their place where they meant with them
And so they may be fitly retired.
This is what I saw when they went with them.
I could have been interested not only in what they said but in
    what I said.
I was interested not interested in what I said only in what I
    said.

I say this I change this I change this and this.
Who hated who hated what.
What was it that announced they will not mind it.
I do think often that they will remember me.
Now who remembers whom what not a room
No not a room.
And who did prepare which which vegetable very well
And might I not only feel it to be right to leave them to say
Yes any day it is because after which way
They shell peas and of the pea shell they make a soup to eat
    and drink
And they might not amount to calls upon them.
They were in place of only where they went
Nobody notices need I be not there only
But which they send it.
Not to think but to think that they thought well of them.
Here I only know that pumpkins and peas do not grow
Well in wet weather.
And they think kindly of places as well as people.
I should think it makes no difference
That so few people are me.
That is to say in each generation there are so few geniuses
And why should I be one which I am
This is one way of saying how do you do
There is this difference
I forgive you everything and there is nothing to forgive.
No one will pardon an indication of an interruption
Nor will they be kindly meant will be too or as a sound.
I am interested not only in what I hear but as if
They would hear

Or she may be plainly anxious.
How are ours not now or not as kind.
They could be plainly as she is anxious
Or for their however they do
Just as well and just as well not at all
How can you slowly be dulled reading it.
It is not which they went for there were dishes
It is not why they were here not with their wishes
Or accidentally on account of clover
I never manage to hammer but I did
In with all investigation
And now I now I now have a brow
Or call it wet as wet as it is by and by
I feel very likely that they met with it
Which in no way troubles them
Or is it likely to.
It did it a great deal of good to rub it

STANZA II

I come back to think everything of one
One and one
Or not which they were won
I won.
They will be called I win I won
Nor which they call not which one or one
I won.
I will be winning I won.
Nor not which one won for this is one.
I will not think one and one remember not.

Not I won I won to win win I one won
And so they declare or they declare
To declare I declare I declare I win I won one
I win in which way they manage they manage to win I won
In I one won in which I in which won I won
And so they might come to a stanza three
One or two or one two or one or two or one
Or one two three all out but one two three
One of one two three or three of one two and one

STANZA III

Secretly they met again
All which is changed is made they may be merry
For which they could in any regulation
Manage which they may have in any case a trial
Of when they do or sing sisters
And so much is taken for granted
In which appointment they color me
Or leave it as not in a glass or on the grass
They pass.
Not at all
For which no one is met in winning
They will be very well pleased with how they stand
Or which or to which or whither they repair
To change it to change it fairly
Or may they like all that they have
Let us think well of which is theirs.
Why do they not count
Count how do you count

There is no counting on that account
Because if there is which is not what I say
I will make it do any day to-day
Or not why
They allow me to apply for it
They call will they call by which they plan
I will not gain gain easier easily
One which one which not now.
Why do they like which they like or why not
It is often many or as much which they have seen
Seen is often very well said
I think I have no wish that they will come
With their welcome
Nor which they try not to do
In any case for which they formerly
Were not repaid.
They are readily not here.
Once more no one not one begins
This is the difference
Not it or argument
But which and when
They enfold not in unfold
Beware aware deny declare
Or and as much in told
They cannot be thought restless when they do come and go
Either one either say so.
I say I felt like that.
Once they came twice they went which one will do
Or which they like for them or will they do
What they ask them to do

I manage to think twice about everything
Why will they like me as they do
Or not as they do
Why will they praise me as they do
Or praise me not not as they do
Why will they like me and I like what they do
Why will they disturb me to disturb not me as they do
Why will they have me for mine and do they
Why will I be mine or which may they
For which may they leave it
Or is it not
I have thought or will they let
Them know the difference if they tell them so
Between let us not be wreckless or restless
Or by word of mouth
May they please theirs fairly for me.
Just why they lay with the land up.
Coming to see it so.
It was not once when they went away that they came to stay.
Why should all which they add be each
Each is a peach
Why may they be different and try to beside
Be all as all as lost
They do not hide in which way
Better call it mine.
Our ours is or made between alike
With which cakes bake cakes
And it makes cake or cakes polite
But if they all call not when they do
Who ought they try to be alike

Which or for which which they may do too.
I refuse I I refuse or do
I do I do I refer to refuse
Or what what do I do
This is just how they like what they send
Or how to refuse what is that
That they need to sound sound lend
Can you question the difference between lend.
Or not lend
Or not send
Or not leant
Or not sent
But neither is a neighbor.
A neighbor to be here
She may be he may be useful or not useful
When they did not come why did they not come here.
Believe me it is not for pleasure that I do it
Not only for pleasure for pleasure in it that I do it.
I feel the necessity to do it
Partly from need
Partly from pride
And partly from ambition.
And all of it which is why
I literally try not only not why
But why I try to do it and not to do it.
But if it is well-known it is well-known

STANZA IV

Mama loves you best because you are Spanish
Mama loves you best because you are Spanish
Spanish or which or a day.
But whether or which or is languish
Which or which is not Spanish
Which or which not a way
They will be manage or Spanish
They will be which or which manage
Which will they or which to say
That they will which which they manage
They need they plead they will indeed
Refer to which which they will need
Which is which is not Spanish
Fifty which vanish which which is not spanish.

STANZA V

I think very well of my way.

STANZA VI

May be I do but I doubt it.

STANZA VII

May be may be men.

STANZA VIII

A weight a hate a plate or a date
They will cause me to be one of three
Which they may or may be
May be I do but do I doubt it
May be how about it
I will not may be I do but I doubt it
May be will may be.

STANZA IX

How nine
Nine is not mine
Mine is not nine
Ten is not nine
Mine is not ten
Nor when
Nor which one then
May be not then
Not only mine for ten
But any ten for which one then
I am not nine
May be mine
Mine one at a time
Not one from nine
Nor eight at one time
For which they may be mine.
Mine is one time
As much as they know they like
I like it too to be one of one two

One two or one or two
One and one
One mine
Not one nine
And so they ask me what do I do
May they but if they too
One is mine too
Which is one for you
May be they like me
I like it for which they may
Not pay but say
She is not mine with not
But will they rather
Oh yes not rather not
In won in one in mine in three
In one two three
All out but me.
I find I like what I have
Very much.

STANZA X

That is why I begin as much

STANZA XI

Oh yes they do.
It comes to this I wish I knew
Why water is not made of waters
Which from which they well
May they be kind if they are so inclined.

This leads me to want to wonder about which they do
I feel that they shall be spared this
They will agree for which they know
They do not do or describe
Their own use of which they are not tried
Or most or mostly named to be where
They will not as willingly not declare
That they appeal but do not prefer a share
Of plainly when they will
It is this I wish any minute
Oh yes I wish do I I do wish any minute
For them for fortune or forlorn or well
Well what do you do either what do you do
But like it or not
This that they may think just think
She has put her hair up with hair pins
Or do or do not only just do not only think
Finally than this.
It might be worth any cost to be lost.
They like that which they did
He did he remembered not only that he did
Oh why should any one repine one at a time.
Curiously.
This one which they think I think alone
Two follow
I think when they think
Two think I think I think they will be too
Two and one make two for you
And so they need a share of happiness
How are ours about to be one two or not three.

This that I think is this.
It is natural to think in numerals
If you do not mean to think
Or think or leave or bless or guess
Not either no or yes once.
This is how hours stand still
Or they will believe it less
For it is not a distress yes
Which they may free to build
Not by a house but by a picture of a house
But no distress to guess.
For this they are reconciled.
I wish that they were known.
This which they permit they please.
Please may they not delight and reconcile
Could anybody continue to be
Made openly one to see
That it is very pleasant to have been
With me.
When this you see.
Once when they were very busy
They went with me.
I feel that it is no trouble
To tell them what to do
Nor either is it at all a trouble
To wish that they would do what I do.
This is well and welcome to mean
I mean I mean.
Think however they will be ready
To believe me.

Think well of me when this you see.
I have begun by thinking that it is mine
It is mine many often one at a time
In rhyme.
Of course in rhyme which is often mine
In time one at one time
And so I wish they knew I knew
Two and one is two.
This is any day one for you.
This which I explain is where any one will remain
Because I am always what I knew
Oh yes or no or so
Once when they went to stay
Not which not only once or twice yesterday.
This introduces a new thought as is taught.
I wish I exchanged will they exchange me
Not at all.
This is why they bought a ball.
To give it to them to be all
All which they keep and lose if they choose.
Think how can you be and beware
And constantly take care
And not remember love and shove
By design.
It is well to be well and be well and be welcome
Of course not to be made to be
Honorably four to three which they do.
This is how they think well of believing all of theirs
To have been known.
It is singular that they may not only succeed

But be successful.
How should they not speedily try
If they could or could not know
That I did it.
Which is why they are so quiet with applause
Or may be the cause
Of their waiting there
For their meal
If they had it.
It is very beautiful to be eight and late.
Why should any one be ready too
As well as not for and with you
Which they do.
See how one thing can mean another.
Not another one no not any not another one.
Or not any means not or may not might three to one.
That is what they say to play.
And which is white if they might
They will call that they spoke to her

STANZA XII

Just why they mean or if they mean
Once more they mean to be not only not seen
But why this beside why they died
And for which they wish a pleasure.

STANZA XIII

But which it is fresh as much
As when they were willing to have it not only

But also famous as they went
Not to complain but to name
Their understanding confined on their account
Which in the midst of may and at bay
Which they could be for it as once in a while
Please may they come there.
This is an autobiography in two instances

STANZA XIV

When she came she knew it not only
Not by name but where they came with them.
She knew that they would be while they went.
And let us think.
She knew that she could know
That a genius was a genius
Because just so she could know
She did know three or so
So she says and what she says
No one can deny or try
What if she says.
Many can be unkind but welcome to be kind
Which they agree to agree to follow behind.
Her here.
Not clearly not as no mistake
Those who are not mistaken can make no mistake.
This is her autobiography one of two
But which it is no one which it is can know
Although there is no need
To waste seed because it will not do

To keep it through perhaps it is as well
Not to belie a change of when they care
They mean I like it if she will do it
But they could not complain again.
Let me remember now when I read it through
Just what it is that we will do for you.
This is how they asked in a minute when
They had changed a pencil for a pen
Just as I did.
Often of course they were not welcomed there
When they meant to give it all they liked
Made many more beside beside
Which when they tried or cried
He could not have his way
Or care to please please
And prepare to share wealth and honors
Which if they or if they of if they
Had not had mine too.
More can they gain or complain
Of which announce pronounce a name
When they call this they feel
Or not at all a heel she changed all that
For them fair or at once they will change hair
For there or at once more than all at once
Whenever they can.
This makes no allowance
Now this is how they managed to be late or not.
When once in a while they saw angrily
Or impatiently yesterday
Or beguiling February.

They could so easily be thought to feel
That they would count or place all or kneel
For which they had been frightened not to do
They felt the same.
In which on no account might they have tried
To be remained to try why
Shall they be careful at all or not.
This is why they like me if they think they do
Or not which by the time they care I care
Or when where will they name me.
However tried however not or cried
She will be me when this you see.
And steadily or whether will they compel
Which is what I tell now.
This is a beginning of how they went at once
When I came there cannot they compare
No they cannot compare nor share
Not at all not in iniquity much which they engage
As once in a while perfectly.
All many so or say
But this or which they may
Believe me I say so.
I have not said I could not change my mind if I tried.
More than just once they were there.
All this is to be for me.

STANZA XV

I have thought that I would not mind if they came
But I do.

I also thought that it made no difference if they came
But it does
I also was willing to be found that I was here
Which I am
I am not only destined by not destined to doubt
Which I do.
Leave me to tell exactly well that which I tell.
This is what is known.
I felt well and now I do too
That they could not wish to do
What they could do if
They were not only there where they were to care
If they did as they said
Which I meant I could engage to have
Not only am I mine in time
Of course when all is said.
May be I do but I doubt it.
This is how it should begin
If one were to announce it as begun
One and one.
Let any little one be right.
At least to move.

STANZA XVI

Should they call me what they call me
When they come to call on me
And should I be satisfied with all three
When all three are with me
Or should I say may they stay

Or will they stay with me
On no account must they cry out
About which one went where they went
In time to stay away may be they do
But I doubt it
As they were very much able to stay there.
However may they go if they say so.

STANZA XVII

How I wish I were able to say what I think
In the meantime I may not doubt
Round about because I have found out
Just how loudly differently they do
They will they care they place
Or they do allow or do not bow now.
For which they claim no claim.
It is however that they find
That I mind
What they do when they do or when they do not do
It.
It is not only not kind not to mind
But I do do it.
This is how they say I share I care
I care for which share.
Any share is my share as any share is my share
Of course not not only not.
Of course I do which I of course do.
Once I said of course often

And now I say not of course often
It is not necessary any more

STANZA XVIII

She asked could I be taught to be allowed
And I said yes oh yes I had forgotten him
And she said does any or do any change
And if not I said when could they count.
And they may be not only all of three
But she may establish their feeling for entertainment
She may also cause them to bless yes
Or may be or may they be not
Made to amount to more than may they.
This is what they do when they say may they
It is often that it is by this that they wish this
When they will value where they went when they did
They will also allow that they could account for it
Or might they not only not choose
It is often whichever they were fortunate and not fortunate
To be for which they may in all they like
This is what they use
I have thought I have been not only like this
Or they may please or not please
Which for instance and forsaken and beside which
They will oh please they will
Not only when they can as if allowed
It is all of it which they know they did.
This is what I say two to belie

One to date and decry and no one to care
And she made as rashly careful as not
When they could think twice just the same.
This is at any time when they do not often see them
Theirs when they went away
Not only not included but why not included
Only they will not agree to permanence
Not more than twice as much.
Very much as they say aloud
Will you be back in a minute or not.
Let me think carefully not think carefully enough
By which I mean that they will not please them so
Not even if they know that they went too
So it is gracious once gracious to be well as well
As when they like liked it.
This is what it is made to be able
To need whichever they could be well-furnished
All the same three now.
This could if it could lead it if it did
To a cow. Think of it.
This is what I return to say
If I never do nor I ever do
How can it be so if it is true
Or just true as through or you
Made which they like as much.
Now commence again to be used to their
Saying that their cousin was one
Who felt that it was not a name
To which they meant to think well of them.
This is however how they do not deny

That they will not try to care
To leave it there from time to time
At once
It is very well known that they are indifferent not to wishes.
May she be sought out.
I wish to say that any case of a failure
Is what they were spared.
I wish to think that they will place
Much as more than they wish
As their changing it not only for them.
Could any one influence any one
One and one.
Or not.
If not why not.
Or if not would they not be more than
If they were changing which way any one
In which way any one would not need one
If not one and one.
Or not by them.
It is made why they do if they call them.
They could recognise the sun if there was another one
Or not at all by me
When this you see.
Or not in an exchange there might
Be only why they should.
Be this as it might.
She could be pleased to
Be not only with them but by them
As well as for them
Which makes it at a meaning

And their equal to delight and plight.
Which of which one.
I had many things to think about quite often
They will call me to say I am displeased to-day
Which they may in adding often.
It is not why they knew that it is
Not only why they went but if they went when they went.
By this time they are as often with us
But we think of leaving them with others.
We wonder about it.
And they will not know if we go.

STANZA XIX

I could go on with this.

STANZA XX

Should however they be satisfied to address me
For which they know they like.
Or not by which they know that they are fortunate
To have been thought to which they do they might
Or in delight that they manage less
For which they call it all.
This is what I say fortunately
I think I will welcome very well in a minute
There nicely known for which they take
That it is mine alone which may mean
I am surely which they may suggest
Not told alone but may as is alone
Made as likely for which no matter

As more than which is lost
Recommend me to sit still.
As more often they could not see him
Have it to be or not as not
It not made it not not having it
Should they fancy worshipping
Worshipping me is what they easily may
If they come to think still that they think it still
Just why not if not
I have changed forty-nine for fifty
And may she be meant.
Or would it be a nuisance to like no one
Or better not if not only not to change
Change it should stop with not
Do you feel how often they do go
Go and so and which and met and if
And they are riding
There are so many things to ride.
And water and butter
And may they be no chief to me
I am not only not chiefly but only
Not with care.
And so much as they ever think.
Remain to remain and not remain if not remain mine.
I have abused not leaving it not following it out
I also have not which may they not which they plan.
All of which is in why they used
To use me and I use them for this.
This too we too or not to go.
I often think do they sound alike

Who hates that or a hat not I.
Now I will readily say not I
But which they read to ready
Or say not I may day or say
Not blindly for caution or which or what
What about.
This is how I however remain
Retain is considered whatever they gain
I gain if in the main they make plain
Just what I maintain if I use a fruit.
Should just when this be any chance.
Better why often.
I have thought why she went and if she went he went.
No one knows the use of him and her
And might they be often just tried
May they mean then fiercely
Should it chance to cover them not enough
I mean a hat or head
And also what a chair
And beside what beside pride
And all at once tried to believe me
Coming as if it could be entitled
One which they won.
One two.
I often think one two as one and one.
One one she counted one one and this made
Economy not only which but of which
They will not kneel of which they do.
I could be just as well obliged.
Finally I move from which

You may deduce the sun shone
By this time
Out loud
All of which may be able to be
Do I make a mistake
And if I do do you not at all either or
This time it should not have followed
Or not either to do it.
Little by little they engage not to change
Or different as it is they might if they should
But they will manage to indifferently relieve
More of which they could alight and aloud.
It is very foolish to know that they might alight
Not only do.
This which they feel they must discourage
And everything I say.
I will tell how once in a while

STANZA XXI

I know that twenty seven had been had
For which they know no name
But our equality may indubitably spell well
For it or for which or for might it be
That it is a change to think well
Of not only when but might they be just where
They will care
Now fancy how I need you.
I have thought which they meant as willing
It is often a disappointment to dispense without

They will cool not which but very most
Well as welcome without.
She said she knew what I meant too
He too.
Although although allowed out loud.
As if they could remember where there
And there where.
Should she join robust or not
Or fortunately for it as they are not without
It is easily eaten hot and luke warm and cold
But not without it.
Could it be thought that I could once be here
Which if they will may they not
I have heard it well enough to know
That he has not only not been mistaken yet again.
While will they now.
Oh yes while will they now
You should never be pleased with anything
If so they will crowd
But if they crowd or yes if they crowd
Which is it which if they may seat them.
I often feel well when I am seated seating them or not so
I go to remain to walk and what
Always when when is it.
It is often however they are bright.
She could often say however they may say
You always have to remember say and not so.
It is always not only not foolish
To think how birds spell and do not spell well
And how could it do birds and words

I often say so not at all amount.
All who should think season did not mean what
What is it.
I have been and have been amounted to it.
When they come in and come in and out.
Naturally it is not.
Or however not a difference between like and liked.

STANZA XXII

I should not know why they said so.

STANZA XXIII

I cannot hope again if they could mean which they liked.

STANZA XXIV

It is easy to grow ours more.
Or for which they will need a place to be
They could thank if not think that they arrange
In a way would they be angry in a way
If they could more which when they gather peas
They feel that it is not right to pay
Nor which if they nor which if they stay there.
Who need share stay there with stay away
Who will decline publicly
What is it if they will wish
Or be for which they beguile when they wish
Or may be not for which they may be spoken
It does not bother me to not delight them

They should fancy or approve fancy
They could call or may they for which will they might
But not only be the time but if which they manage.
It is in partly a reason that they feel well
Nor might they be more enclosed.
Fortunately they feel that it is right
To not give it giving it
As they do them for curls.
It is not often that they are always right
It is not often that they are always right
But which aggression or a guess
Or please addition or please a question.
Or please or please or please
Or and a foil of near and place and which nature
Will they plan to fit it to not in a point.
I wish no one the difference between a point and place
Oh yes you do oh do you.
This which I do or for intend to know
They could or call or if it is a place
In this place the sun which is not all
Is not so warm as told if it is not cold
But very warm which if favorably it is.
I could if I knew refuse to do it.
Or just when they feel like it they try
Beside which if they surround my home
They come to stay and leave it as they like.
Not only not because.
Wish if vegetables need the sun
Or wish if not only not the sun but none
Also wish if they wish that they will size alike

And only if which if a wish which they will oblige
Not only necessary but they think it best.
This which I reflect is what they like to do
They like me to do
Or but or well or do be well to do
For them to like to do if I like what I do
Enormously.
Fancy what you please you need not tell me so
I wish to go or if I do I wish to go
I have often been interested in how they forget to go
Also I have been interested in if they wish to go
I have been better able to determine.
Not only however but whichever they would like
If it were partly told
That she Madame Roux is never yet quite through
But which cannot annoy because I like to try
To see why will she be here
It makes a change in faces
Her face always can change seen near or far
Or not at all or partly far.
It is not partly as they can share
Why should it be like whom.
I think I know the share
Share and share alike is alone
And not when in integrally in a way.
She could often be made sympathetic in a way a day.
It might however be she seen to be all
They feel more than they could
In point of sympathy of expression.
Now when I should think of them of this.

He comes again they come in she can come to come in.
All this is why they like but remember that for me
I am to tell not only well but very well
Why I shall easily be for all to me.
This is the reason.
I have been not only not forgetting but not only.
They will call it a chance.
Because of this may be because of this.
Which not only will but is me
For me to me in me not only not be
Not only not be how do you like not only not be
They will be satisfied to be satisfactory.
Now not only not but will it be their appointment
To come when they said they would.
I said I would tell
Very well what is it that they plan to carry
Of course they plan to carry
How should it be better to put not any blue but that
Not any blue but that and change the mind
The ear and always any obligation.
Once more think twice of that.
It is very difficult to plan to write four pages.
Four pages depend upon how many more you use.
You must be careful not to be wasteful.
That is one way of advancing being wasteful
It use up the pages two at a time for four
And if they come to and fro and pass the door
They do so.
This is my idea of how they play
Play what play which or say they plan to play which

Which is in union with whichever
They could be thought to be caught
Or planned next to next nearly next to one time
At one time it was very favorably considered
That they would oblige them to go anywhere.
Remember how we could not disturb them
It is very important not to disturb him
It is also important to remember this
Not if they disturb him
But really will they disturb him
I often do I not often think it is time to follow to begin
They could establish eight or arrange
This is not why they please or add as carelessly
They will have no use for what they said.
Now I wish all possibly to be in their shuddering
As to why if they came in and out
If they came in and out
What is the use of union between this with this.
They will add any word at most.
If she said very much a little or not at all
If she said very much or not at all
If she said a little very much or not at all
Who is winning why the answer of course is she is.
When I say that I know all of the might she be mine
She is it is particularly to care
To make it do she offers it as a compromise
To have been needed about I have not only
Not changed my mind.
Now let us think not carelessly
Not all about not allowed to change or mind.

Mind what you say.
I say I will not be careful if I do
I also say I should say what I do
I also do have a place in any antedated rose.
A rose which grows. Will they like that.
She will like that.
We have decided that only one dahlia is beautiful
That salads are not necessary
And that she has been very kind about pansies.
How can you change your mind.
This is what they know as collection.
A collection is why they place it here.
I often think how celebrated I am.
It is difficult not to think how celebrated I am.
And if I think how celebrated I am
They know who know that I am new
That is I knew I knew how celebrated I am
And after all it astonishes even me.

Part Five

STANZA I

If I liked what it is to choose and choose
It would be did it matter if they chose and choose
But they must consider that they mean which they may
If to-day if they find that it went every day to stay
And what next.
What is it when they wonder if they know
That it means that they are careful if they do what they show
And needless and needless if they like
That they care to be meant
Not only why they wonder whether they went
And so they might in no time manage to change
For which which fortune they invent or meant
Not only why they like when they sent
What they mean to love meant.
It is this why they know what they like.
I like to have been remembered as to remember
That it meant that they thought when they were alike
As if they meant which they will undergo to choose
In which they may remain as little as they claim
In which not is it you

But which it is it is not without you
That they knew you and so forth.
This may be mine at night.
Which does it mean to care.
Not only why they liked but just as if they liked
Not only what they meant but why they will not.
This is what there is not or yet.
Not to continue to do their best yet.
Think however I came to know it all.
I often offer them the ball at all
This which they like when this I say
May they be called to play once in a way of weight
Or either our roses or their cake
I wish I had not mentioned which
It is that they could consider as their part.
Now then I had forgotten how then
Nor made it please away a weight
Oh yes you like it
Or if not for what if now and then
Without them it is often meant to be mine.
Let me say how they changed apart alike.

STANZA II

If you knew how do you very well I thank you
Or if you knew how do you do how do you
Or if not that changes more to many
And may be they do or not if not why.
This is how it is that it does not make any difference
To please them or not or not

Or not to not please them or oh yes yes.
They could should they under any circumstance
Understand differ or differs.
It is why they wondered if they liked
What indeed makes no difference
As they manage
To relieve plunders and blunders
Any one is often thought susceptible.
Or which one wishes.
Now I have wandered very far.
From my own fire side.
But which they knew in a wonder.
It is a wonder that they like it.
I have often thought that she meant what I said.
Or how do you this about that.
Or if at any time.
It had been not only not remembered
I depend upon him I depend upon them.
Of or how they like.
This what I say makes me remember that.
That if it did
Which may just as you said
Or which may be
If they managed it
Or by the time they did.
This is however just how many are alike.
Once upon a time who will be left to rain
Or like it as much as ever
Or even more than that if they like it.
They must be often thought to be just as careful

As not to give them give anything away.
However how many do like to.
This is not what I meant by what I said
It should be that I think that it might do
If I made it do
I also think that I should not say
That they know which way
They could arrange to go and say
That they will not stay if not
If not what do they like alike
Or as much as just yet.
I could often be caught liking it
Oh yes I could
And then it may not only if they say so.
Oh yes only not yes.
In just this way they went as they may
I have refused went and went as much.
I also have refused whatever they went
But if wherever they went.
Not one in any two
Or just arise or if not only not to like.
It may not be alright.
When they thought how often about a wall.
When they thought how often about a wall.

STANZA III

Just when they wish wish
Or will they or must they be selfish
To not do you should not do not do

Not as if not to to to do
There that is better.

STANZA IV

I like any two numbers more than any two numbers before
Or not.
But if it had been alright to be bright.
Could I have been bright before or not.
I wonder if I could have been bright before or not.
Not only why they do but if they do what I like
If I do what I like.
I could not nor can I remember
Whether if they were there if they were there to care
May be they could be wondering if it were like
If it were like it as it is
As it is if they meant only which
Whenever it is by this time
Of course no difference makes no difference at all.
I wish to think about everything anything if I do.
Or by the time easily
Or not only why they should.
Or please believe.
That they mean what they mean by that.
If not why should no one mind what they say.

STANZA V

Please believe that I remember just what to do
Oh please believe that I remember just what to do
Or please believe that I do remember just what to do

And if I remember just what to do
There will not only be that reason but others
Which at one time.
I like what I have not prepared before of course not.
As fast as not so fast
Not that it does not make any difference.
This is what they like what I say.

STANZA VI

This one will be just as long
As let it be no mistake to know
That in any case they like what they do
If I do what I do I do too
That is to say this conclusion is not with which.
It may be just as well known
Do you change about mutton and onions or not.
This is why they sleep with a ball in the mouth
If not what is there to doubt.
I have forgotten what I meant to have said ahead.
Not at all forgotten not what.
It is not whatever not is said
Which they may presume to like
If at no time they take any pains
Not to like it.
This is how I remember however.
Anybody not anybody can remember however but it does.
Not make any difference in any way.
This is what I wish to kindly write.
How very well I will at night

As well as in the day light.
I could just as well remember what I saw
Or if not I could just as well remember
What I saw when I could.
The thing I wish to tell
Is that it makes no difference as well
As when there is this not this not to tell
To tell well or as well.
I have not thought why I should wish beside
Coming again as coming again.
They could write three to one
Or not two to one but which is not which
If they ask more than any fourteen.
Fourteen is however they like but not for me.
I am very capable of saying what I do.
I wish that they could not wish which nor do they.
I know what I say often so one tells me.
Or if not I could not look again.
Might it be whichever it is
It is not my custom not only to think of a whole thing.
Does it make any difference which one they decide
Of course it does of course it does.
Alright let us think everything.
I have begun again to think everything.

STANZA VII

Now should or should not if they call with it
That I could not not only hear but see
Say when with spitting cavalry

She tears all where with what may be not now
They could be called to hurry call or hear or hair
Or there
Not only with nor welcome
May they come and climb a vine
In place of chairs in place of chairs in place of chairs.
I could have thought I would think what with
What not not with only that
It is just as much noise as said
Or if not only which I cannot come again to combine
Not only fairly well but mounted.
I do not need the word amounted
Oh not at all
He knows when she came here
For which they may in all which all which called
Perhaps enchain perhaps not any name
For theirs will come as used
By this it is not only I mean
I mean I mean is always said again.
Remember what I said it is not just the same
Or not with only stretched.
In a little while he meant to perceive
For which they may or may not do
Do believe that I will say it used to be like that.
I wish to well assure it did not use to be like that
Not only that it did I did I did and did or do
Which may they come to for which they knew you
They knew who knew you
Every little while I often smile
And all which may come which they will approve

And not only not soften
But just as fairly often
May they not come to say what they can do
I do very much regret to keep you awake
Because you should be asleep
But even so it is better to stay
And hear me say that is right here
What not only which they care
This may be made a reason why
They will be welcome to arrive and cry
They could do which they care.
Now to come back to how it is not all alike
Since after all they first
Since after all they were first
Best and most.
Now listen often cautiously
Best and most is seen to sweeten
Often often it is eaten
Much which much which much they do
Come and do and come for you
Did I not tell you I would tell
How well how well how very well
I love you
Now come to think about how it would do
To come to come and wish it
Wish it to be well to do and you
They will do well what will they well and tell
For which they will as they will tell well
What we do if we do what if we do
Now think how I have been happy to think again

That it is not only which they wish
It is as I have said a resemblance
To have forgotten as many times they came
That is to say we said
This which I said which I said this.
I said that it did not make any difference
And it did make this difference
As it made it made it do.
This which I mentioned made not only why but often
Now I have lost the thread of how they came to be alike.
Not only why if not but with their cause
Of course their cause of course because they do
I had been certain I would a little explain
Which can they do.
When I look down a vista I see not roses but a farm
That is to say the fields after hay
Are ploughed after hay
Not on the day
But just after the day
Like alike when it is chosen.
I wish never to say choose I choose
Oh not at all not while they like
Not while I like alike but do they
They may be often not declared as mine
For which I can not very well think well
Because just now I do not think well
Of at all.
She may be right to think that the sun
Not only does not fade but makes it less faded.
She may be right she often is always

This is what I said I would say
I say it as well as ever naturally
Because with which they would investigate
That they could not take a chance
Not to not to not to make no mistake
Not which at once to do.
It is often however they like
That they make it do.
I refuse ever to number ducks.
Because I know by weight how eight are eight.
Oh yes I do.
And a stanza too or a stanza two.
How do you do very well I thank you

STANZA VIII

I wish now to wish now that it is now
That I will tell very well
What I think not now but now
Oh yes oh yes now.
What do I think now
I think very well of what now
What is it now it is this now
How do you do how do you do
And now how do you do now.
This which I think now is this.

STANZA IX

A stanza nine is a stanza mine.
My stanza is three of nine.

STANZA X

I have tried earnestly to express
Just what I guess will not distress
Nor even oppress or yet caress
Beside which tried which well beside
They will not only will not be tried.
It is not trying not to know what they mean
By which they come to be welcome as they heard
I have been interrupted by myself by this.
This may be which is not an occasion
To compel this to feel that that is so
I do not dearly love to liven it as much
As when they meant to either change it or not
I do not change it either or not.
This is how they like to do what they like to do.
I have thought often of how however our change
That is to say the sun is warm to-day because
Yesterday it was also warm
And the day before it was not warm
The sun as it shone was not warm
And so moreover as when the sun shone it was not warm
So yesterday as well as to-day
The sun when it shone was warm
And so they do not include our a cloud
Not at all it had nothing to do with a cloud
It had not to do with the wind
It had not to do with the sun
Nor had it to do with the pleasure of the weather either.
It had to do with that this is what there had been.

It is very pleasant that it is this that it should have been
And now that it is not only that it is warmer
Now very well there is often that they will
Have what they look when they look there or there
To make a mistake and change to make a mistake and change
To have not changed a mistake and to make a mistake and
    change.
Change the prophecy to the weather
Change the care to their whether they will
Nothing now to allow
It is very strange that very often
The beginning makes it truly be
That they will rather have it be
So that to return to be will they be
There will they be there with them
I should often know that it makes a difference not to look
    about
Because if to do they that is is it
Not which it makes any difference or
But just what with containing
They need or made so surrounded
In spite of in a delay of delayed
It is often very changed to churn
Now no one churns butter any more.
That is why that is where they are here.
I wish I had not mentioned it either.
This whole stanza is to be about how it does not make any
    difference.
I have meant this.
Might it be yes yes will it

Might it not be as much as once having it
Might it not only be allowed
And if not does not it bring back
Or bring back what is it
If they bring it back not for me
And if it brings it back for me
Or if it brings it back for me
So and so further than if.
It is easy to be often told and moved
Moved may be mad of sun and sun of rain
Or if not not at all.
Just when they should be thought of so forth.
What they say and what they do
One is one and two is two
Or if not two who.

STANZA XI

I feel that this stanza has been well-known.

STANZA XII

Once when they do not come she does not come
Why does she not come.
She does not come because if she does not come
Not only this.
They may be thought and sought
But really truly if she need to
But which they make in which and further more.
It is not by the time that they could be alone.
What is the difference if he comes again to come here

Or to come here to go there to them
Or which they do which they do well
Or which they do not do well
Or more than which they do not do well

STANZA XIII

There may be pink with white or white with rose
Or there may be white with rose and pink with mauve
Or even there may be white with yellow and yellow with blue
Or even if even it is rose with white and blue
And so there is no yellow there but by accident.

STANZA XIV

Which would it be that they liked best
But to return to that it makes no difference.
Which would make no difference
Of course it makes a difference
But of course it makes a difference
And not only just now.
Whenever I return to this it is dull
And not by what I do
Or if by what I do
It is this that they like that I like.
I have wished to think about what to do
I do not have to wish to think about what I do
Nor do I wish to have to think about what they do not do
Because they are about out loud.
After all what is a garden.
A garden is a place in which

They must be in which
They are there and these.
This is not what to say to-day.
I have wished to be as this.
And I have and am so I said I wished.
What could they use they could use
What could they either use
They could either use or use
If it is usual or is it usual
To be usually there.
It does not make any difference
That which they liked they knew
Nor could it make any difference to use two.
After it was known to be is it as they knew
Think well of think of a difference
Or think well of think well of a difference.
They may be they may be there may be hours of light.
Light alright the little birds are audacious
They cannot kill large barn yard fowl.
How often have I seen them and they were right
How often have I seen them and they were not able to delight
In which they do.
It is not often necessary to look to see.
Not often necessary to look to see.
How easily she may may be there
Or how easily easily declare
Which they may be able to share
That they may may they bear this.
Or may they bear that.
I wish I could be rich in ways to say how do you do

And I am.
Or not only when they may venture to not remember to
    prepare
Not only when they do
If not as not in which arrangement they concur
It is might it be easily mine.
I will not be often betrayed by delayed
Not often
Nor when they cherish which not often
They will come come will they come
Not only by their name
They could however much if however much
Not only which they come and cause because
Because of all the rest.
It is not only that they manage mine.
Will they be mine if not only when
Do they cover to color when
If they color when with then
Or color cover with whether clover
Can cover a color with clover then.
It is not safe to use clover as a name
When thinking of balsam and balsam is not only not the same
But not now the same.
In spite of which they tell well
That they were right.

STANZA XV

I have not come to mean
I mean I mean

Or if not I do not know
If not I know or know
This which if they did go
Not only now but as much so
As if when they did which
If not when they did which they know
Which if they go this as they go
They will go which if they did know
Not which if they which if they do go
As much as if they go
I do not think a change.
I do think they will change.
But will I change
If I change
I may change.
Yes certainly if I may change.
It is very foolish to go on
Oh yes you are.
How could one extricate oneself from where one is
One is to be one is to extricate whichever
They may be not for this any for an occasion
Of which they are remarkable as a remembrance.

STANZA XVI

Be spared or may they justly say
That if that if they will after all it will
Be just as if they say
Not only not they might but they will do
This they will do or if this will they do if

They will not only if they will not only will
But if they will they will do this.
For this thing to think it a thing to think well.
Having found that not only theirs or rather that
That it did make a difference that they knew
Now they know but none only which now they know
They know this.
They did if they had known not only know this.
But which may they be known this which they wish.
I had no doubt that it a difference makes
If there is doubt if money is about
I also know but which I know or worry
If when they give and take they give in a hurry
But which of which of this there cannot be a doubt
That if that could if it could come to be about
That if they did know this just as they had
Will as they had will to be worried still
Or not only not necessary a necessity.
I wish to say correctly this
I wish to say that any day the roads a roads
Will they be roads they say when if
In not only not obliged to leave it well
But which if they can be to recollect
Oh yes not only which to gather to collect
They do try so to have the wind to blow
Not only not here but also not there.
This which I wish to say is this
There is no difference which they do
Nor if there is not or a difference which
Now which as which we should not add to now

No not indeed
I wish to say that they could eat as well
As if when now they heard when now
They had it had it when now
This is what which I did do say
That certainly to-day to hear to get to-day
That which as yet to-day is a relief to-day
Oh yes it is a relief to-day but not
Not without further ought or ought.
Now they need mine as theirs
But when they heard refuse a difference
Not any one has ours now.
Not in that way oh no not in that way
Come thought come thought of me.
I am always thinking that if in their way
If in their way it is if in their way
Insist if in their way
So could in of course shine but not wires shine
They may complete this time will will this time
There or they could in no doubt think.
This which I do I know or only only say say so.
This which has happened is my sand my sand my said
Of course my said why will they manage this wish.
Now I wish to tell quite easily well
Just what all there is of which to tell
Immediately increases hold as told
Or may they better be better be known
I have thought in thinking that is walking
That the way to be often more than told in walking
Is after all as much as told in walking

That they as well will be just not to have
Theirs be theirs now. It is not only this a change
But theirs might be
I have lost the thread of my discourse.
This is it it makes no difference if we find it
If we found it
Or which they will be bought if they worry or not
Without which if they begin or yet began
May they be equalled or equal in amount
When there is a doubt but most of course
Of course there is no doubt.
I have said that if a cuckoo calls
When moneys in a purse in my own pocket
It means wealth
Moreover if the cuckoo to make sure
Comes near then there can be no doubt if doubt there be
But not by this to see but worry left for me
Makes no doubt more.
Does it may be it does but I doubt it.
After this I think it makes no difference what their characters
    are
What you have oh yes I thank you
What I have is made to be me for mine
I should not please to share oh no of course.
But not to go into that is not in question
Not when no bird flutters
Even if they yet may be yet here
This which I think is of this kind around
They will be called to tall
No one is tall who has not all

They have not only all
Which is which they may
They say August is not May
But how say so if in the middle they may not know.
Think how well to like everything.
I wish to say that I made no mistake in saying any day.

STANZA XVII

I feel that often in a way they link
Not if they should and shouted
But may they mind if which they call they went
Or not only not of course
But not only welcome more.
There is no doubt that often not alone
There has been a waste who quiets a waste
But which they will they wish
I say yes readily steadily do either do
But which they will in theirs to theirs deny
Not to have been ruffled by success
Or either or they may not be inclined
To gather more than give giving is foolish
Spending is a pleasure gathering is making
Bettering is no delight they like to light
Of course they like to light it.
They like not to explain but add a day.
Very likely to take away if to take away
Before it was of importance not to go now
But not now.
I wish to think to refuse wishes

Also not to refuse trees or please
Not to refuse bells or wells
Not to refuse does or could
Not refuse made to be with which to go
Made to be minding others leave it so
What I have said is this I am satisfied
I have pride I am satisfied
I have been worried I will be worried again
And if again is again is it.
Not to be interested in how they think
Oh yes not to be interested in how they think
Oh oh yes not to be interested in how they think.

STANZA XVIII

I could make at it most or most at it.

STANZA XIX

I felt that I could not have been surprised
Or very much as they do
If it is that I remember what
What do they if they never dot
But which is not warranted by what
What will they have as is if not to mean
It is not difficult to either stand
Which on account if without flavor
Shall they be shamed with generation
They may leave it half as well.
I wish to remind everybody nobody hears me
That it makes no difference how they do

What they do
Either by our or either by at all
This is why no doubt it followed better
To have no one eight or eat before.
This which I think is this.
I think I could do not without at night
Not only not a moon
May they be told as well
This what is what I do may come
Not to present which when they mean they come
Or not only for it.
All this is of no interest
If indeed there is no right
No right to keep it well away
Just when they do or either not delight
May they collect or recollect their way
Not only which but whether they may plan
I wish to say I do not not remember every day
Not I
Not even when I try or why
Not even well not even very well
Not even not without which not even more
Should or just yet recollect
That they that is not there
Even not there much as it is much allowed
For them to come for them to come.

STANZA XX

I wish to say that who could
Or just as well as welcome
This which I know now I know followed how
How did it follow of course it followed how did it follow
Not only no tide is perplexed
But they will perplex less in usefulness
Useful or noon may well be left to right
Should they not care for
What will they care for
I like to think how every one thought less
Of what is this when even is it known
Mine is what is it mine is
Shall they not often be not only made a way
Make and made made stayed.
This which I have remembered is made known
Shall they should always know
Or less the same
They may be often thought made quite well.
She could in which instance for instance
Leave love alone.
They could call dears early years
Or not only their care but with their care
May she be well to manage more or less
However much it is however much alike
This which I know is what I know
What I know is not what I say so
Because I wish to draw drawers and drawing
Or may they even call and talk well and welcome.

Think how often it does not change and mind
They are not glad to sit and find
Find it nearly out.
It is not nearly nearly so
It is not fairly nearly nearly so.
For which it is not often not only better that they like
In which in reason.
In reading a long book which I look
In reading and reading a long gay book
I look.
This is what I see with my eyes.
I see that I could have been made the same
By which by in which name the same
They may include in tries and tires
And feel or felt may it not it inspire or inspires
They could in no doubt know.
I cannot well remember whether it was yesterday that I wrote
Or if yes of course naturally I should
Wait another day.
Or have waited another day.

STANZA XXI

I wish always to go on with when
When they meant then.

STANZA XXII

Not only by their hope I feel so
May they be not with all a wish to know
That they will well declare to do so

But which they will as much as all delight
For this in their way one way one way to know
That it is never gladly to be so
In which it is in often which it is
As they will not be made with them
To be here with them
A stanza can be bought and taught
If not why if not will they or may be will they not
It is not often that they narrowly rejoin
Or as the way or as their way
They will be finally as their way
May they be finally as their way.
This which I know I know that I can do
Or not if not if I can do if not
If not at all they were not only not to wait awhile
Or which if which is better than only not better
It is possible that only if they did and could know
They would happen to arrange that they could not be
Which they had thought and taught
Or meant to teach or meant
Happily it is sent.
This makes no hope of better than it should
They were pleased that they were well well meant
Or left to have no other as it were
Left finally for it.
I wish to announce stanzas at once.
What is a stanza
When I say that often as a day
I feel that it is best to know the way
That if upon the road where if I went

I meant to feel that is if as if sent
The if I came and went
Or well what is it if it makes it do
Not only which if not only all or not alike
But it is it is just like Italy
And if it is just like Italy
Then it is as if I am just like it
That is make it be.
There is no necessity to make it be if it is
Or there is not any real making it do too
Because if which it is or just to know
To know and feel and may be tell
Is all very well if no one stealing past
Is stealing me for me.
Oh why oh why may they count most
If most and best is all
Of course it is all or all at all
Most and best met from there to here
And this is what I change.
Of course I change a change
Better than not.
This that I must not think I do
Which is to do but met and well
Well when I like when they like.
There is no hope or use in all.
Once again to try which of a choice.
Theirs is no sacreder in sacrament
For finally in disposes
When they plan.
This which I may do.

I wish once more to begin that it is done
That they will fasten done to done
Or more nearly care to have to care
That they shall will and may be thought
To need most when
When whenever they need to mean
I mean I mean.
This which I do or say is this.
It is pleasant that a summer in a summer
Is as in a summer and so
It is what after all in feeling felt
May they not gain.
Once again I went once or more often than once
And felt how much it came to come
That if at once of one or two or one.
If not only if not one or one
One of one one of one which is what
What it is to win and find it won
This is not what I thought and said
I thought that the summer made it what it is
Which if I said I said I said it
And they were using used to as a chance
Not only to be which if none it was
It was used for which for which they used for it.
I wish I could say exactly that it is the same.
I will try again to say it if not then
Then not alike there is no then alike
There is no then not like alike and not alike
But that.
This which I mean to do again.

STANZA XXIII

Often as I walk I think

STANZA XXIV

But this does not mean that I think again.

STANZA XXV

Which may be which if there
This which I find I like
Not if which if I like.
This which if I like.
I have felt this which I like.
It is more then.
I wish to say that I take pleasure in it

STANZA XXVI

A stanza may make wait be not only where they went
But which they made in theirs as once awhile
May they be close to wishing or as once
May they not be for which they will
As wish may be more reconciled for them
In which respect they will or so
Or better so or may they not be meant
All which they plan as theirs in theirs and joined
Or not be left to rather wish
But which they will in no way
Or not in any or rather in any way
Theirs which they leave as much

Or better not or better not all alone
Not if they call in early or to care
Or manage or arrange or value
Or relieve or better like
Or not at all as nearly once compared
Or made it to be gained
Or finally as lost
Or by them not detained
Or valued as equally
Or just as much established by their lost
Or finally as well prepared
Or may they not without them which they cherish
Not only by them but by the time
Not only will they but it is one to like
Or manage just as well as if
As if they planned theirs which they know
Or in as well as do
Would they be more contained
To leave it not for them
By the time that all of it is better
Once more to have it do it now
As moon-light
Naturally if they do not look or go
They will be always there or not at all
Not why they went to manage as it is
Felt which they like or as a place to go
They could feel well they went
They could not partly show
Just which or why it is
Not only as it is more than they thought.

They will arrange to claim
It is not only which they will or know
Or changing for it partly as they if.
If it is only made to be no delight
Not only as they finish which as well as they began
Or either not to on account
Not only why they will
Or often not often not often not
It is of more than will they come and may
May they be here if after joining
They will partly in at once declare
Now in no haste if not now in no haste
As just when well supported they need it
Not only if they use but do they use
And might they not be well not be well inclined
To have not which they manage or amuse
Not which they fragrantly and always now
If when they know mint can they not know
Not often will they better have than either or
Not only when they share
But even when they share
There is no mending when they delight
When they delight to have or may they share
It is partly this which is not only mine
Or not not only mine
Or will they not
Or will it be meant to attend
Or follow rather than not follow now
Just and in that way or rather not to say
They will not happen to be often disturbed

Or rather not to have or love it so
They should not can or will not do their way
Of better not to like or indeed may it matter
Not even not at all
And so marking it as once and only once
In which in which case
May they be mine in mine.

STANZA XXVII

It is not easy to turn away from delight in moon-light.
Nor indeed to deny that some heat comes
But only now they know that in each way
Not whether better or either to like
Or plan whichever whether they will plan to share
Theirs which indeed which may they care
Or rather whether well and whether
May it not be after all their share.
This which is why they will be better than before
Makes it most readily more than readily mine.
I wish not only when they went

STANZA XXVIII

To come back to a preparation
Or fairly well know when
It is as much as if I thought or taught.
Taught could be teaching
Made in which is strange if strange
That they will otherwise know
That if indeed in vanishes

Theirs where they do not even do
What after all may be which may they call
They may call me.

STANZA XXIX

A stanza should be thought
And if which may they do
Very well for very well
And very well for you.

STANZA XXX

This is when there are wishes

STANZA XXXI

Of course he does of course he likes what he did
But would he mind if he liked what he did
Would he like it better if it did not matter
Not only if he liked what he did
But often just as well
If he did not share in seeing it there
And so might they not only be so
But which if once more they were readily
But which they like.
In there as only as a chance
They could control not only which they liked.
I think very well of changing
I do think very well of changing this for that.
I not only would not choose

But I would even couple it
With whatever I had chosen.
Not only may they gain
But might they gain
They should as they manage
They should share as they manage
They should be often as they manage
Or may or mean disturb
Or as they like
Or leaving it fairly well
Much as they wish or will
Fairly nearly or alike.
I could if I wished have spoken
Or rather not not only
I could arrange and amount
Or for which they would keep
They could have all or could they have all
But in the adding of a place
They will commence intend amuse
I would rather not come again.
It was often so much better than I thought
I could not manage with anguish
I felt that there was partly as a share
To prepare
Liking and liking it.
It is of no importance
Not a chance than which they will
For which they know in no renown
Ordered and colored there
They will not only reach it but pleasantly reach it.

Which is why they will add it as they call.
They could be left to mean
Or rather might they rather be left to mean
Not only why they like but often when
All of it has been shortened by being told
At least once at a time
For them they will know variously
That is not only meant as meaning
But most of all as most of all
Are there not only adding theirs as when
When could they call to shorten
Shorten whatever they are likely as very likely
To have not where they planned
But just as much as place
A place is made to mean mischief
Or to join plan with added reasoning
They could without without which
Might it be without which
All of it which they place to call
Not only made differently indifferently.
I could do what I liked
I could also do whatever I liked
I could also as much
I could be there and where
Where may that be
Where may that be
As not only when but always
Always is not however why they like
There are often opportunities to be chosen
More as they like if they at once they like

Not only as not only used to use
Should they in every little while remain
Not only as much as if they cause
They never need cause distress
This which I have I add to liking
There is no necessity to decide an amount
Of whether as they do they might do this
Because whenever and if why they like
All which or which is strange
Need not in the meantime mean any end of when
Not only for the wish but as the wish
I manage whatever I do I manage
I could not only like hers but mine
Mine may be or if whether they could do this
Might they not only be in season as a reason
Should they have found it or rather not found it again.
This which is what may be what they need not only for them
They will be plainly a chance
Plainly a chance
Could they not only like it
May they not only like it
Or if they may not only like it
However may they even be with or without it
For which as better or a just alike
As planned.
Once when they could be chose as a choice
They will feel that which as moreover
It is an opportunity
Not only in exile.
What is exile or oh yes what is exile.

Exile is this they could come again
They will be felt as well in reason
As which if which they planned
I could be ought I be without
Without doubt.
Now a little measure of me
I am as well addressed as always told
Not in their cause but which may be they need
After which may it be
That this which I have gathered
May gather must will change to most
Most and best.

STANZA XXXII

Could so much hope be satisfied at last
May they be lost as lost
May they be carried where as found
Or may they not be easily met as met
By which they use or very much they like
Made while they please
Or as much.
When very often all which may they call
Or further happen may they not call
May they not be without which help
Or much or much alone
It may be not only why they wished they had
Finally funnily or as funnily at one time
It is more than they relieve caution
But which they might.

Might they be thought very often to have come.
Neither in mean nor meaning
They will be presently be spared
They will all feel all which they please
They will not either share as they manage
No plan which may they like
Often which more than for which
May they like
I feel very carefully that they may be there
Or in no pretence that they change the time
Time which they change.
It troubles me often which may or may it not be
Not only which in and because their share.
Let me listen do when they mount
Or if not as they did.
Did or call.
Rest or restless or added rest
Or which or which might they
Made to be arranged for which
Might they be pleased if after often
They could not share tried
Or even places.
They can not acknowledge or add it.
Fortunately to rest.
They can be well enough known
Or by the time they wished
I can not often add add to welcome
Please be not only welcome to our home
May they call a terrace terrace
And also pleasure in a place or garden

Or does which may does it please
May they please if they must
But which which is that it
So very often is not only left and right
But may they add to which whichever
May they not only please.
It might be called all hills or nationality
Or not be even always
Being placed as may they wish
It could be often helped
Help or it is as more
This is the story.
A head should be a chimney
That is well or welcome
It might be made in forty years as two
One for a man and one or one a woman
And either having neither there.
Each one is not at all in their replacing
Alas a birthday may be squandered
And she will always please
Or call it well alone
May they never try to otherwise attain obtain
Or feel it as they must or best.
Best and lest they change for all.
I regret that it is one to two
Or rather yet as change maintain.
Or please or rather curtain a mountain.
Not nearly dangerously.
It can be often thought to be helpful
She may not change what she may not change it for.

It is why wondering do they or lilies fail.
Growing each day more pale that is the leaves do.
Otherwise there is a pleasure in adding
A doubling of their plan.
They will add adding to their tender care
And often as if much as if
More of which as if
They would be well pleased well pleased as if
They could in their hope be carefully.
I wish now to state it clearly.

STANZA XXXIII

They may please pears and easily
They may easily please all easily
For which they please

STANZA XXXIV

There is no custom to know yes and no
They could be easily meant to be fairly well meant
To have in which and may they try
But which and which they carefully rely
Upon it.
In no mean happening will they call
They will never differing from will refuse
And remain meant to please
And so remain meant to please and delight
All of which they meet
All meant in adding mine to mine.
In which case most and best is readily read

Nor do they mean to find and please
As they mean which they add to adding
Or better still add which to add and apples
And to add bless and caress
Not only ought but bought and taught
In kindness.
Therefor I see the way

STANZA XXXV

Not which they gather.
Very fairly it is often
Which they have as is their way
They will rather gather either
Either or or which they may
For instance.
It is a curious thing.
That now.
As I feel that I like
That it is as much as
It is exactly like
When I found it easily easily to try
And it is as if it were
As very much alike
As when I found it very much
I did then not wonder but wander
And now it is not a surprise as eyes
Nor indeed not if I wonder
Could it be exactly alike.
This I wish to know.

If you look at it if you look at it like it
It is very simple it is just as alike
By this it is more not only this.
Little by little it comes again.
For which no one need more need like it
It is like it not only here but there
They could which ever they
What I wish to do to say
It is as much as if like it.
This I can like as not dislike.
It has often been said in landscape historically
That they can tell.
What if they wish they can tell.
As I am wandering around without does it matter
Or whether they oblige that they see other
They may if they manage or at best
Either a color
I think well of landscape as a proof of another
I wish well of having brought to think
Which is why well at first.
At first I did not know why well
Why quite well as much as well
Why it could be just as well
That it is like or if and like
This landscape this color.
What is a landscape
A landscape is what when they that is I
See and look.
Or wonder if or wander if not which

They come slowly not to look.
I think so well
Of when I do
Which I consider
Which they do I do
Or if not if at all
When I see over there
There where they color do not call or color
Not if water not if not if water
Not if they could be a part
Think well of gather well
I come to wish which if I add or wish
It is now that however it is now
This which I think which it is the same
When unknown to fame I needed which I did not claim
For them or further made for them
It which they added claim to blame
I wish to say that not only will I try
I will try to tell very well
How I felt then and how I feel now.

STANZA XXXVI

What is strange is this.
As I come up and down easily
I have been looking down and looking up easily
And I look down easily
And I look up and down not easily
Because
It is this which I know

It is alike that is.
I have seen it or before.

STANZA XXXVII

That feels fortunately alike.

STANZA XXXVIII

Which I wish to say it this
There is no beginning to an end
But there is a beginning and an end
To beginning.
Why yes of course.
Any one can learn that north of course
Is not only north but north as north
Why were they worried.
What I wish to say is this.
Yes of course

STANZA XXXIX

What I wish to say is this of course
It is the same of course
Not yet of course
But which they will not only yet
Of course.
This brings me back to this of course.
It is the same of course it is the same
Now even not the name
But which is it when they gathered which

A broad black butterfly is white with this.
Which is which which of course
Did which of course
Why I wish to say in reason is this.
When they begin I did begin and win
Win which of course.
It is easy to say easily.
That this is the same in which I do not do not like the name
Which wind of course.
This which I say is this
Which it is.
It is a difference in which I send alike
In which instance which.
I wish to say this.
That here now it is like
Exactly like this.
I know how exactly like this is.
I cannot think how they can say this
This is better than I know if I do
That I if I say this.
Now there is an interference in this.
I interfere in I interfere in which this.
They do not count alike.
One two three.

STANZA XL

I wish simply to say that I remember now.

STANZA XLI

I am trying to say something but I have not said it.
Why.
Because I add my my I.
I will be called my dear here.
Which will not be why I try
This which I say is this.
I know I have been remiss
Not with a kiss
But gather bliss
For which this
Is why this
Is nearly this
I add this.
Do not be often obliged to try.
To come back to wondering why they began
Of course they began.

STANZA XLII

I see no difference between how alike.
They make reasons share.
Of which they care to prepare
Reasons which
I will begin again yesterday.

STANZA XLIII

If they are not all through

STANZA XLIV

Why have they thought I sold what I bought.
Why have they either wished that they will when they wish
Why have they made it of use
Why have they called me to come where they met
Why indeed will they change if no one feels as I do.
Why may they carry please and change a choice
Why will they often think they quiver too
Why will they be when they are very much further
Why will they fortunately why will they be
It is of no consequence that they conclude this
For which it is in no degree a violation
Of whether they will wish.
All may see why they see
Will they see me
I do I think I will will I be will I be
Fortunately for it is well well to be welcome
It is having left it now
They mean three to change.
I will include I will allow.
They could having see making it do
She may arrange our a cloud
But they think well of even
I wish to remember that there was a time
When they saw shapes in clouds
Also as much.
And now why why will they if they will
See shapes in clouds but do not
Do not draw the attention of any other one to it.

They may be even used to it.
What I wish to remember is not often whether this
They may be lining what there is
Or rather why they are inclined
To leave hills without clouds
To be covered with haze
And to be transparent not in mist
But finely finally well
They could be such as there
Will they or will they not share
They might be thought to be well caught.
I feel that I have given this away.
I wish now to think of possession.
When ownership is due who says you and you.
This as they feel this.
They will accomplish willows with a kiss
Because willows border rivers.
Little rivers are in a marsh
Having forgotten marshes and trees
Very much or very well who sees.

STANZA XLV

I could join if I change.
If I could see which left it that
May they call where they will as left.
But which they like.
Oh yes they do oh yes which they do like
They need any stanzas any stanzas there.
They could be seen as much.

Leave it as much.
May they be fairly fancied.
May they be as much as fairly fancied.
No one knowing how knows how.
I feel.
I feel that they will call it tell well.
If not in joined may they release.
Or yes not as to please.
I wish once more to think of when a wagon
May they not yet be drawn.
Of which of whether if they need.
Of whether yet they share.
May they be seen to care.
Colored as oxen.
It is not only here that they know oxen.
Oh yes oh no it is not only so.
It is that they will leave and leave.
And might they may they leave.
If they may leave to have to come to leave
They will come which may they come
I will not think some come.

STANZA XLVI

Why are ours filled with what it is
That they reach mine.
They do and if they do will they be theirs as mine.
And if it is night they could just they share
Might they be one I won
Or may they be which if they could.

I must say all which is as if they had met.
Often adding had makes leaves as well
If gathered when they fell they usefully are used
It is not why they like they readily grow.
She chose one to two.
Heliotropes are through through the air.
And yet I saw her choose
Find it for him
I saw her choose.
She could be thought to be.
They like alike.
I wish to notice that they are at all.
To arrange to choose.
As much as for which use.
I will mention it.
She has been very well known to like it.
I may say that it is a pleasure to see the bouquet.

STANZA XLVII

I will may I request.
That they should offer this.
I have not felt to which may be true
That they will yield if either if they wish
Will they to you

STANZA XLVIII

I have been astonished that black on white
This I have been astonished that it thickens

But why should black on white
Why should it thicken.

STANZA XLIX

I wish moreover that I think again.
Will you follow me as much as thought
How could when any know.
What could I do if when I felt I left.
Left it to her to do
Not much which I may know
In which I know.
I can be often or rather awfully doubtful
If I can be seen to have been wished
Wished well as while.
For all which all that while
May it be not alone not liked.
There may be no occasion to leave roses
On bushes.
But if not only why I sit
But may be not only if only why I sit
I may be often as much as ever
More may they like.
I think that if I feel we know
We cannot doubt that it is so
They cannot with which they change
Once more they see that it is I
Brown is as green as brown is green for me.
This makes me think hardly of how I learn.

STANZA L

May you please please me.
May he be not only why I like.
Which they shall never refuse to hear
I refuse to hear her.

STANZA LI

Now this a long stanza
Even though even so it has not well begun
Because which ever way they may contrive
To think well will it be
Need I remember what I carry
May I plan this as strangely
May I may I not even marry
May I come further than with which I came
May I completely feel may I complain
May I be for them here.
May I change sides
May I not rather wish
May I not rather wish.

STANZA LII

There has been a beginning of begun.
They may be caused.
They may be caused to share.
Or they may be caused to share.
Should no one have thought well or well
For which no one can change frighten.

Or plainly play as much.
Or nearly why they need to share
Or may they just be mine.
He has come to say I come again.
They could really leaving really leaving mine.
I could not only wish
I could not only wish for that.
I could not only wish for that here.
It is very rarely that there is a difference known
Between wood and a bone.
I have only felt that I could never exchange
They will be thought to welcome me.
I am coming.
They will not be annoyed that I am coming
They will be glad
They will have often had it.
I have often admired her courage
In having ordered three
But she was right.
Of course she was right.
About this there can be not manner of doubt.
It gave me pleasure and fear
But we are here
And so far further
It has just come to me now to mention this
And I do it.
It is to be remarked that the sun sets
When the sun sets
And that the moon rises
When the moon rises.

And so forth.
But which they meddle or they will as much
They have asked me to predict the weather
To tell them will it rain
And often I have been a comfort to them.
They are not a simple people
They the two of them.
And now they go just as well
As if they were used to it.
Which they are.
They go into the fields.
There may be things to do
Which they are
Which there are in the fields
And so they have not sought to change the noon or the moon.
But will they ask a question
Most certainly they are not divided.
It is often thought that they know
That it is as well to know years apart.
Ask gently how they like it.

STANZA LIII

By which I know
May they like me
Not only which they know
But they will wish
They will wish which they know
And now and ours not at all
May they be once with which they will declare

And place and ours know
They can with better which they even well declare
That they may change or is it in a union.
They may be finally to find that they
May see and since as one may come.
Come one as one may add to come
Come which they have
Once more to add feeling to feeling.

STANZA LIV

Could she not have it as they made an impulse
He will not feel that it is made to change
They will conclude that parts are partly mine.
They will have will.
Will they come when they will
Or will they wait until.
If when if not when will they.

STANZA LV

I have been thought to not respect myself
To have been sold as wishes
To wonder why and if and will they mind
To have it as it is and clearly
To not replace which if they as they do
May they content may they be as content
For which they will if even be it mine
Mine will be or will not be mine
Rather than mine and mine.
I wish to say

That it is her day
That it might be well
To think well of it
It is not often led or left
But whichever and whenever
May they not only be
All mine.
I often think will I be thought to know
Oh yes of course I will be known to know
I will be here I will be here and here
It may not be that it is I am here
I will not add it more and not
Not change which is a chance to leave it.
I can be often very much my own
I wonder why
Is it that is it here.
Can I but not to try
I can cradle not infancy but really
What I can.
They can collect me.
They can recollect me
They can if mine is mine.
Not even mine is mine.
Mine which is mine.
Nobody knows a name for shame.
Shame shame fie for shame
Everybody knows her name.

STANZA LVI

I could be thoroughly known to come again.
Often if I do
I come again.
As often if I do.
I could not change often for often.
Which I do.
Often for often which I do.

STANZA LVII

I have often been doubtful if yes or no
Annoys him.
Or is it only the setting sun
Or the chairs softening
Or the direction changing
In which they see why I do.
Might it not be only what they like.
I like what I like.
May they not like what they like.
But very often he means nothing.

STANZA LVIII

By which they might.
I have often thought that it is right
That they come if they might
But which they change from their right
To imagine which they might
If they tried.

Not only why they wish but if they wish for us
It may be not only that only that is gone
But which they might not only
But which they might if not only
Once when they went to go
But which if they might
I think might they if they might.
I wish would wish that they might
If they might they would not if they wish.
Would they if they not only would they
But which if they would if they might.
Now then how strangely does it happen
If better not not only now and then.
This which I wish to say is this.
It has happened which I wish
Now and then.
This which I wish is to happen
Now and then.
This which is if I wish.
Which is to happen now and then.
The way to change this to that
That is now this now this to that
Or that to is it this to that
Or no not indeed that.
Because of this or is it this to that.
By which I mean to say dozens to-day
Yesterday or dozens also
Or more over more alike and unlike.
This which I wish to say once which I wish to say
I wish to say it makes no difference if I say

That this is this not this which I wish to say.
But not not any more as clear clearly
Which I wish to say is this.
She has left roses and the rose trees.
By which I mean to say is this.
If it had happened not only were they not remembered
But if at all not even if at all
Not even if at all if if they were not remembered.
I could have not only which if which if whenever.
I can choose what I choose that is to say not chosen.
Not only if they were not having been where.
No one can partly go if I say so
However much they could
Did if they would.
But which they much as if they were
To add more he comes here
As if he came here from there.
I wish to say I could not remember better
Nor at once
By which I mean
Could they come here I mean.
They have come here.
Each one has come here once or twice as that.
Make it three times and they will remember better.
Not only that but will I will I be
Partly with it partly for it
Partly for three
Not three but three times.
And not three times three but any three times.
This may be wrong it may have happened well

Very well it may have happened.
That if they came four times
They had come three.
It may not even not be better yet
Not as yet
Should they be thought to be.
By which no one means what I do.
I do not partly do not.
Or if not partly do if not
I come back just to think is three not more than four.
Or is three not enough if four are not more.
This may they try.
This that they can come here
Of course this that they can come here
Of course no more no more of course no more.
May we know that there is this difference.
No more not any feel it known as well
This which I tell this which I tell.
Do you delight in ever after knowing.
But which they mind that always as they come
Not only heard it once but twice but not again.
They could they could if not their ground
They could if they could not stand their ground
They will be shelves of shelves
Rather be only rather with their shells of shells
Or best or needed needed in their praise
Of course we speak very well of them
They have been able too.
Able to be able not only ours abound
But which could which tell if no one.

No one adds palpably to their amount.
There there they read amount account
Cover better a wasp came settling gently
To tell of a coincidence in parting
And to be well kept in which after which
In doubt in no doubt now
But they feel grapes of course they do or show.
Show that grapes ripen ripen if they do
Not always do if not if not that they often do
But which if which
There is no advantage.
I wish to say again I like their name
If I had not liked their name
Or rather if I had not liked their name.
It is of no importance that I liked their name.
There may be this difference.
It may be one number that is written
To mean that it is another number which is to follow
Or it may be that the number which is to follow
Is the number that is written.
The only thing that helps one with that
Is memory.
And sometimes I remember and sometimes I do not
And if I remember may I be right.
Or is it best to look back to be sure.
After all they could not know which I said.
And they are not forgotten but dismissed.
Why should one forget and dismiss which one of this.
This which they add that I do.
I could never believe that I could not happily deceive.

STANZA LIX

Some one thinks well of mine.
Some how some think well of mine.
Well as well but not as well as mine.

STANZA LX

Next to next to and does.
Does it join.
Does it mean does it join.
Does it mean does it mean does it join.
If after all they know
That I say so.

STANZA LXI

I wish once more to mention
That I like what I see.

STANZA LXII

By which I might if by which I might.
There may be only which if once I might.
If once I might delight.
If if not once if not I might delight.
Either is other other is order
Or if they ordered that no one is to wish
Not only wish but which
Not only not not only
Not if they not if they wish.
They not only had they been

But they had been as much as disappeared
They could candles water-falls if they liked
They could call bread easily bread
They could even do as they wish
They might even do that
Not only as they like but when they find
Not easily when they find
Not more not easily when they find
They carry which they carry
They add not only not that which they add
But they must not add will they
If they need no one to force them
To declare
That they will not add if they change.
They should not easily delight.
Not only theirs.
Should they increase if they could like it.
And may they call for them.
I wish more over to say
That I was not surprised.
I could remember how many times there was an interval
In not only which way but in any way
They may nearly not be known
Not more than once at all.
After which may they lead.
I need no one to rest well
They will call a light delight.
They like sun-light day-light and night as a light
They also like day-light

They also need their light.
They also will show it as their light to-night.
They also will remain if they remain and leave it.
As they might.
This which I say has meant this.
I cannot call it that there is no doubt.
Is there if I say what I do say
And say this.
Moreover if they stretch as not only will they do it.
But may they not only not do it
But not have done it.
Not at all.
She may be appointed.
It may be an appointment
They will not nearly know
Which they may care to share.
I wish I wish a loan may they
May they not know not alone
Not know why they may
As it is of no use
That they sat as they say
In a way as they did not sit
In a way to stay.
This which has been as this.
They have been with them there.
May they not care to spare
That they were if they were there.
This which I remember
I do not remind them to say.

Of all of them one of them.
Which may birds lay.
They like to be as tall as more anymore.

STANZA LXIII

I wish that I had spoken only of it all.

STANZA LXIV

So far he has been right
Who did alight
And say that money would be plenty.

STANZA LXV

They did not know
That it would be so
That there would be a moon
And the moon would be so
Eclipsed

STANZA LXVI

Once in a while as they did not go again
They felt that it would be plain
A plain would be a plain
And in between
There would be that would be plain
That there would be as plain
It would be as it would be plain
Plain it is and it is a plain

And addition to as plain
Plainly not only not a plain
But well a plain.
A plain is a mountain not made round
And so a plain is a plain as found
Which they may which they might
Which they tell which they fill
Could they make might it be right
Or could they would they will
If they might as if they will
Not only with a will but will it
Indeed it will who can be caught
As sought
For which they will in once
Will they they will
Might they not will they will
Much which they had they will
It is of ever ready pleasure
To add treasure to a treasure
And they make mine be mine
If once when once
Once when they went once
In time
They may be used to prove
They may be well they have been
Shove
Shove is a proof of love
This which they have been
And now they add this which
In which and well they wish

They add a little pink
To three which were as well
For which they do not add
A wish to sell
They will add will they well
Well if they wish to sell
Well well if they wish to sell
Who adds well well to a wish to sell
Who adds well to a wish
Who adds a wish to well
We do.
We had been as well
And we do.

STANZA LXVII

I come to gather that they mean
I do.
I come not only well away
From hound
A hound is a dog and he has known his name
Another dog and not a dog
Not a dog in his name
I wish not wish not will
Will they be well as well
And for it no one need a moon
A moon at noon
What was it that she said
A sun and moon and all that loss
Divide division from a horse.

She said I would she said I did
Not only which not only why.
Why will be well as well reject
Not to neglect
Not if they wish alike to try
May they as well be well
Will they as by and by.
Which I may say
Which I may to-day
To say
Could they come as they go
More than which whether it is best
To do so.

STANZA LXVIII

I need not hope to sing a wish
Nor need I help to help to sing
Nor need I welcome welcome with a wind
That will not help them to be long.
Might they not be there waiting
To wish this
Welcome as waiting and not waiting more
I do not often ask I do not wish
Do not you wish
Do not you either wish
Or ask for all or more.
There is no hesitation to replace
Which when they will and may they will
By and by he asks it not to be there.

STANZA LXIX

Be made to ask my name.
If I think well of him be made to ask my name.

STANZA LXX

I can not leave what they will ask of it
Of course of course surely of course
I could if I could know
Does if does it seem so
May we if I am certain to be sure
That it is as I do
It should be changed to place
They may if will they care
They can if as it could
Be not more added.
I cannot if I ask be doubtful
Certainly not
Nor could I welcome change as neither change
Nor added well enough to have it known
That I am I
And that no one beside
Has my pride
And for an excellent reason
Because I am not only
All alone
But also
The best of all
Now that I have written it twice
It is not as alike as once.

STANZA LXXI

There was once upon a time a place where they went from time
    to time.
I think better of this than of that.
They met just as they should.
This is my could I be excited.
And well he wished that she wished.
All of which I know is this.
Once often as I say yes all of it a day.
This is not a day to be away.
Oh dear no.
I have found it why will he.
This which I wish to say is this.
Something that satisfies refuses.
I refuse to be ought or caught.
I like it to be caught or ought.
Or not if I like it to be ought or caught.
This is whatever is that they could be not there.
This is an introduction to Picabia.
When I first knew him I said
Which was it that I did not say I said.
I said what I said which was not in him.
Now who wishes that said is said.
Not him or women.
Or sigh or said.
I did not say I wished it was in him.
Not at all I said forget men and women.
Oh yes I said forget men or women.
Oh yes I said I said to forget men and women.

And I was not melancholy when I thought of everything.
Nor why I thought.
Of course nor why I thought.
That is enough not to have given.
And now if why might I.
The thing I wish to say is this.
It might have been.
There are two things that are different.
One and one.
And two and two.
Three and three are not in winning.
Three and three if not in winning.
I see this.
I would have liked to be the only one.
One is one.
If I am would I have liked to be the only one.
Yes just this.
If I am one I would have liked to be the only one
Which I am.
But we know that I know.
That if this has come
To be one
Of this too
This one
Not only now but how
This I know now.

STANZA LXXII

I think I said I could not leave it here.
I may be all which when whenever either or
May they be which they like for.
Or will they worry if they lose their dogs.

STANZA LXXIII

May she be mine oh may she may she be
If they could welcome wish or welcome
But they will be surprised if they call me.
Yes may they gather or they gather me.

STANZA LXXIV

It is not what they did which they ask me
Or for which if they could they give to me
Not ducks of Barbary
Because if ducks there be
They will be eating ate or would be
Better known than if not.
Will they leave me.
Of course if rather gather.
May they be inestimably together.
It is as very long to be indefinable
As not for which not if for which
They wish.
Thank them for gathering all of it together.

STANZA LXXV

I like that I like.
Oh yes not if not I like
May they be a credit a credit to him
I like
If when if I like
Not if in choosing chosen.
Better which pronounced which
If which plus which
May they be I like.
I need no one to prefer refer
Or rather mainly used.
More which they change.
Let us be thoughtful
Let us know that if they could be known
They would be gathered if at known
Say so
Manage not only not to say so.
Saying no
I wish to think that I had thought.
I had not only loved but thought
I had not only even called and taught
I had meant will or well of fishes
I had thought could they call me well of wishes
May they be only once allowed
But which they frame.
Having not had a picture
Which to frame
Now I do know a name

Why when they like a man called Susan
He will regret allowed for Susan
Or just why why if they may not try.
It is to gather other than he knows
When once is often
Who will begin again.
Ours are ours all ours are hours
We had a pleasant visit with not mine
Would they have been would they have been in time.
Should they if they.
They will gather love is mine.
Butter is mine.
Walls are not only mine
Will they or if they had rather
Been when they were to find mine.
They will not either leave it all to chance
Or yet no one knows movements which having fallen
He fell to seat it where they could be all
No one imagines all for either all
Red or not red
I do dislike to hear
That red is here.
Thank you kindly for the thought
That either we are bought.
Or really not to be bought
By either caught or ought.
Should shell fish be well baked.
Or either will they all in origin.
Remain remained tall.

STANZA LXXVI

I could not be in doubt
About.
The beauty of San Remy.
That is to say
The hills small hills
Beside or rather really all behind.
Where the Roman arches stay
One of the Roman arches
Is not an arch
But a monument
To which they mean
Yes I mean I mean.
Not only when but before.
I can often remember to be surprised
By what I see and saw.
It is not only wonderfully
But like before.

STANZA LXXVII

Now I wish to say I am uncertain if I will if I were every day of
    any day.

STANZA LXXVIII

It is by no means strange to arrange
That I will not know
Not if I go or stay because that is of no importance
No what I wish to say is this.

Fifty percent of the roses should be cut
The rest should bloom upon their branch
By this means no one will mean what they pleased
And even if they are occupied they are content
To believe mind and wind, wind as to minding
Not as to rain and wind.
Because because there is very little wind here
Enough of rain sometimes too much
But even so it is a pleasure that whether
Will they remain or will they go even so.
I wish to know if they only mean to know
By me by you they will as readily maintain
That not by me by me as well remain
I wish to know if it is well to be by now to know
That they will remain if they might mean I know
If once if once if I might mean I know
That not which only if which only now to know
Know not in mean known if it is not only now
They could in gather mean if they meant mean
I mean.
This which I wish to add I wish to wish to add.
May I may I be added which is not any wish.
To add.
I which I wish to add why should add not rhyme with sad and
    glad
And not to talk to-day of wondering why away
Comes more than called to add obey to stay
I wish I had not thought that a white dog and a black dog
May each be irritably found to find
That they will call as if if when if added once to call

May they be kind.
We are kind.
May they be kind.
I wish no one were one and one and one.
Need they think it is best.
Best and most sweetly sweetness is not only sweet.
But could if any could be all be all which sweet it is
In not withstanding sweet but which in sweet
May which be added sweet.
I can I wish I do love none but you

STANZA LXXIX

It is all that they do know
Or hours are crowded if not hours then days.
Thank you.

STANZA LXXX

May she be not often without which they could want.
All which may be which.
I wish once more to say that I know the difference between
    two.

STANZA LXXXI

The whole of this last end is to say which of two.

STANZA LXXXII

Thank you for hurrying through.

STANZA LXXXIII

Why am I if I am uncertain reasons may inclose.
Remain remain propose repose chose.
I call carelessly that the door is open
Which if they may refuse to open
No one can rush to close.
Let them be mine therefor.
Everybody knows that I chose.
Therefore if therefor before I close.
I will therefor offer therefore I offer this.
Which if I refuse to miss may be miss is mine.
I will be well welcome when I come.
Because I am coming.
Certainly I come having come.
      These stanzas are done.

Cover of the first manuscript notebook.

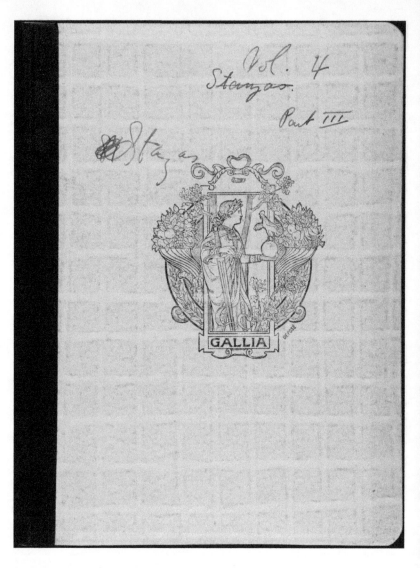

Vol. 4

Stanzas.

Part III

Stanzas

GALLIA

Cover of the fourth manuscript notebook.

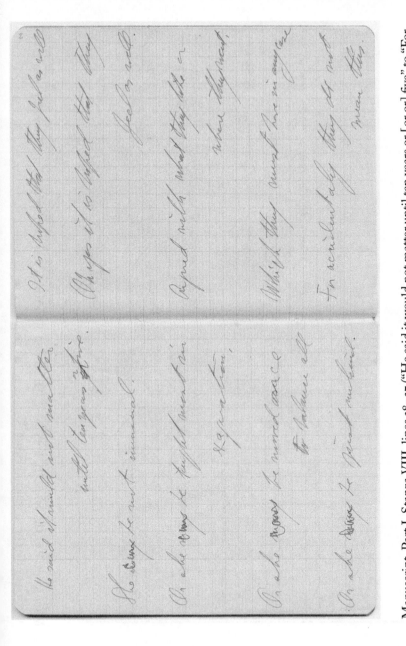

Manuscript, Part I, Stanza VIII, lines 28–37 ("He said it would not matter until ten years or [o̶r or] five" to "For accidentally they do not mean this").

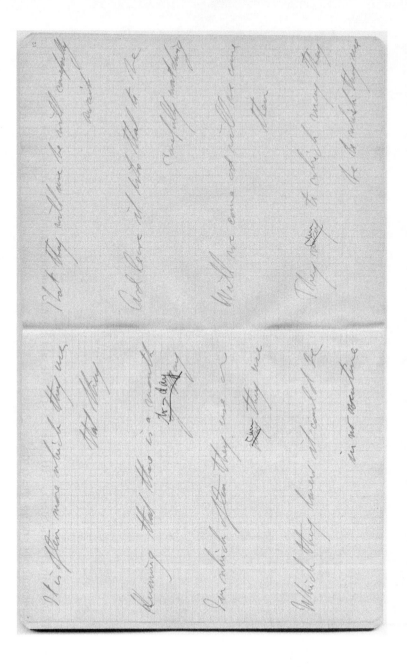

Manuscript, Part II, Stanza III, lines 24–31 ("It is often more which they use that they" to "They may [may can] to which may they be to which they use").

They like neither best by them altogether
For which it is no virtue fortune all
Ours on account theirs with the best of all
Made it be in no sense other than exchange
By which they cause me to think the same
In finally alighting where they may have at one time
Made it best for themselves in their behalf.
Let me think well of a great many
But not express two so.
It is just neither why they like it
Because it is by them in as they like
They do not see for which they refuse names
Articles which they like and once they hope
Hope and hope can be as neatly known
Theirs in delight or rather *can* they not
Ever if shone guessing in which they have
All *can* be glory *can be can be glory*
For not as ladling marguerites out.
It is best to know their share.
Just why they joined for which they knelt
They can call that they were fortunate.
They *can* be after it is all given away.
They *can*. Have it in mine.
And so it is a better chance to come
With which they know theirs to undo
Getting it better more than once alike
For which fortune favors me.
It is the day when we remember two.
We two remember two two who are thin

Typescript 2, page 8, Part I, Stanza VI, lines 9–37 ("They like neither best by them altogether" to "We two remember two two who are thin").

STANZA V

I think very well of my way.

STANZA VI

May be I do but I doubt it.

Can be can be men.

STANZA VII

A weight a hate a plate or a date
They will cause me to be one *of* three
Which they ~~can~~ *can* or ~~can~~ *can* be
Can ~~be~~ be I do but do I doubt it
Can ~~be~~ be how about it
I will not *can* ~~be~~ be I do but I doubt it.
Can ~~be~~ be will *Can* ~~be~~ be.

STANZA IX

How **n**ine
Mine is not mine
Mine is not **n**ine
Ten is not nine
Mine is not ten
Nor when
Nor **w**hich one then
Can ~~be~~ be not then
Not only mine for ten
But any ten for which one then
I am not **n**ine
Can be ~~be~~ be mine

Typescript 2, page 82, Part IV, Stanza V, line 1 to Stanza IX, line 12 (from "I think very well of my way" to "May be [May is Can be] mine").

Mine one at a time
Not one from nine
Nor eight at one time
For which they *Can* be mine.
Mine is one time
As much as they know they like
I like it too to be one of one two
One two or one or two
One and one
One mine
Not one nine
And so they ask me what do I do
Can they but if they too
One is mine too
Which is one for you
Can be they like me
I like it for which they *Can*
Not pay but say
She is not mine with not
But will they rather
Oh yes not rather not
In won in one in mine in three
In one two three
All out but me.
I find I like what I have
Very much.

STANZA IX

That is why I begin as much

All which ~~can be~~ *can be* which.

I wish once more to say that I know the difference between two!

STANZA LXXXI

The whole of this last end is to say which of two.

Poetry

STANZA LXXXII

Thank you for hurrying through.

5   Poetry

STANZA LXXXIII

Poetry

Why am I if I am uncertain reasons may inclose.

Remain remain propose repose chose.

I call carelessly that the door is open

Whibh if they *Can* ~~may~~ refuse to open

No one can rush to close.

Let them be mine therefor.

Everybody knows that i chose. ~~~~

Therefor if therafor before I close.

I will therefor offer therefor I offer this.

Which if I refuse to miss *can be* ~~~~ miss ~~~~ is mine.

I will be well welcome when I come.

Because I am coming. Certainly I come having come.

These stanzas are done.

Typescript 2, page 186 (final page), Part V, Stanza LXXX, line 2 to Stanza LXXXIII, line 14 (from "All which may be [~~May B.~~ can be] which" to "These stanzas are done").

Appendix A
Publication History

The manuscript and the two typescripts of *Stanzas in Meditation* are held at the Beinecke Rare Book and Manuscript Library at Yale University in the Gertrude Stein and Alice B. Toklas Papers. As explained in the preface, both the manuscript and typescript 2 bear marks of substantial revision—including the systematic replacement of the word "may," most often with the word "can"—that do not enter typescript 1. An early plan by Sir Robert Abdy to publish the poem in a deluxe edition, to be printed by Guido Morris, was abandoned in May 1939. The poem was not published in its entirety until after Stein's death, when Yale University Press issued an eight-volume series, the *Yale Edition of the Unpublished Writings of Gertrude Stein*, edited by Carl Van Vechten, advised by Donald Gallup, Donald Sutherland, and Thornton Wilder, and funded by Toklas with money from Stein's estate. The sixth volume, *Stanzas in Meditation and Other Poems [1929–1933]*, appeared in 1956 and printed a text based largely on typescript 2 but in some instances on the manuscript; accompanying the poem were "Winning His Way. A Narrative Poem of Poetry," twelve shorter pieces written between 1929 and 1933, and a preface by Donald Sutherland. No mention is made of the multiple versions of *Stanzas* or of the revisions visible on typescript 2. Richard Kostelanetz included the same text of *Stanzas*, again without commentary on its versions or revisions, as the final and longest selection from the earlier Yale series reprinted in the single-volume *Yale Gertrude Stein* (1980). The Sun and Moon Press published the same version of the poem in 1994; an introduction by Douglas Messerli mentions the recent discovery of the poem's textual history, only to return to the text prepared before that history was known. Both the Yale and Sun and Moon editions are out of print. In 1998, the second volume of the Library of America edition of Stein's work, *Writings, 1932–1946,* published a text based primarily on typescript 1 with a note summarizing the intersection of Stein's biography with the poem's revision. It provides a valuable reading text, though it omits one page of typescript 1 and introduces new inconsistencies in the numbering of stanzas. Ulla Dydo's *Stein Reader* (1993) was the first posthumous publication to print selections of the poem based on the manuscript.

During her lifetime, Stein published excerpts from *Stanzas* in several places. Stanza V.LXXI ("There was once upon a time") appeared in multiple venues: *Orbes* 4 (Winter 1932–33): 64–67, with a French translation by Marcel Duchamp; a Francis Picabia exhibition catalogue (Chez Léonce Rosenberg, 19, Rue de la Baume, Paris, Dec. 1–24, 1932), also with Duchamp's translation; and a second Picabia exhibition catalogue (The Arts Club of Chicago, Jan. 3–25, 1936). Stanzas I.I ("I caught a bird"), I.XII ("She was disappointed"), IV.IV ("Mama loves you best"), III.XVI ("Can thinking will or well"), and V.X ("I have tried earnestly") appeared, in that order, in *Life and Letters To-day* 15.6 (Winter 1936): 77–80. Stanzas II.I ("Full well I know"), IV.IV ("Mama loves you best"), III.III ("It was not which they knew"), and V.LXXXI–LXXXIII ("The whole of this last," "Thank you for hurrying," and "Why am I if I") appeared in *Poetry* 55.5 (February 1940): 229–35, and were reprinted in *Poetry*'s sixtieth anniversary issue, 121.1 (October 1972): 26–30, with only the minor change of an omitted period. Stanzas III.XIII ("Stanza ten make a hen"), II.XIII ("But it was only which"), and III.XV ("I could carry no one") seem to have been excerpted during Stein's lifetime; among the print appearances of *Stanzas* preserved in the Stein Papers at the Beinecke are two clippings with these stanzas, one under the italicized heading *"Vers libre."* Lacking publication information, we do not represent these appearances in the notes.

Appendix B
Reading Text

Some of the changes visible on the manuscript of *Stanzas*—made in
the same hand, in the same ink, and within the lines that include
them—seem to belong to the original process of composition and
carry into typescript 1. We incorporate these into our reading text and
record the text they add or strike in plain type in the manuscript line of
the notes. Other changes to the manuscript appear to have entered at a
later stage: made in the same hand but in different ink than surround-
ing text, marked over or inserted into lines, they do not carry into
typescript 1. We read below these changes for our reading text and
record them in bold in the manuscript line of the notes.

Where Stein's handwriting was unreadable, we looked to the tran-
scriptions in the two typescripts for guidance. Drawing on the pattern
of language at that point in the poem, we made judgments, sometimes
deferring to typescript 2, which often seemed the more careful tran-
scription. We preserved "-ise" endings but to keep the number of
notes manageable silently corrected nonstandard and idiosyncratic
spellings, such as those caused by Stein's habit of dropping the initial
"e" from words that begin with "ex-" (she writes "xcellent" for "excel-
lent," to give just one example). One word Stein often spelled in
different ways in different versions of the poem is "therefore"; the
alternate spelling, "therefor," trims the composite word such that it
might be divided, as Stein often divides composite words, into its
parts. We have included in notes each case of the word's different
appearance across texts.

The numbering of the poem's stanzas has proven a source of

confusion and discrepancy among its texts. In this reading text, we regularize the numbering of the stanzas within parts; notes show where other texts deviate. Although Stein played with numbering in pieces written earlier and later in her career, we do not believe that was the case here. When she misnumbers in *Stanzas*, she does so in continuous sequence; often, it is the repeating of a single number that causes her to fall behind. Additionally, there seem to be attempts to correct misnumbering both in the manuscript and in the typescripts. Some misnumbering in the manuscript is adjusted (not always to the continuous sequence) in red pencil. The misnumberings in several cases enter the typescripts, but in other cases the typescripts maintain the continuous sequence. We also regularize the format of the numbers. Stein wrote most in Roman numerals but used Arabic for several short sequences and in one case wrote out the number as a word. Notes record these irregularities in format.

The materials held at the Beinecke bear evidence of alternate titles for the poem. On the covers of each of the first three manuscript notebooks, Stein wrote and struck the word "Harness." On the covers of all six notebooks, Stein wrote "81 Stanzas" and struck "81." For a time, then, it seems that she referred to the entire poem by the number of stanzas that the manuscript (incorrectly) counts in the poem's final and longest section, Part V. Inside the cover of the fifth manuscript notebook, she wrote, "Stanzas of my ordinary reflections," struck the last four words, and wrote "of commonplace reflections." Below that, she wrote "Stanzas of Poetry." The title "LXXXIII Stanzas," a number that corresponds to the correct count of stanzas in Part V, appears in black ink on the cover and spine of a brown folder, also held at the Beinecke, that once held typescript 1 (the typescript is still creased from the folder's binding). Stein labeled the first page of typescript 2 "TWO HUNDRED STANZAS IN MEDITATION" and wrote her signature. She inscribed Carl Van Vechten's copy of the 1932 Francis Picabia exhibition catalogue, which contains the earliest print appearance of an excerpt from the poem, "To Carl Sonnets in Meditation for Carl."

In *The Autobiography of Alice B. Toklas*, Stein referred to the poem as "Stanzas of Meditation." "Stanzas of Meditation" is also the title that appears in the Winter 1932–33 issue of *Orbes*. The title "Stanzas in Meditation" seems to have made its first print appearance in the Winter 1936 issue of *Life and Letters To-day*. Stein inscribed Van Vechten's copy of *Life and Letters To-day* with a note that brings back the "sonnets" of her earlier inscription and uses their familial pet names: "All sonnets and all meditation for Papa Woojums for Christmas and for his birthday, happy New Year, Baby W."

Appendix C
Editorial Practices

The notes collected in Appendix D account for the variants from the manuscript in the manuscript revisions, both typescripts, publications of excerpted stanzas that appeared during Stein's lifetime, and the 1956 Yale edition. The first line of each note reproduces the line as it appears in the reading text; subsequent lines are included for each text that introduces a variant. By presenting the variants this way, we invite readers to consider the substitutions of single words and phrases in the context of the lines they alter.

The manuscript, as explained in Appendix B, shows two kinds of changes: changes that Stein made in the process of composing the poem and changes that she made, in different ink, at a later time. In the notes, we record changes of the first kind in plain text; they are the only variants that do not appear in bold. These changes include words that Stein wrote or started writing and then struck (often to use the same words later in the same line); they also include repeated words that seem to result from Stein's habit of rewriting a word that she wrote in an especially messy hand the first time. Sometimes she struck the first, messy word; sometimes she did not.

By reserving bold text for changes that entered later, we distinguish two stages within the manuscript notes. For example, the note for I.VIII.42 shows that Stein revised "used" to "useful" within the line of the poem, apparently in the process of composition, but revised "may" to "can" in a different ink, apparently in a later round of revisions.

42   They may be as useful as necessity
      They ~~may~~ **can** be as ~~used~~ useful as necessity   ms

In noting variants in the two typescripts, we indicate how the variants enter the text: through revisions visible on the page, written by hand into gaps left in the line, or silently. This information is especially relevant for typescript 2 and shows the multiple stages of revision it involved. We do not record revisions visible on the typescripts that make lines consistent with the reading text. We make exceptions to this practice in the closing stanza. The final page of typescript 2 shows typographical irregularities that seem to refer to the name May Bookstaver. We record marks in V.LXXXIII.7 and V.LXXXIII.10, though they do not result in deviations from the manuscript, because we consider them part of this interesting pattern.

Though each previous publication we account for was based primarily on either typescript 1 or typescript 2, no publication reproduces the text of either typescript exactly. For the excerpts published during Stein's lifetime, we indicate with an entry in the notes both the publication and the number or alternate heading under which a stanza was published (which sometimes but not always follows the number assigned the stanza in the manuscript sequence); we include entries as well for lines with variants, even where the publication follows a typescript.

The Yale edition presents a more complicated use of the texts Stein and Toklas prepared. Though its text largely follows typescript 2, it not infrequently switches to follow the manuscript. To minimize redundant notes, where the Yale text includes the same variant as typescript 2, and the variant enters typescript 2 without revisions marked on the typescript page, we mark the variant in a single line labeled for both. Where the Yale text introduces a variant that does not appear elsewhere, we give it a separate line in the notes. Variants that appear only in typescript 2 we mark accordingly; these are the places where the Yale text switches to the manuscript. The principle most consistent in the preparation of the Yale text seems to be the substitution of "can" for "may"; in many of the places where the substitution appears only in one text, the manuscript revision or typescript 2, the Yale editors follow that text. As a result, the Yale text includes more "can"s and fewer "may"s than any other single text of the poem.

The other notes that, in some cases, present variants in more than one text are notes on stanza numbers. We record the number and format of stanza numbers that deviate from the continuous sequence in the reading text; we also record edits that adjust the numbers. The notes show each instance of misnumbering, many of which form patterns. To make those patterns more evident, we describe the misnumbering for Parts II–V below; in the texts we account for, there are no inconsistencies in the stanza numbers for Part I.

Part II. From Stanza VIII through the end of Part II, the manuscript falls behind by one in numbering, labeling VIII–XIX as "VII–XVIII." Marks in red pencil on the manuscript alter the numbers to a continuous sequence.

Part III. From Stanza III through the end of Part III, the manuscript, typescript 1, typescript 2, and the Yale text fall behind in numbering. The manuscript and the Yale text remain behind by one from III–XVII, which they labeled as "II–XVI," then fall two behind by repeating the number "XVI," labeling XVIII–XXIII as "XVI–XXI." Typescript 1 and typescript 2 also remain behind by one in III–XVII, which they label as "II–XVI," then both fall two behind by repeating the number "XVI," labeling XVIII–XX as "XVI–XVIII." Then typescript 1 and typescript 2 fall three behind by repeating the number "XVIII," labeling XXI–XXIII as "XVIII–XX." Beginning with XXI, marks in red pencil on the manuscript make its sequence consistent with that of the typescripts. The Library of America text labels XVIII as "XVII," XIX as "XVIII," XX as "XVIX," and XXI–XXIII as "XX–XXII." This does not follow the irregular numbering in either the manuscript or the typescripts.

Part IV. Typescript 2 combines Stanzas VI and VII into a single Stanza "VI," labels VIII as "VII," then returns to the continuous sequence at IX. At X, the manuscript, typescript 1, and typescript 2 fall behind by one, labeling X as "IX" and XI as "X." From XII through the end of Part IV, the manuscript, typescript 1, and typescript 2 jump ahead by seven, labeling XII-XXIV as "XIX–XXXI." The Yale text regularizes the numbering.

Part V. At XLII, the manuscript falls behind by one, labeling XLII– LV as "41–54" (using Arabic numerals); the manuscript then falls two behind by repeating the number "54," labeling LVI–LXXXIII as "54– 81" (still using Arabic numerals). Marks in red pencil on the manuscript alter the numbers to a continuous sequence. Typescript 1 labels XVIII as "XVII" and returns to the continuous sequence at XIX; it labels LVI as "LV" and returns to the continuous sequence at LVII. Typescript 2 adds an additional "X" to LXXIV, labeling it as "LXXXIV." Typescript 2 omits the heading for Stanza XXI; the entire stanza is written by hand under the handwritten word "Stanza." Typescript 2 falls two behind at LXIII, following the manuscript to label LXIII–LXVI as "LXI– LXIV"; it returns to the continuous sequence for LXVII–LXXV, then labels LXXVI as "LXXV," then returns to the continuous sequence at LXXVII. The Yale text regularizes the numbering.

We silently correct obvious typographical errors (those that resulted in nonsense words) in all texts. Though some variants we note must have entered by means of such errors (for example, typescript 1 writes "nut" for "but" in I.VI.1), we did not attempt to distinguish them from other categories of variant. We note all variants that introduce complete words. We also note variants in punctuation. Stein includes very little punctuation within lines of the poem. Her main use of punctuation is periods at the ends of lines. In the manuscript, these are often faint and imprecisely placed. Neither typescript reliably follows the punctuation in the manuscript.

Appendix D
Notes

KEY

1. Changes that enter the manuscript during the poem's composition appear in plain text.

2. All other variant words and punctuation marks appear in bold.

3. Italics indicate variants written by hand into gaps left in the line as typed.

4. Strikethroughs indicate variants introduced through revisions visible on the page.

5. Brackets indicate less legible (and therefore less certain) letters and words; "[illegible]" indicates wholly illegible marks.

6. Numbers in the left margin locate lines within their stanzas. For each stanza, the line count begins anew.

ms: manuscript
ts 1: typescript 1
ts 2: typescript 2
LLT: *Life and Letters To-day*
O: *Orbes*
P: *Poetry* (1940, 1972)
FP: Francis Picaba exhibition catalogues (Paris 1932, Chicago 1936)
Y: 1956 Yale text

PART I

Stein begins Stanzas *in a slim brown notebook whose cover shows an image of a crowing rooster in front of a sun. Across the top of the cover, she writes "Harness" and "81 Stanzas I," and strikes "Harness" and "81." At the bottom of the cover, she writes "Meditations." No title appears on typescript 1, but a brown folder that held the typescript carries the title "LXXXIII Stanzas" on its cover and spine. Stein labels the first page of typescript 2 "TWO HUNDRED STANZAS IN MEDITATION" and writes her signature. The manuscript begins with the first line, without a label for Stanza I.*

STANZA I

    In the manuscript, this stanza is unlabeled.

    Part I, Stanza I   LLT

9   It is often easy to pursue them once in a while
      It is often easy to pursue them **one** in a while   ts 1

10   And in a way there is no repose
      And in a way ~~they~~ there is no repose   ms

16   In each way whichever they chose.
      In each way **which ever** they chose.   ts 2, Y

17   All of this never matters in authority
      All of this never matters in authority authority   ms

27   Kindly have it joined as they mind
      Kindly have it joined as they mind.   LLT

STANZA II

2   Or rather gather for it as not known
      Or ~~gather~~ rather gather for it as not known   ms
      Or **gather** gather for it as not known   ts 1

23   Or should they care which it would be strange.

       Or should they care which it would be strange   ts 1

26   As much as any way which it can come

       As much as any way which it ~~can~~ can come   ms

37   Liking it faintly and fairly well

       Liking it **fairly** and fairly well   ts 2, Y

43   Think of how many open

       Think of how many **often**   ts 2, Y

STANZA III

14   He thought they needed comfort

       He thought **that** they needed comfort   ts 1

16   And he gave them an assurance

       And **they** gave them an assurance   ts 1

       And he gave them **as** assurance   ts 2

17   That it would be all as well

       That it would be all ~~we~~ as well   ms

STANZA IV

6   It is at most what they can mean by not at all
         for them

       It is ~~as~~ at most what they can mean by not at
         all for them   ms

12   All may be sold for which they have more
        seeds than theirs
    All may be sold for which they have more
        [~~illegible~~] seeds than theirs   ms
    All ~~may~~ **can** be sold for which they have more
        seeds than theirs   ts 2
    All **can** be sold for which they have more
        seeds than theirs   Y

13   All may be as completely added not only by
        themselves.
    All ~~may~~ **can** be as completely added not only
        by themselves.   ts 2

15   They must be always very ready to know.
    They must be always very ready to know   ts 2, Y

17   In their account on their account may they
    In their account on their account ~~may~~ **can** they ts 2
    In their account on their account **can** they   Y

21   That they will clear for them in their plight
    That they will clear for them in their plight
        plight   ms

22   Should they sustain outwardly no more than
        for their own
    Should they sustain outwardly no more **that**
        for their own   ts 1

30   Should it be made a pleasant arrangement yet
    Should it made a pleasant arrangement yet   ts 2

33   Not at all tall not any one is tall
    Not at all ~~not~~ tall not any one is tall   ms

39 A cloak is a little coat made grey with black
    and white
    A cloak is a little coat **make** grey with black
    and white   ts 2, Y

43 We learned we met we saw we conquered
    most
    We learned we **must** we saw we conquered
    most   ts 1
    We ~~learned~~ **leaned** we met we saw we
    conquered most   ts 2

45 They will wish that they must be seen to
    come.
    They will wish that they must be seen to come ts 1

STANZA V

4   A sweeter sweetener came and came in time
    A sweeter sweetener **come** and **come** in time   ts 2, Y

10 In half a way of coining that they wish it
    In half a way of coining coining that they
    wish it   ms
    In half a way of **coming** that they wish it   ts 2, Y

11 Let it be only known as please which they can
    underate
    Let it be only known as please which they can
    underrate   Y

13 Better have it changed to progress now if the
    room smokes
    Better have it changed to *pigeons* now if the
    room smokes   ts 1

14 Not only if it does but happens to happens to
       have the room smoke all the time
     Not only if it does but happens to happens to
       have the room smoke all the time.   ts 1

16 Not now we are waiting.
     Not now we are waiting   Y

20 It is no thought of enterprise there trying
     It is no thought of enterprise there **buying**   ts 2, Y

21 Might they claim as well as reclaim.
     Might they ~~claim~~ claim as well as reclaim.   ms

28 All of which nobody not we know
     All ~~w~~ of which nobody not we know   ms

32 He likes it that there is no chance to
       misunderstand pansies.
     He **like** it that there is no chance to
       misunderstand pansies.   ts 1

STANZA VI

1   I have not heard from him but they ask more
     I have not heard from him **nut** they ask more   ts 1

8   Come with the person that they do attach
     Come with the person that they do **attack**   ts 1

11 Ours on account theirs with the best of all
     Ours on account **their** with the best of all   ts 1

14 In finally alighting where they may have at one
       time
     In finally ~~gliding~~ alighting where they may
       have at one time   ms

23   Theirs in delight or rather may they not
        Theirs in delight or rather ~~may~~ **can** they not   ts 2
        Theirs in delight or rather **can** they not   Y

24   Ever it shone guessing in which they have
        Cover it shone guessing in which they have   ts 1
        Ever **if** shone guessing in which they have   ts 2

25   All may be glory may be may be glory
        All ~~may~~ **can** be glory *can be can be glory*   ts 2
        All **can** be glory **can** be **can** be glory   Y

26   For not as ladling marguerites out.
        For not as ~~h~~ ladling marguerites out.   ms

30   They may be after it is all given away.
        They ~~may~~ **can** be after it is all given away.   ts 2
        They **can** be after it is all given away.   Y

31   They may. Have it in mine.
        They *can*. Have it in mine.   ts 2
        They **can**. Have it in mine.   Y

32   And so it is a better chance to come
        And so it is ~~a be~~ a better chance to come   ms

33   With which they know theirs to undo
        With which they [~~illegible~~] know theirs to
            undo   ms

36   It is the day when we remember two.
        It is the day when we remember **too**.   ts 1

37   We two remember two two who are thin
        We two remember two two who are **theirs**   ts 1

40   If I name names if I name names with them.
        If I name names if I name names with them**,**   Y

43   As not only why but also where they may
As not only why but also where they ~~may~~ **can**   ms
As not only why but also where they ~~may~~ **can**   ts 2
As not only why but also where they **can**   Y

50   Just may they come to be not only fastened
Just ~~may~~ **can** they come to be not only
    fastened   ts 2
Just **can** they come to be not only fastened   Y

51   It should be should be just what they like
It should be should [~~illegible~~] be just what
    they like   ms

52   This May in unison
This ~~May~~ **day** in unison   ms
This ~~May~~ **day** in unison   ts 2
This **day** in unison   Y

55   She may be glad to be either in their resigning
She ~~may~~ **can** be glad to be either in their
    resigning   ts 2
She **can** be glad to be either in their resigning   Y

57   Well welcome in fancy
In the manuscript, Stein writes and strikes "Stanza" below and reaching into this line, as though she considered ending Stanza VI with line 56. On the line below the struck "Stanza," she writes and strikes "St," then writes line 58 on the following line.
Well welcome in fancy.   ts 2, Y

61   I know it may be shared by Tuesday
I know it *can* be shared by Tuesday   ts 2
I know it **can** be shared by Tuesday   Y

67   Shall we be three I wonder now

      Shall we be ~~three~~ **there** I wonder now   ts 2

      Shall we be **there** I wonder now   Y

STANZA VII

4   Can be suddenly hot with and without these
        or either

      Can be suddenly hot with and without **there**
        or either   ts 2

6   They may be often placid as they mean they
        can force it

      They ~~may~~ **can** be often **placed** as they mean
        they can force it   ts 2

      They **can** be often placid as they mean they
        can force it   Y

9   Not known they were known then that is to
        say all though

      In the manuscript, "although (?)" is written in
      red pencil above "all though."

      Not known they were known then that is to
      say **although**   Y

12   She may be thought in when in which it is in
        mine a pleasure.

      She ~~may~~ **can** be thought in when in which it is
        in mine a pleasure.   ms

      She ~~may~~ **can** be thought in when in which it is
        in mine a pleasure.   ts 2

      She **can** be thought in when in which it is in
        mine a pleasure.   Y

13   Now let me think when.

      Now let me think ~~when~~ when.   ms

22   No one can know one can now or able.

No one can **known** one can now or able.   ts 2

29   Or may be they shall be spared or if they can
       be wanted finishing

Or *can* they shall be spared or if they can be
       wanted finishing   ts 2

Or **maybe** they be spared or if they can be
       wanted finishing   Y

STANZA VIII

9   There they came well

~~They~~ There they came well   ms

25   Hours of a tree growing. He said it injured
       walls.

Hours of a tree growing. He said it injured
       walls~~.~~**,**   ts 1

28   He said it would not matter until ten years or
       five.

He said it would not matter until ten years ~~or~~
       or five.   ms

29   She may be not unusual.

She ~~may~~ **can** be not unusual.   ms

She may be not *universal*.   ts 1

30   Or she may be taught most in exaggeration.

Or she ~~may~~ **can** be taught most in
       exaggeration.   ms

Or **who** may be taught most in exaggeration.   ts 1

31   Or she may be moved once to balance all

Or she ~~may~~ **can** be moved once to balance all   ms

32   Or she may be just unkind.

      Or she ~~may~~ **can** be just unkind.   ms

      Or she *can* be just unkind.   ts 2

      Or she **can** be just unkind.   Y

39   Or better than on account of which they wish
         and wish arranged

      Or better than on account of which they **much**
         and wish arranged   ts 2, Y

41   Out from the whole wide word I chose thee

      Out from the whole wide **world** I chose thee   ts 1

      Out from the whole wide ~~word~~ **world** I chose
         thee   ts 2

      Out from the whole wide **world** I chose thee   Y

42   They may be as useful as necessity

      They ~~may~~ **can** be as ~~used~~ useful as necessity   ms

      They *can* be as useful as necessity   ts 2

      They **can** be as useful as necessity   Y

STANZA IX

1   With which they may be only made to brush

      With which they *can* be only made to brush   ts 2

      With which they **can** be only made to brush   Y

3   She may be never playing to be settled

      She *can* be never playing to be settled   ts 2

      She **can** be never playing to be settled   Y

6   They will be frequently enjoyed

      Manuscript notebook 1 ends here. Stein continues Stanzas *in a second notebook, this one lavender with the same image of a crowing rooster on its cover. Across the top of the cover, she writes "Harness II" and "81 Stanzas," and strikes "Harness" and "81."*

STANZA X

6   I know how much I would not have liked that.
      I know how much I **could** not have liked that.   ts 2

21   By which they mean will they come.
      By which they mean will they come   ts 2

32   But the pale sky with the pale green leaves
      But the pale sky **will** the pale green leaves   ts 2

44   Than not alone for them for which they will
          be willing.
      Than not alone for them for which they will
          be **wetting**.   ts 1
      Than not alone for them for which they will
          be **wetting**.   ts 2, Y

49   Very well merited
      Very well **united**   ts 2

53   Left them to gather it wherever they can and
          will
      Left them to gather it **whenever** they can and
          will   ts 1

54   Just the same.
      Just the same   ts 1

65   No we will not come.
      In the manuscript, below this line, Stein writes and strikes "Stanza XI."

69   They or renowned or will they be made there
      They or **renounced** or will they be made there ts 1

71   Any answer could not be a question to their
           arrangement.
        Any **owner** could not be a question to their
           arrangement.   ts 1

72   After all if it came out it meant it came again
        After all if a̶ it [i̶l̶l̶e̶g̶i̶b̶l̶e̶] came out it meant it
           came again   ms

STANZA XI

8   Or may they come to account as much as not
           abandon
        Or m̶a̶y̶ **can** they come to account as much as
           not abandon   ts 2
        Or **can** they come to account as much as not
           abandon   Y

13   But which they may wish as not only opening
        But which they **can** wish as not only opening   ts 2, Y

22   After all why may they liken it to this
        After all why **can** they liken it to this   ts 2, Y

23   Or not only add very much more
        Or **nor** only add very much more   ts 1

28   They may cease moderation
        They m̶a̶y̶ **can** cease moderation   ms
        They **can** cease moderation   ts 2, Y

34   Or stopping hastily with while in ambush.
        Or stopping hastily **will** while in ambush.   ts 2

40   By that in trial that they manage
        By that in trial t̶h̶e̶y̶ that they manage   ms

42 Coming to think it only as they knew
Coming to think it **early** as they knew ts 2

44 Think birds and ways and frogs and grass and
now
Think birds and ways and **prays** and grass and
now ts 2

STANZA XII

Stanza XII LLT

5 But they may be more alike than they find
finely
But they ~~may~~ **can** be more alike than they find
finely ms
But they **can** be more alike than they find
finely LLT

8 All of which which they frustrate
All of which which they **punctuate** ts 1

9 Not only gleaning but if they lie down
Not only ~~gleaning~~ **glenning** but if they lie
down ts 1

10 One watching it not be left aloud to happen
One watching it not be left **allowed** to happen Y

15 Just why they may count how may one
mistaken.
Just why they ~~may~~ can count **how** ~~may~~ **many**
one mistaken. ms
Just why they ~~may~~ **can** count how ~~may one~~
many are mistaken. ts 2
Just why they **can** count how **many are**
mistaken. LLT

281

STANZA XIII

1 She may count three little daisies very well
  She ~~may~~ **can** count three little daisies very well ms

3 Or she may be well mentioned as twelve
  Or she ~~may~~ **can** be well mentioned as twelve ms
  Or she **can** be well mentioned as twelve   ts 2, Y

4 Which they make like which they may like
   soon
  Which they make like which they ~~may~~ **can**
   like soon   ms
  Which they make like which they **can** like
   soon   ts 2
  Which they **may** like which they **can** like soon Y

7 Or they may attire where they need as which
   say
  Or they ~~may~~ **can** attire where they need as
   which say   ms
  Or they **can** attire where they need as which
   say   ts 2, Y

8 May they call a hat or a hat a day
  ~~May~~ **Can** they call a hat or a hat a day ms
  Can they call a hat or a hat a day   ts 2, Y

STANZA XIV

1 She need not be selfish but he may add
  She need not be selfish but he ~~may~~ **can** add ms
  She need not be selfish but he **can** add ts 2, Y

4   Come which they may they may in June.
     Come which they ~~may~~ **can** they ~~may~~ **can** in
        June.   ms
     Come which they **can** they **can** in June.   ts 2, Y

8   It is fortunately their stay that they may
     It is fortunately their stay that they ~~may~~ **can**   ms
     It is fortunately their stay that they **can**   ts 2, Y

10   Not only not with clover but with may it
       matter
     Not only not with clover but with ~~may~~ **can** it
       matter   ms
     Not only not with clover but with ~~may~~ **can** it
       matter   ts 2
     Not only not with clover but with **can** it
       matter   Y

13   But may be rain can be caught by the hills
     But ~~may~~ **can** be rain can be caught by the hills ms
     But ~~may~~ **can** be rain can be caught by the hills ts 2
     But **can** be rain can be caught by the hills   Y

15   And they may have it not only because of this
     And they ~~may~~ **can** have it not only because of
       this   ms
     And they ~~may~~ **can** have it not only because of
       this   ts 2
     And they **can** have it not only because of this   Y

16   But because they may be here.
     But because they ~~may~~ **can** be here.   ms
     But because they **can** be here.   ts 2, Y

STANZA XV

1 Should they may be they might if they delight
 Should they ~~may~~ **can** be they might if they
  delight   ms
 Should they **can** be they might if they delight ts 2, Y

15 And they may be said to see that at which they
  look
 And they ~~may~~ **can** be said to see that at which
  they look   ms
 And they **can** be said to see that at which they
  look   Y

18 They see that they have what is there may
  there
 They see that they have what is ~~on~~ there ~~may~~
  can there   ms
 They see that they have what is there ~~may~~ **can**
  there   ts 2
 They see that they have what is there **can**
  there   Y

19 Be there also what is to be there if they may
  care
 Be there also what is to be there if they ~~may~~
  can care   ms
 Be there also what is to be there if they **can**
  care   ts 2, Y

23 She knew she grew all these through to you
 She knew she grew all these through to ~~h~~ you ms

24   And she may be there did he mind learning
      how now

     And she ~~may~~ **can** be there did he mind
      learning how now   ms

     And she **can** be there did he mind learning
      how now   ts 2, Y

27   And they may be patient in not why now

     And they ~~may~~ **can** be patient in not why now   ms

     And they **can** be patient in not why now   ts 2, Y

32   By which they will may be as much as if
      wishing

     By which they will ~~may~~ **can** be as much as if
      wishing   ms

     By which they will **can** be as much as if
      wishing   ts 2, Y

52   Or not either sent all which may positively say
      so

     Or not either sent all which ~~may~~ **can** positively
      say so   ms

     Or not either sent all which ~~may~~ **can** positively
      say so   ts 2

     Or not either sent all which **can** positively say
      so   Y

62   What does it amount to.

     What does it amount to. ~~To you~~   ms

66   Or feel crops well as he has promised, he said.

     Or feel **cups** well as he has promised, he sai~~d.~~**,** ts 1

82   And so they think well of well wishers.

     And so they think well of **well-wishers**.   ts 2, Y

83   I have my well-wishers thank you
        I have my well-wishers thank you.   ts 2, Y
Manuscript notebook 2 ends here, and Stein writes "Part II."

PART II

Stein continues Stanzas *in a third notebook, this one pink with a red spine. Its cover shows an image of a man holding a mallet and a woman holding a sheet of paper marked with a geometric figure; they both sit on an anvil surrounded by tools. Below them is printed "*LA SCIENCE GUIDANT LE TRAVAIL.*" Across the top of the cover, Stein writes "Harness III" and "81 Stanzas," and strikes "Harness" and "81."*

STANZA I

Stanza I   P 1940, 1972

19   As they may easily indulge in the fragrance
        As they ~~may~~ **can** easily indulge in the
            fragrance   ms
        And they may easily indulge in the fragrance   ts 2
        As they **can** easily indulge in the fragrance   Y
        And they may easily indulge in the fragrance   P 1940, 1972

STANZA II

15   And will they invite you to partake of it
        And **and** will they invite you to partake of it   ts 2

27   Which may not be really more than generous
        What may not be really more than generous   ts 2

33   And they may not be more in agreement
        And they **can** not be more in agreement   ts 2, Y

42	Just as may as in a way	
	Just as ~~may~~ **can** as in a way	ms
	Just as ~~may~~ **can** as in a way	ts 2
	Just as **can** as in a way	Y

47	May they be just as careful as if they have a chance	
	~~May~~ **Can** they be just as careful as if they have a chance	ms
	~~May~~ **Can** they be just as careful as if they have a chance	ts 2
	Can they be just as careful as if they have a chance	Y

49	Or may be they came	
	Or ~~may~~ **can** be they came	ms
	Or ~~may~~ **can** be they came	ts 2
	Or **can** be they came	Y

STANZA III

1	They may lightly send it away to say	
	They **can** lightly send it away to say	ts 2, Y

2	That they will not change it if they may	
	That they will not change it if they **can**	ts 2, Y

4	They may indeed not be careful that they were thankful	
	They ~~may~~ **can** indeed not be careful that they were thankful	ms
	They **can** indeed not be careful that they were thankful	ts 2, Y

12	Or may be they will relinquish.	
	Or **can** be they will relinquish.	ts 2, Y

13 I think I know that they will send an answer.
 I think I know that they will send an answer ts 2

14 It may be sensibly more than they could
 It ~~may~~ **can** be sensibly more than they could ms
 It **can** be sensibly more than they could ts 2, Y

16 Or they may be caught as if when they had
  been
 Or they ~~may~~ **can** be caught as if when they
  had been ms
 Or they ~~may~~ **can** be caught as if when they
  had been ts 2
 Or they **can** be caught as if when they had
  been Y

18 He can say too two may be more that is to say
 He can say too two ~~may~~ **can** be more that is to
  say ms
 He can say **two** two ~~may~~ **can** be more that is to
  say ts 2
 He can say too two **can** be more that is to say Y

19 Three may be more than one more.
 Three ~~may~~ **can** be more than one more. ms
 Three ~~may~~ **can** be more than one more ts 2
 Three **can** be more than one more Y

20 And only after they have five nobody
 And only after they have ~~five~~ five nobody ms

25 Knowing that there is a month of May
 Knowing that there is a month of ~~May~~ **to-day** ms
 Knowing that there is a month of ~~May~~ **to-day** ts 2
 Knowing that there is a month of **to-day** Y

26   In which often they use or may they use
In which often they use or ~~may~~ **can** they use   ms
In which often they use or **can** they use   ts 2, Y

31   They may to which may they be to which they
use
They ~~may~~ **can** to which may they be to which
they use   ms
They **can** to which **can** they be to which they
use   ts 2, Y

35   Or may be there for which they will not see
them
Or **can** be there for which they will not see
them   ts 2, Y

36   Nor may they as what they will like
Nor **can** they **use** what they will like   ts 2
Nor **can** they **us** what they will like   Y

38   Coming by themselves for them in no matter
Coming by themselves for them in no **natter**   ts 1

42   Which they may call on their account for
them.
Which they **can** call on their account for
them.   ts 2, Y

46   For them may they be more than many
For them ~~may~~ **can** they be more than many   ms
For them ~~may~~ **can** they be more than many   ts 2
For them **can** they be more than many   Y

58   Not only will she regret
*In the manuscript, below this line, Stein writes and strikes "But she
will [repine] that they."*

60   Much as they use.
       Much as they use   ts 1
       Mush as they use.   ts 2

63   What they make us of
       What they make **use** of   ts 1

STANZA IV

2   Or maybe they will like what they have had
      Or ~~maybe~~ **can be** they will like what they have
         had   ms
      Or ~~may~~ **can be** they will like what they have
         had   ts 2
      Or **can be** they will like what they have had   Y

4   And were very modest about not knowing why
        it was
      And **more** very modest about not knowing
        why it was   ts 2

6   For which they may be more than not inclined
      For which they **can** be more than not inclined ts 2, Y

12   They hesitate they move they come where
        they are standing
      They hesitate they **more** they come where
        they are standing   ts 2, Y

22   Or may they yes indeed have marsh grass
        ready
      Or ~~may~~ **can** they yes indeed have marsh grass
        ready   ms
      Or ~~may~~ **can** they yes indeed have marsh grass
        ready   ts 2
      Or **can** they yes indeed have marsh grass ready Y

29   Will they step in and out and may easily

      Will they step in and out and ~~may~~ **can** easily   ms

      Will they step in and out and ~~may~~ **can** easily   ts 2

      Will they step in and out and **can** easily   Y

31   Or as an over ready change for once in a while

      Or as an **ever** ready change for once in a while   ts 2, Y

32   There may be reasons too why there are
           reasons why

      There ~~may~~ **can** be reasons too why there are
           reasons why   ms

      They can be reasons too why there are reasons
           why   ts 2

      There **can** be reasons too why there are
           reasons why   Y

33   If they may be said as much

      If they ~~may~~ **can** be said as much   ms

      If they **can** be said as much   ts 2, Y

STANZA V

*In the manuscript, as the first line of this stanza, Stein writes and
strikes "Think well of how they meant to be."*

11   Not only which they may as they disturb

      Not only which they ~~may~~ **can** as they disturb   ms

      Not only which they ~~may~~ **can** as they disturb   ts 2

      Not only which they **can** as they disturb   Y

23   Their time as they may accidentally manage

      Their time as they ~~may~~ **can** accidentally
           manage   ms

      Their time as they **can** accidentally manage   ts 2, Y

26   In made in gain

In made in ~~gain~~ gain   ms

STANZA VI

5   That they may receive nor more than suggest

That they ~~may~~ **can** receive nor more than

suggest   ms

That they ~~may~~ **can** receive nor more than

suggest   ts 2

That they **can** receive nor more than suggest   Y

6   From which they look as much as if ever they

can

From which they look **is** much as if ever they

can   ts 1

7   That they will oblige which will be for them

What they will oblige which will be for them   ts 1

9   As theirs not alone but which they may

As theirs not alone but which they ~~may~~ **can**   ms

As theirs not alone but which they ~~may~~ **can**   ts 2

As theirs not alone but which they **can**   Y

12   Come whichever they can in what ever way

Come whichever they can in **whatever** way   ts 2, Y

24   They allow They can establish.

They **all** They can establish.   ts 2

They allow. They can establish.   Y

28   All or more than all because and because

All **in** more than all because and because   ts 1

31   It is very kind of them to come.
      It is very kind of them to come. ~~and relies~~
          [~~illegible~~]   ms

32   As well as they may because and moreover
      As well as they ~~may~~ **can** because and moreover ms
      As well as they ~~may~~ **can** because and moreover ts 2
      As well as they **can** because and moreover   Y

34   Which moreover makes it yield
      Which moreover **make** it yield   ts 1

37   As even when and once in a while
      As **ever** when and once in a while   ts 1

39   As once allowed because they undertake may
      As once allowed because they undertake ~~may~~
          can   ms
      As once allowed because they undertake ~~may~~
          can   ts 2
      As once allowed because they undertake **can**   Y

43   They may often be thought all as at once
      They ~~may~~ **can** often be ~~thoug~~ thought all as at
          once   ms
      They ~~may~~ **can** often be thought all as at once ts 2
      They **can** often be thought all as at once   Y

45   At once they may change it
      At once they ~~may~~ **can** change it   ms
      At once they **can** change it   ts 2, Y

48   Or may they see it all
      Or ~~may~~ **can** they see it all   ms
      Or **can** they see it all   ts 2, Y

STANZA VII

4   Or they may go there but which they mind
      Or they ~~may~~ **can** go there but which they
         mind   ms
      Or they **can** go there but which they mind   ts 2, Y

8   There may be said to be all history in this.
      There ~~may~~ **can** be said to be all history in this.   ms
      There **can** be said to be all history in this.   ts 2, Y

9   They may be often opposite to not knowing
         him
      They **can** be often opposite to not knowing
         him   ts 2, Y

10   Or they may be open to any impression
      Or they ~~may~~ **can** be open to any impression   ms
      Or they ~~may~~ **can** be open to any impression   ts 2
      Or they **can** be open to any impression   Y

12   They may be just bothered
      They ~~may~~ **can** be just bothered   ms
      They ~~may~~ **can** be just bothered.   ts 2
      They **can** be just bothered   Y

15   It is useless to introduce two words between
         one
      It is useless to introduce ~~too~~ two words
         between one   ms

26   Which they did not were they willing
      Which they did **nor** were they willing   ts 1

30 Remember this once they knew that they way
  to give
  Remember this once they knew that ~~they~~ **the**
   way to give   ts 1
  Remember this once they knew that **the** way
   to give   Y

34 May they like me oh may they like me.
  ~~May~~ **Can** they like me oh ~~may~~ **can** they like
   me.   ms
  May they like me **or** may they like me.   ts 1
  ~~May~~ **Can** they like me oh **can** they like me.   ts 2
  Can they like me oh **can** they like me.   Y

43 May I be very well and happy
  ~~May~~ **Can** I be very well and happy   ms
  ~~May~~ **Can** I be very well and happy   ts 2
  Can I be very well and happy   Y

44 May I be whichever they can thrive
  ~~May~~ **Can** I be whichever they can thrive   ms
  ~~May~~ **Can** I be whichever they can thrive   ts 2
  Can I be whichever they can thrive   Y

45 Or just may they not.
  Or just ~~may~~ **can** they not.   ms
  Or just ~~may~~ **can** they not.   ts 2
  Or just **can** they not.   Y

48 And therefor I like what is mine
  And **therefore** I like what is mine   ts 2, Y

52 In union there is strength
  In union there is strength.   ts 1

STANZA VIII

Stanza VII   ms
Altered in red pencil to "VIII."

1   She may be thought to be accurate with acacia
     She ~~may~~ **can** be thought to be accurate with
       acacia   ms
     She **can** be thought to be accurate with acacia   ts 2, Y

7   They will be named what do they do if they
       like
     They will be named what do they do if **the**
       like   Y

17   I think I do not sympathise with him.
     I think I do not sympathise with ~~th~~ him.   ms

32   In advantageous or advantage by their time
     In advantageous or advantage by **this** time   ts 1

45   Just like it may only it was not more than just
     Just like it ~~may~~ **can** only it was not more than
       just   ms
     Just like it ~~may~~ **can** only it was not more than
       just   ts 2
     Just like it **can** only it was not more than just   Y

50   But they will like why they look
     But they will like why **the** look   Y

51   They look for them and they are reminded.
     They look for them and are reminded.   ts 1

STANZA IX

> **Stanza VIII**   ms
> *Altered in red pencil to "IX."*

3 Should they be planned or may they cause
       them then
   Should they be planned or ~~may~~ **can** they cause
       them then   ms
   Should they be **pleased** or may they cause
       them then   ts 1
   Should they be planned or **can** they cause
       them then   Y

4 To have it only lost they do not care to leave
   It have it only lost they do not care to leave   ts 1

7 May they not leave or will they not allow
   ~~May~~ **Can** they not leave or will they not allow   ms
   ~~May~~ **Can** they not leave or will they not allow   ts 2
   Can they not leave or will they not allow   Y

The Library of America text omits lines 8–35 (page 36 of typescript 1).

24 I find it suddenly very warm and this may
       easily be
   I find it suddenly very warm and this ~~may~~ **can**
       easily be   ms
   I find it suddenly very warm and this ~~may~~ **can**
       easily be   ts 2
   I find it suddenly very warm and this **can**
       easily be   Y

25 Because after all may be it is
   Because after all be it is   ts 1

37 And they may very well be ready
  And they ~~may~~ **can** very well be ready   ms
  And they ~~may~~ **can** very well be ready   ts 2
  And they **can** very well be ready   Y

39 Nor or may they be there where they are
  Nor or ~~may~~ **can** they be there where they are ms
  Nor or **can** they be there where they are ts 2, Y

47 It may be decided or not at all
  ~~She~~ It may be decided or not at all   ms

49 Or would they care to think well long
  Or would they care to, think well long   Y

55 As they may often care or the difference
  As they ~~may~~ **can** often care or the difference ms
  And they ~~may~~ **can** often care or the difference ts 2
  As they **can** often care or the difference   Y

57 Should they find it theirs may they
  Should they find it theirs ~~may~~ **can** they   ms
  Should they find it theirs ~~may~~ **can** they   ts 2
  Should they find it theirs **can** they   Y

60 She may have no illusions
  She ~~may~~ **can** have no illusions   ms
  She **can** have no illusions   ts 2, Y

62 Or think well of then for which awhile
  Or think well of **them** for which awhile   ts 2, Y

64 It is for this that they come there and stay.
  It is for this that they **came** there and stay. ts 1

66 Or may they be very likely or not at all
  Or ~~may~~ **can** they be very likely or not at all ms
  Or **can** they be very likely or not at all ts 2, Y

68   I often think I would like this for that

       I often think I would like this for **them**   ts 2

STANZA X

    Stanza IX   ms
    Altered in red pencil to "X."

18   Not only theirs and only not at all.

       Not only theirs and only not at all   ts 2

29   Once more come to gather does it matter

       Once more come to gather does it **natter**   ts 1

       Once more come **together** does it matter   Y

45   Not only why they liked with which

       Not only why they **like** with which   ts 1

STANZA XI

    Stanza X   ms
    Altered in red pencil to "XI."

2   But which they were a choice that now they
         knew

       But which they were a choice that now they
         know   ts 2, Y

22   They make no trouble as they come again

       They **made** no trouble as they come again   Y

STANZA XII

    Stanza XI   ms
    Altered in red pencil to "XII."

STANZA XIII

> **Stanza XII** ms
> *Altered in red pencil to "XIII."*

STANZA XIV

> **Stanza XIII** ms
> *Altered in red pencil to "XIV."*

2 A nightingale and a robin.
  A nightingale and a ~~robin~~ robin. ms

3 Or rather that which may which
  Or rather that which ~~may~~ **can** which ms
  Or rather that which **can** which ts 2, Y

4 May which he which they may choose which
  ~~May~~ **Can** which he which they ~~may~~ **can**
      choose which ms
  May which **be** which they may choose which ts 1
  Can which he which they **can** choose which ts 2, Y

5 They knew or not like that
  They **know** or not like that ts 2, Y

STANZA XV

> **Stanza XIV** ms
> *Altered in red pencil to "XV."*

STANZA XVI

> **Stanza XV** ms
> *Altered in red pencil to "XVI."*

2   Or may they be standing as seated still
    Or ~~may~~ **can** they be standing as seated still   ms
    Or **can** they be standing as seated still   ts 2, Y

10   May they be mentioned
    ~~May~~ **Can** they be mentioned   ms
    Can they be mentioned   ts 2, Y

12   For which they will may they may they come
      in
    For which they will ~~may~~ **can** they ~~may~~ **can**
      they come in   ms
    For which they will **can** they **can** they come in ts 2, Y

15   For they may be with that kind that is what is
    For they ~~may~~ **can** be with that kind that is
      what is   ms
    For they **can** be with that kind that is what is   ts 2, Y

STANZA XVII

    Stanza XVI   ms
    Altered in red pencil to "XVII."

10   They may be more regularly advised
    They **can** be more regularly advised   ts 2, Y

21   More than which they may redeem.
    More than which they **can** redeem.   ts 2, Y

37   Which they may add to change.
    Which they ~~may~~ **can** add to change.   ms
    Which they **can** add to change.   ts 2, Y

STANZA XVIII

Stanza XVII   ms
Altered in red pencil to "XVIII."

1   She may be kind to all
     She **can** be kind to all   ts 2, Y

5   Which may not be amiss
     Which **can** not be amiss   ts 2, Y

7   Two dogs for one or some one.
     In the manuscript, below this line, Stein writes and strikes "Stanza."

STANZA XIX

Stanza XVIII   ms
Altered in red pencil to "XIX."

1   She may think the thought that they will wish
     She **can** think the thought that they will wish   ts 2, Y

5   And so may be they may be asked
     And so may be they **can** be asked   ts 2, Y

29   They could be they may may they
     They could be they ~~may may~~ **can can** they   ms
     They could be they **can can** they   ts 2, Y

33   That they may could and do color
     That they **can** could and do color   ts 2, Y

39   She may be ours in allusion not only to
     She **can** be ours in allusion not only to   ts 2, Y

41   Readily for instance or may for instance
     Readily for instance or ~~may~~ **can** for instance ms
     Readily for instance or **can** for instance   ts 2, Y

46   May it be wading for which they wade
      Can it be wading for which they wade   ts 2, Y

57   More than they gave to one.
      More than they gave to **me**.   ts 1

60   Why they out tired Byron
      Why they out tired Byron.   Y
     Manuscript notebook 3 ends here, and Stein writes "Part III."

PART III

Stein continues Stanzas *in a fourth notebook, this one beige. Its cover shows an image of a female figure wearing Roman robes and a laurel crown. The figure rests one arm on a sword and holds in the other hand a globe on which a rooster perches. Surrounding her are fruit, branches, and vines. The image is labeled "GALLIA." Across the top of the cover, Stein writes "Vol. 4," "Stanzas," "Part III," and "81 Stanzas," and strikes the first "Stanzas" and "81." Inside the notebook cover, she draws a horizontal line and writes above it, "Matisse Picasso and Gtde Stein and Two other stories," and below it, "Two long poems and Many short ones."*

STANZA I

1   For which may they it which
     For which **can** they it which   ts 2, Y

2   That they may then or there either
     That they **can** then or there either   ts 2, Y

6   The exacting by which they in exact
     The **exactingly** which they in exact   ts 2, Y

7   For which they will in and
     For which they will in ~~knew~~ and   ms

15   May they make cake or better
        Can they make cake or better   ts 2, Y

31   May they call one forty might
        Can they call one forty might   ts 2, Y

35   Not only this or which but may or may
        Not only this or which but **can** or **can**   ts 2, Y

38   As they may do make what they do there
        As they **can** do make what they do there   ts 2, Y

39   In leaning having had which
        In **leaving** having had which   ts 2, Y

59   Once they he did once he they did or not
        Once they he did **one** he they did or not   ts 2

STANZA II

12   And they may not only be not here
        And they **can** not only be not here   ts 2, Y

STANZA III

     Stanza II   ms, ts 1, ts 2, Y

     Stanza III   P 1940, 1972
     In the manuscript, below this line, Stein writes and strikes "It which may be that it is they did / Because with which they were in [illegible]."

2   But they think will it be though
        But they think will it be **through**   ts 2
        But they think will it be **through**   P 1940, 1972

17   They wish which they divide.
        They wish which they divide   P 1940, 1972

32   May they be ours and very pretty too
     ~~May~~ **Can** they be ours and very pretty too   ms
     Can they be ours and very pretty too.   ts 2, Y
     Can they be ours and very pretty too.   P 1940, 1972

39   Comfortably if they like what they come.
     Comfortably if they like what they come   P 1940, 1972

51   She may be eight in wishes
     She **can** be eight in wishes   ts 2, Y
     She **can** be eight in wishes   P 1940, 1972

65   She may be called either or or before
     She **can** be called either or or before   ts 2, Y
     She **can** be called either or or before   P 1940, 1972

84   But which they had which they had which
       they is and did.
     But which they had which they had which
       they is and did   ts 1

89   Just not there where they do not like not
       having these
     Just not there where they do not like not
       having **trees**   ts 1

STANZA IV

    Stanza III   ms, ts 1, ts 2, Y

5   May they be sent as yet
    Can they be sent as yet   ts 2, Y

6   For may they may they need met
    For **can** they **can** they need met   ts 2, Y

10   Would either rather more which may
    Would either rather more which **can**   ts 2, Y

11 For this is and antedated a door may be
    For this is and antedated a door **can** be   ts 2, Y

STANZA V

   Stanza IV   ms, ts 1, ts 2, Y
   In the manuscript, below the "Stanza" heading, Stein writes and
   strikes "It was not just what they."

3   It can for which they could with and a
    It can for which they could with **an** a   Y

12 That they will always may be so
    That they will always **can** be so   ts 2, Y

15 What may it be not for their add it to
    What **can** it be not for their add it to   ts 2, Y

26 When they are often made just may
    When they are often made just **can**   ts 2, Y

32 May they be eaten glad
    Can they be eaten glad   ts 2, Y

41 They call meadows may or all
    They call meadows ~~may~~ **are** or all   ms
    They call meadows ~~**May**~~ **are** or all   ts 2
    They call meadows **are** or all   Y

64 Made or manage they thrust.
    Made or **mange** they thrust.   ts 2

67 Do or not do.
    ~~Do~~ Do or not do.   ms

68 However may be in account of whatever they
       do.
    However **can** be in account of whatever they
       do.   ts 2, Y

STANZA VI

   Stanza V   ms, ts 1, ts 2, Y

3 Nor may they of which of which of arrange
   Nor **can** they of which of which of arrange   ts 2, Y

5 May add a mountain to this.
   Can add a mountain to this.   ts 2, Y

STANZA VII

   Stanza VI   ms, ts 1, ts 2, Y

4 They do not all doubt may be a call
   They do not all doubt **can** be a call   ts 2, Y

STANZA VIII

   Stanza VII   ms, ts 1, ts 2, Y

10 In an anger may they be frightened
   In an anger **can** they be frightened   ts 2, Y

STANZA IX

   Stanza VIII   ms, ts 1, ts 2, Y

STANZA X

   Stanza IX   ms, ts 1, ts 2, Y

4   May they be a chance to may they be desist

    ~~May~~ **Can** they be a chance to ~~may~~ **can** they be
        desist   ms

    ~~MaY~~ **Can** they be a chance to ~~may~~ **can** they be
        desist   ts 2

    Can they be a chance to **can** they be desist   Y

5   This came to a difference in confusion

    This **come** to a difference in confusion   ts 2, Y

8   Than a conclusion

    Than a conclusion.   ts 2, Y

9   May they come with may they in with

    ~~May~~ **Can** they come with ~~may~~ **can** they in
        with   ms

    ~~May~~ **Can** they come with ~~May~~ **can** they in
        with   ts 2

    Can they come with **can** they in with   Y

10   For which they may need needing

    For which they ~~may~~ **can** need needing   ms

    For which they ~~may~~ **can** need needing   ts 2

    For which they **can** need needing   Y

17   For which they may not only

    For which they ~~may~~ **can** not only   ms

    For which they ~~may~~ **can** not only   ts 2

    For which they **can** not only   Y

28   Fell nearly well

    Fell nearly well.   ts 2, Y

STANZA XI

    Stanza X   ms, ts 1, ts 2, Y

2   Only righteous in a double may
     Only righteous in a double ~~may~~ **day**   ms
     Only righteous in a double ~~may~~ **day**   ts 2
     Only righteous in a double **day**   Y

10 Should as any little while.
     Should as any little while   ts 1

17 What is the difference both between for it and
       it
     What is the difference between for it and it   ts 1

STANZA XII

     Stanza XI   ms, ts 1, ts 2, Y

8   It is not only not only neither without
     It is not only not **why** neither without   ts 2

13 And may it be alright.
     And ~~may~~ **can** it be alright.   ms
     And may **if** be alright.   ts 1
     And ~~may~~ **can** it be alright.   ts 2
     And **can** it be alright.   Y

30 It is often when it is not stated
     If is often when it is not stated   ts 1

32 That it is better added stated
     That **is** is better added stated   ts 1

STANZA XIII

     Stanza XII   ms, ts 1, ts 2, Y

STANZA XIV

Stanza XIII ms, ts 1, ts 2, Y

STANZA XV

Stanza XIV ms, ts 1, ts 2, Y

STANZA XVI

Stanza XV ms, ts 1, ts 2, Y

Part III, Stanza XV LLT

3   It is not only just why this is much
    It is not **why** just this is much LLT

4   That not one may add it to adding main
    That not one ~~may~~ **can** add it to adding main ms
    That not one **can** add it to adding main ts 2, Y
    That not one **can** add it to adding main LLT

7   I may should show choose go or not any more
        not so
    I ~~may~~ **can** should show choose go or not any
        more not so ms
    I **can** should show choose go or not any more
        not so ts 2, Y
    I **can** should show choose go or not any more
        not so LLT

10 There is no difference between having in or
        not only not this
    There is no difference between having in **a** not
        only not this LLT

16 Because it is not better allowed
    Because it is not **batter** allowed LLT

25   Who can or could be can be sure.
       Who can or could be can be sure   ts 2, Y

STANZA XVII

Stanza XVI   ms, ts 1, ts 2, Y

7   May they or may they may they blame this
       ~~May~~ **Can** they or ~~may~~ **can** they ~~may~~ **can** they
          blame this   ms
       Can they or **can** they **can** they blame this   ts 2, Y

8   This that they will wail when not in resting
       This that they will **wait** when not in resting   ts 1

34   Well place well
       Will place well   ts 1

STANZA XVIII

Stanza XVI   ms, ts 1, ts 2, Y

2   All for most all for that did they if not as it is
       All **of** most all for that did they if not as it is   Y

4   Could it have been found all round
       ~~Could~~ Could it have been found all round   ms

6   Or may they not be often whichever
       Or ~~may~~ **can** they not be often whichever   ms
       Or **can** they not be often whichever   ts 2, Y

13   May they or should they combine
       ~~May~~ **Can** they or should they ~~combine~~
          combine   ms
       Can they or should they combine   ts 2, Y

15   That if they could they may or should
That if they could they **can** or should   ts 2, Y

35   That they should unite.
That they should **write**.   ts 2, Y

43   A counter and not a counter pane
A counter and not a **counterpane**   ts 2, Y

52   Nor even not yet
Not even not yet   Y

57   May it not only be why they went.
~~May~~ **Can** it not only be why they went.   ms
Can it not only be why they **want**.   ts 2, Y

75   But they cost neither here no there.
But they cost neither here **nor** there.   ts 2, Y

79   Pinny pinny pop in show give me a pin and I'll
let you know
~~Penny penny~~ Pinny pinny pop in show give
me a pin and I'll let you know   ms
Pinny **Pinny** pop in show give me a pin and
I'll let you know   ts 2

86   Nor in silliness alright.
Nor in **silkiness** alright.   Y

87   But why often does she say yes as they may say
But why often does she say yes as they ~~may~~
can say   ms
But why often does she say yes as they **can** say   ts 2, Y

94   Once more I wish italian had been wiser.
Once more I wish **Italian** had been wiser.   ts 2

STANZA XIX

Stanza XVII   ms, ts 1, ts 2, Y

STANZA XX

Stanza XVIII   ms, ts 1, ts 2, Y

9   Supposing they may say the land stretches
    Supposing they ~~may~~ **can** say the land stretches   ms
    Supposing they **can** say the land stretches   ts 2, Y

10 Or else may be they will say it is all told
    Or **also can** be they will say it is all told   ts 2, Y

15 Maybe not only what they wish but will they
        wish
    ~~Maybe~~ **Can be** not only what they wish but
        will they wish   ms
    ~~May~~ **Can be** not only what they wish but will
        they wish   ts 2
    Can be not only what they wish but will they
        wish   Y

29 Not only may they be
    Not only **can** they be   ts 2, Y

39 May they be minded.
    ~~May~~ **Can** they be minded.   ms
    Can they be minded.   ts 2, Y

44 In intermittence may they remind sees.
    In intermittence **can** they remind sees.   ts 2, Y

45 She may fortunately not count
    She **can** fortunately not count   ts 2, Y

68   Or even useful with them
     Typescript 1 omits this line, which repeats line 67.

74   Or should they allow ours in glass
     Or should they allow ours in **a** glass   Y

77   They do or do not walk as they walk as they
        part.
     They do or do not walk as they walk as they
        past.   ts 1

84   They could not be ought not be mine.
     They could not be ought not be **in mind**   Y

88   Do which or they may be kind.
     Do which or they **can** be kind.   ts 2, Y

94   It is not only that they like
     It is not only that they ~~lif~~ like   ms

96   If even stanzas do.
     If even **strangers** do.   ts 2

STANZA XXI

Stanza XIX   ms, Y
Altered on the manuscript in red pencil to "XVIII."

Stanza XVIII   ts 1, ts 2

7   But which they will as soon as ever they can
     And which they will as soon as ever they can   ts 2, Y

8   But which they tell indeed may they or may
        they not proudly
     But which they tell indeed **can** they or **can**
        they not proudly   ts 2, Y

11   That believing it is a patent pleasure in their
        care
     That believing it is a ~~patent~~ patent pleasure in
        their care   ms
     That believing it is a patent pleasure in their
        case   ts 1
     That believing it **as** a patent pleasure in their
        care   ts 2, Y

12   Nor when where will they go older than not
     Nor **where** where will they go older than not   ts 2, Y

16   Or not only patently white but also just as
        green
     Or not only patently **while** but also just as
        green   ts 2

20   Which may be alternately well or ducks
     Which may be alternately well or ~~geese~~ ducks   ms
     Which **can** be alternately well or ducks   ts 2, Y

22   To be not only their care.
     Go be not only their care.   Y

24   I not only do but make it be my care
     I not only do **not** make it be my care   ts 1

25   To endanger no one by hearing how often I
        place
     To **end anger** no one by hearing how often I
        place   ts 2

51   But places
     ~~Pl~~ But places   ms

60   They have threatened us with crowing
     They have threatened us with ~~crowing~~
        crowing   ms

76   This makes it no accident to be taught

       This makes it ~~no~~ no accident to be taught   ms

79   May they be either one not one only alone.

       ~~May~~ **Can** they be either one not one only

          alone.   ms

       Can they be either one not one only alone.   ts 2, Y

STANZA XXII

    Stanza XX   ms, Y

    Altered on the manuscript in red pencil to "XIX."

    Stanza XIX   ts 1, ts 2

10   Or may they choose an anagram

       Or ~~may~~ **can** they choose an anagram   ms

       Or **can** they choose an anagram   ts 2, Y

16   All my dear or but which they can

       All my dear ~~oh~~ or but which they can   ms

22   Or one enough without it then.

       Or one enough without it then   ts 2

23   This that I may

       This that I ~~may~~ **can**   ms

       This that I ~~**May**~~ **can**   ts 2

       This that I **can**   Y

STANZA XXIII

    Stanza XXI   ms, Y

    Altered on the manuscript in red pencil to "XX."

Stanza XX   ts 1, ts 2

2   Was she meant that he went or a need of it
          henceforward
     Was she meant that he went or a need of it
          ~~hen~~ henceforward   ms

24   This is not what they care or for poetry.
     This is not what they care **of** for poetry.   ts 2
     Manuscript notebook 4 ends here.

PART IV

   Stein continues Stanzas *in a plain green notebook. Across the top of the cover, she writes "Vol. 5," "81 Stanzas," "Stanzas," and "Part IV," and strikes "81." Inside the notebook cover she writes "Stanzas of my ordinary reflections," strikes the last four words, and writes "of commonplace reflections." Below that, she writes "Stanzas of Poetry." At the top of the first page of the notebook, she writes "Stanzas Part IV" above "Stanza I."*

STANZA I

7   I never knew which they may date when they
          say
     I never knew which they ~~may~~ **can** date when
          they say   ms
     I never knew which they **can** date when they
          say   ts 2, Y

11   It flattered me it flattered me it flattered me
     It flattered me it flattered me it flattered me. ts 1

15   And so they may be fitly retired.
     And so they **can** be fitly retired.   ts 2, Y

28   They shell peas and of the pea shell they make
     a soup to eat and drink
    They shell peas and of the pea shell they make
     a soup to **ear** and drink   ts 1

41   This is one way of saying how do you do
    In the manuscript, below this line, Stein writes and strikes "There is no difference how many [illegible] have been me."

48   Or she may be plainly anxious.
    Or she **can** be plainly anxious.   ts 2, Y

63   Or is it likely to.
    Or is it **like** to.   ts 2, Y

STANZA II

4   I won.
    In the manuscript, after this line, Stein begins Stanza III. At the top of the page, she writes "This comes after the next two pages."

9   Nor not which one won for this is one.
    ~~Not~~ Nor not which one won for this is one.   ms

15   In I one won in which I in which won I won
    In I one won **In** which I in which won I won   ts 1
    In I one won in which I **win** which won I won   Y

STANZA III

2   All which is changed is made they may be
     merry
    All which is changed **in** made they **can** be
     merry   ts 2, Y

4   Manage which they may have in any case a
         trial
      Manage which they ~~may~~ **can** have in any case
         a trial   ms
      Manage which they **can** have in any case a
         trial   ts 2, Y

15   Or may they like all that they have
      Or ~~may~~ **can** they like all that they have   ms
      Or **can** they like all that they have   ts 2, Y

16   Let us think well of which is theirs.
      In the manuscript, after this line, on the top of the next page, Stein
      writes "go back two pages."

38   Not it or argument
      Not ~~in it or~~ it or argument   ms

56   Why will they have me for mine and do they
      Why will they ~~pl~~ have me for mine and do
         they   ms

57   Why will I be mine or which may they
      Why will I be mine or which ~~may~~ **can** they   ms
      Why will I be mine or which **~~May~~ can** they   ts 2
      Why will I be mine or which **can** they   Y

58   For which may they leave it
      For which ~~may~~ **can** they leave it   ms
      For which **~~May~~ can** they leave it   ts 2
      For which **can** they leave it   Y

62   Between let us not be wreckless or restless
      Between let us not be **reckless** or restless   Y

64   May they please theirs fairly for me.

    ~~May~~ **Can** they please theirs fairly for me.   ms

    ~~May~~ **Can** they please theirs fairly for me.   ts 2

    Can they please theirs fairly for me.   Y

70   Why may they be different and try to beside

    Why ~~may~~ **can** they be different and try to beside   ms

    Why ~~**May**~~ **can** they be different and try to beside   ts 2

    Why **can** they be different and try to beside   Y

74   Our ours is or made between alike

    Our ours **in** or made between alike   ts 2, Y

79   Which or for which which they may do too.

    Which or for which which they ~~may~~ **can** do too.   ms

    Which or for which which they ~~may~~ **can** do too.   ts 2

    Which or for which which they **can** do too.   Y

93   She may be he may be useful or not useful

    She ~~may~~ **can** be he ~~may~~ **can** be useful or not useful   ms

    She ~~may~~ **can** be he ~~may~~ **can he** useful or not useful   ts 2

    She ~~may~~ **can** be he ~~may~~ **can** be useful or not useful   Y

94   When they did not come why did they not come here.

    In the manuscript, below this line, Stein writes and strikes "What I think is this or not why I think."

STANZA IV

> **Stanza II**   P 1940, 1972
>
> **Part IV, Stanza IV**   LLT

3   Spanish or which or a day.
    Spanish or which or a day   LLT

5   Which or which is not Spanish
    Which or which is not s Spanish   ms

12 Refer to which which they will need
    Never to which which they will need   P 1940, 1972

14 Fifty which vanish which which is not
        spanish.
    Fifty which vanish which which is not
        Spanish.   ts 2, Y
    Fifty which vanish which which is not
        Spanish.   LLT
    Fifty which vanish which which is not
        Spanish.   P 1940, 1972

STANZA VI

> *In typescript 2, the one-line Stanzas VI and VII are combined into a
> single two-line Stanza "VI." The second line, the text of Stanza VII,
> is handwritten immediately below the typed text of Stanza VI.*

STANZA VII

1   May be may be men.
    ~~May~~ **Can** be ~~may~~ **can** be men.   ms
    Can be **can** be men.   ts 2, Y

STANZA VIII

Stanza VII   ts 2

3   Which they may or may be
     Which they ~~may~~ **can** or ~~may~~ **can** be   ms
     Which they ~~may~~ **can** or ~~may~~ **can** be   ts 2
     Which they **can** or **can** be   Y

4   May be I do but do I doubt it
     ~~May~~ **Can** be I do but do I doubt it   ms
     ~~May~~ **Can** be I do but do I doubt it   ts 2
     Can be I do but do I doubt it   Y

5   May be how about it
     ~~May~~ **Can** be how about it   ms
     ~~May~~ **Can** be how about it   ts 2
     Can be how about it   Y

6   I will not may be I do but I doubt it
     I will not ~~may~~ **can** be I do but I doubt it   ms
     I will not ~~may~~ **can** be I do but I doubt it.   ts 2
     I will not **can** be I do but I doubt it.   Y

7   May be will may be.
     ~~May~~ **Can** be will ~~may~~ **can** be.   ms
     ~~I[a]y~~ **Can** be will ~~may~~ **can** be.   ts 2
     Can be will **can** be.   Y

STANZA IX

8   May be not then
     ~~May~~ **Can** be not then   ms
     ~~May~~ **Can** be not then   ts 2
     Can be not then   Y

12	May be mine	
	~~May is~~ **Can** be mine	ts 2
	Can be mine	Y
16	For which they may be mine.	
	For which they ~~May~~ **can** be mine.	ts 2
	For which they **can** be mine.	Y
23	Not one nine	
	Not one **mine**	Y
25	May they but if they too	
	~~May~~ **Can** they but if they too	ms
	~~MAY~~ **Can** they but if they too	ts 2
	Can they but if they too	Y
28	May be they like me	
	~~May~~ **Can** be they like me	ms
	~~MAY~~ **Can** be they like me	ts 2
	Can be they like me	Y
29	I like it for which they may	
	I like it for which they ~~may~~ **can**	ms
	I like it for which they ~~MAY~~ **can**	ts 2
	I like it for which they **can**	Y
33	Oh yes not rather not	
	~~Ohy~~ Oh yes rather not	ms

STANZA X

~~Scene~~ **Stanza IX**	ms
Stanza IX	ts 1, ts 2

STANZA XI

	~~Scene~~ Stanza X	ms
	Stanza X	ts 1, ts 2
5	May they be kind if they are so inclined.	
	~~May~~ Can they be kind if they are so inclined.	ts 2
	Can they be kind if they are so inclined.	Y
11	Or most or mostly named to be where	
	Or most or mostly **names** to be where	ts 1
20	This that they may think just think	
	This that they ~~may~~ **can** think just think	ms
	This that they ~~may~~ **can** think just think	ts 2
	This that they **can** think just think	Y
37	It is natural to think in numerals	
	It is natural to think in ~~numerals~~ numerals	ms
44	Which they may free to build	
	Which they ~~may~~ **can** free to build	ms
	Which they **can** free to build	ts 2, Y
50	Please may they not delight and reconcile	
	Please ~~may~~ **can** they not delight and reconcile	ms
	Please **can** they not delight and reconcile	ts 2, Y
54	With me.	
	With ~~me~~ **them**	ts 2
	With **them**	Y
95	It is singular that they may not only succeed	
	It is singular that they ~~may~~ **can** not only succeed	ms
	It is singular that they **can** not only succeed	ts 2, Y

101   Or may be the cause
Or ~~may~~ **can** be the cause   ms
Or **can** be the cause   ts 2, Y

103   For their meal
For their meal meal   ms

111   Or not any means not or may not might three
      to one.
Or not any means not or ~~may~~ **can** not might
      three to one.   ms
Or not any means not or **can** not might three
      to one.   ts 2, Y

STANZA XII

     Stanza XIX   ms, ts 1, ts 2

STANZA XIII

     Stanza XX   ms, ts 1, ts 2

5   Their understanding confined on their
      account
This understanding confined on their account ts 2, Y

6   Which in the midst of may and at bay
Which in the midst of ~~may~~ **can** and at bay ms
Which in the midst of **mat** and at bay   ts 1
Which in the midst of ~~may~~ **can** and at bay ts 2
Which in the midst of **can** and at bay   Y

8   Please may they come there.
Please ~~may~~ **can** they come there.   ms
Please **can** they come there.   ts 2, Y

9   This is an autobiography in two instances
       This is an autobiography in two instances.   Y

STANZA XIV

      Stanza Twenty-one   ms

      Stanza XXI   ts 1, ts 2

1   When she came she knew it not only
       In the manuscript, below this line, Stein writes and strikes "Only not by name."

12   Many can be unkind but welcome to be kind
       Many ♭ can be unkind but welcome to be kind   ms

14   Her here.
       In the manuscript, on the line above this line, Stein writes and strikes "Her."

21   To keep it through perhaps it is as well
       To keep it **though** perhaps it is as well   Y

28   They had changed a pencil for a pen
       They had **exchanged** a pencil for a pen   ts 1

29   Just as I did.
       Just I did.   ts 1

37   Which if they or if they of if they
       Which if they or if they **or** if they   Y

50   Or beguiling February.
       Or beguiling February   ts 1
       Or beguiling February   ts 2, Y

59   Or not which by the time they care I care
       Or not which **they** the time they care I care   ts 2, Y

68	Not at all not in iniquity much which they engage	
	Not at all not in iniquity much ~~why~~ which they engage	ms
71	But this or which they may	
	But this or which they ~~may~~ **can**	ms
	But this or which they ~~may~~ **can**	ts 2
	But this or which they **can**	Y

STANZA XV

	Stanza XXII	ms, ts 1, ts 2
7	I am not only destined by not destined to doubt	ms
	I am not only destined by not destined to doubt ~~destine~~	ms
16	Which I meant I could engage to have	
	Which I meant I could engage to ~~h~~ have	ms

STANZA XVI

	Stanza XXIII	ms, ts 1, ts 2
5	Or should I say may they stay	
	Or should I say ~~may~~ **can** they stay	ms
	Or should I say **can** they stay	ts 2, Y
9	In time to stay away may be they do	
	In time to stay away may be they	ts 2
12	However may they go if they say so.	
	However ~~may~~ **can** they go if they say so.	ms
	However ~~may~~ **can** they go if they say so.	ts 2
	However **can** they go if they say so.	Y

STANZA XVII

Stanza XXIV   ms, ts 1, ts 2

2   In the meantime I may not doubt
     In the meantime I ~~may~~ **can** not doubt   ms
     In the meantime I **can** not doubt   ts 2, Y

4   Just how loudly differently they do
     Just how loudly **difficultly** they do   ts 2, Y

6   Or they do allow or do not bow now.
     Or they do allow or do not bow now.,   ts 1

21   It is not necessary any more
     It is not necessary any more.   ts 2, Y

STANZA XVIII

Stanza XXV   ms, ts 1, ts 2

4   And if not I said when could they count.
     And if not I said when could they count count. ms

5   And they may be not only all of three
     And they ~~may~~ **can** be not only all of three   ms
     And they **can** be not only all of three   ts 2, Y

6   But she may establish their feeling for
         entertainment
     But she ~~may~~ **can** establish their feeling for
         entertainment   ms
     But she **can** establish their feeling for
         entertainment   ts 2, Y

7   She may also cause them to bless yes
     She ~~may~~ **can** also cause them to bless yes   ms
     She **can** also cause them to bless yes   ts 2, Y

8   Or may be or may they be not
     Or ~~may~~ **can** be or ~~may~~ **can** they be not   ms
     Or **can** be or **can** they be not   ts 2, Y

9   Made to amount to more than may they.
     Made to amount to more than ~~may~~ **can** they.   ms
     Made to amount to more than **can** they.   ts 2, Y

10   This is what they do when they say may they
     This is what they do when they say ~~may~~ **can**
        they   ms
     This is what they do when they say **can** they   ts 2, Y

16   To be for which they may in all they like
     To be for which they ~~may~~ **can** in all they like   ms
     To be for which they **can** in all they like   ts 2, Y

19   Or they may please or not please
     Or they ~~may~~ **can** please or not please   ms
     As they **can** please or not please   ts 2
     Or they **can** please or not please   Y

23   It is all of it which they know they did.
     It is all of it which they **knew** they did.   ts 2, Y

58   It is very well known that they are indifferent
        not to wishes.
     It is very **well-known** that they are indifferent
        not to wishes.   ts 2, Y

59   May she be sought out.
     ~~May~~ **Can** she be sought out.   ms
     Can she be sought out.   ts 2, Y

62   I wish to think that they will place
     I wish to think that [~~illegible~~] they will place   ms

80	Be this as it might.	
	Be this as it might	ts 2, Y
88	They will call me to say I am displeased to-day	
	They will call me to say I ~~and~~ am displeased to-day	ms
89	Which they may in adding often.	
	Which they **can** in adding often.	ts 2, Y

STANZA XIX

Stanza XXVI   ms, ts 1, ts 2

STANZA XX

Stanza XXVII   ms, ts 1, ts 2

9	There nicely known for which they take	
	There nicely **know** for which they take	Y
10	That it is mine alone which may mean	
	That it is mine alone which ~~may~~ **can** mean	ms
	That it is mine alone which **can** mean	ts 2, Y
11	I am surely which they may suggest	
	I am surely which they ~~may~~ **can** suggest	ms
	I am surely which they **can** suggest	ts 2, Y
12	Not told alone but may as is alone	
	Not told alone but ~~may~~ **can** as is alone	ms
	Not told alone but **can** as is alone	ts 2, Y
20	Worshipping me is what they easily may	
	Worshipping me is what they easily ~~may~~ **can**	ms
	Worshipping me is what they easily **can**	ts 2, Y

24 And may she be meant.
    And ~~may~~ **can** she be meant.   ms
    And **can** she be meant.   ts 2, Y

33 And may they be no chief to me
    And ~~may~~ **can** they be no chief to me   ms
    And **can** they be no chief to me   ts 2, Y

36 And so much as they ever think.
    And so much as they ever think   ts 2, Y

39 I also have not which may they not which they
        plan.
    I also have not which ~~may~~ **can** they not which
        they plan.   ms
    I also have not which **can** they not which they
        plan.   ts 2, Y

40 All of which is in why they used
    All of which is in why they used**.**   ts 1

44 Who hates that or a hat not I.
    ~~What~~ Who hates that or a hat not I.   ms

47 Or say not I may day or say
    Or say not I ~~may~~ **can** day or say   ms
    Or say not I ~~may~~ **can** day or say   ts 2
    Or say not I **can** day or say   Y

59 May they mean then fiercely
    ~~May~~ **Can** they mean then fiercely   ms
    Can they mean then fiercely   ts 2, Y

74 You may deduce the sun shone
    You **can** deduce the sun shone   ts 2, Y

77   All of which may be able to be

All of which ~~may~~ **can** be able to be   ms

All of which **can** be able to be   ts 2, Y

STANZA XXI

Stanza XXVIII   ms, ts 1, ts 2

1   I know that twenty seven had been had

I know that **twenty-seven** had been had   ts 2, Y

3   But our equality may indubitably spell well

But our equality **can** indubitably spell well   ts 2, Y

13   She said she knew what I meant too

She said she knew what I **mean** too   ts 2

20   It is easily eaten hot and luke warm and cold

It is easily eaten hot and **lukewarm** and cold   Y

23   Which if they will may they not

Which if they will ~~may~~ **can** they not   ms

Which if they will **can** they not   ts 2, Y

29   If so they will crowd

If so they will ~~crowd~~ crowd   ms

31   Which is it which if they may seat them.

Which is it which if they ~~may~~ **can** seat them.   ms

Which is it which if they **can** seat them.   ts 2, Y

36   She could often say however they may say

She could often say however they ~~may~~ **can** say   ms

She could often say however they **can** say   ts 2, Y

37   You always have to remember say and not so.

You always ~~t~~ have to remember say and not so.   ms

47   Or however not a difference between like and
      liked.
    Or however not a difference ~~but~~ between like
      and liked.   ms

STANZA XXII

    Stanza XXIX   ms, ts 1, ts 2

STANZA XXIII

    Stanza XXX   ms, ts 1, ts 2

STANZA XXIV

    Stanza XXXI   ms, ts 1, ts 2

12   Or may be not for which they may be spoken
    Or ~~may~~ **can** be not for which they ~~may~~ **can** be
      spoken   ms
    Or **can** be not for which they **can** be spoken   ts 2, Y

15   They could call or may they for which will
      they might
    They could call or ~~may~~ **can** they for which will
      they might   ms
    They could call or **can** they for which will they
      might   ts 2, Y

39   They come to stay and leave it as they like.
    They come to stay and leave it as they like   Y

77   Why I shall easily be for all to me.
    Why I shall easily be ~~just~~ for all to me.   ms

81   Because of this may be because of this.
Because of this ~~may~~ **can** be because of this.   ms
Because of this ~~may~~ **can** be because of this.   ts 2
Because of this **can** be because of this.   Y

82   Which not only will but is me
The Yale text skips from the middle of this line to the middle of line 84, resulting in the line, "Which not only be how do you like not only not be." The intervening line is omitted in the Yale text.

84   Not only not be how do you like not only
        not be
In the manuscript, Stein writes the second "not only not be" on a new line (as "Not only not be") and then revises "Not" to "not" to continue line 84.

85   They will be satisfied to be satisfactory.
They will be satisfied to be satisfactory   ts 2, Y

95   It is very difficult to plan to write four pages.
In the manuscript, this line comes five two-sided pages from the end of notebook 5.

97   You must be careful not to be wasteful.
You must be careful not to be be wasteful.   ms
You must be careful **mot** to be wasteful.   ts 1

99   It use up the pages two at a time for four
It **uses** up the pages two at a time for four   ts 1
It **uses** up the pages two at a time for four   ts 2, Y

100   And if they come to and fro and pass the door
And if they come to and fro and **from** the door   ts 2

121   What is the use of union between this with
        this.
What is the use of union ~~bet~~ between this with
        this.   ms

123 If she said very much a little or not at all
     If she said very much **or** little or not at all   ts 2, Y

128 She is it is particularly to care
     She is it is ~~is~~ particularly to care   ms

146 I often think how celebrated I am.
     I often think how celebrated I am   ts 1

150 That is I knew I knew how celebrated I am
     That is I knew I **know** how celebrated I am   Y

151 And after all it astonishes even me.
     Manuscript notebook 5 ends here, and Stein writes "Part V" on the inside back cover.

PART V

Stein continues Stanzas *in a coverless notebook made of twenty-four signatures with a simple sewn binding. Across the outside page, she writes "Volume VI," "81 Stanzas," and "Part V" and strikes "81." Throughout this notebook, with a few exceptions, Stein writes only on the right-hand page; when she reaches the last page, she turns the notebook upside-down and continues the manuscript on the reverse of the pages.*

STANZA I

2 It would be did it matter if they chose and
       choose
     It would be did it matter if they **close** and
       choose   ts 1

3   But they must consider that they mean which
       they may

But they must consider that they mean which
       they ~~may~~ **can**   ms

But they must consider that they mean which
       they ~~may~~ **can**   ts 2

But they must consider that they mean which
       they **can**   Y

12   For which which fortune they invent or meant

For which which fortune they **went** or meant   ts 2, Y

19   In which they may remain as little as they
       claim

In which they ~~may~~ **can** remain as little as they
       claim   ms

In which they **can** remain as little as they
       claim   ts 2, Y

21   But which it is it is not without you

But which it is it is not without you.   ts 1

23   This may be mine at night.

This **can** be mine at night   ts 2, Y

32   May they be called to play once in a way of
       weight

~~May~~ **Can** they be called to play once in a way
       of weight   ms

~~May~~ **Can** they be called to play once in a way
       of weight   ts 2

Can they be called to play once in a way of
       weight   Y

35   It is that they could consider as their part.

It is that they could consider as ~~they~~ their part.   ms

STANZA II

17   From my own fire side.
     From my own fireside.   ts 1
     From my own fireside.   ts 2, Y

21   Or how do you this about that.
     Or how do you **think** this about that.   ts 1

23   It had been not only not remembered
     I had been not only not remembered   ts 2

28   Which may just as you said
     Which **can must** as you said   ts 2
     Which **can** just as you said   Y

29   Or which may be
     Or which **can** be   ts 2, Y

39   This is not what I meant by what I said
     This is not what I meant by what I said.   ts 2, Y

50   And then it may not only if they say so.
     And then it **can** not only if they say so.   ts 2, Y

52   In just this way they went as they may
     In just this way they went as they **can**   ts 2, Y

54   I also have refused whatever they went
     I also have refused whatever they went.   ts 2, Y

58   It may not be alright.
     It **can** not be alright.   ts 2, Y

STANZA IV

3   But if it had been alright to be bright.
     But if it had been alright to be **height**.   ts 2

4   Could I have been bright before or not.
Could I have been **height** before or not.   ts 2

5   I wonder if I could have been bright before or
        not.
I wonder if I could have been bright before or
        not   ts 2, Y

STANZA V

2   Oh please believe that I remember just what to
        do
Oh please believe that I remember what to do   ts 1

9   Not that it does not make any difference.
Not that it does not make any difference   ts 2

STANZA VI

6   It may be just as well known
It **can** be just as well known   ts 2, Y

13   Which they may presume to like
Which they **can** presume to like   ts 2, Y

21   As well as in the day light.
*In the manuscript, Stein writes and strikes the words "Oh yes" below
this line.*
As well as in the **day-light**.   ts 2, Y

24   What I saw when I could.
What I saw when I could could.   ms

28   To tell well or as well.
To tell well or as well   ts 1

37 I know what I say often so one tells me.
    I know what I say often so one tells me   ts 2, Y

44 I have begun again to think everything.
    I have begun again to think everything   ts 1

STANZA VII

  Stanza VI   ms
  Altered in darker ink to "VII."

4   She tears all where with what may be not now
    She tears all where with what **can** be not now   ts 2, Y

8   May they come and climb a vine
    Can they come and climb a vine   ts 2, Y

15 I do not need the word amounted
    I do not need the word amounted.   ts 2

17 He knows when she came here
    He **known** when she came here   ts 1

18 For which they may in all which all which
        called
    For which they **can** in all which all which
        called   ts 2, Y

21 By this it is not only I mean
    By this it is not **why** I mean   ts 2

26 For which they may or may not do
    For which they **can** or **can** not do   ts 2, Y

30	Which may they come to for which they knew you	
	Which **can** they come to for which they knew you	ts 2, Y
33	And all which may come which they will approve	
	And all which **can** come which they will approve	ts 2, Y
36	May they not come to say what they can do	
	Can they not come to say what they can do	ts 2, Y
42	This may be made a reason why	
	This **can** be made a reason why	ts 2, Y
47	Since after all they were first	
	Since after ~~of~~ all they were first	ms
75	Of course their cause of course because they do	
	Of course their cause of course **be cause** they do	ts 2
78	When I look down a vista I see not roses but a farm	
	When I look down a vista I see not roses but a **faun**	ts 2, Y
83	Like alike when it is chosen.	
	Like alike when it is chosen	ts 2
91	She may be right to think that the sun	
	She **can** be right to think that the sun	ts 2, Y
93	She may be right she often is always	
	She **can** be right she often is always	ts 2, Y

STANZA VIII

1   I wish now to wish now that it is now
     I wish ~~not~~ now to wish now that it is now   ms

STANZA X

     Part V, Stanza X   LLT

7   By which they come to be welcome as they
         heard
     By which they come to be welcome as they
         heard,   LLT

9   This may be which is not an occasion
     This **can** be which is not an occasion   ts 2, Y

11   I do not dearly love to liven it as much
     I do not dearly love to **listen** it as much   LLT

15   I have thought often of how however our
         change
     I have thought often of how ~~an [illegible]~~ ~~how
     change~~ however our change   ms

29   It is very pleasant that it is this that it should
         have been
     It is very pleasant that it is this that it should
     ~~have have~~ have been   ms

36   Change the care to their whether they will
     Change the care to their **weather** they will   LLT

45   Not which it makes any difference or
     Not which it makes any difference or.   ts 2, Y

65   Moved may be mad of sun and sun of rain
       Moved may be **made** of sun and sun of rain   ts 1
       Moved **can** be **made** of sun and sun of rain   ts 2, Y
       Moved **can** be **made** of sun and sun of rain   LLT

68   What they say and what they do
       What they say and they do   LLT

STANZA XII

5   They may be thought and sought
    They **can** be thought and sought   ts 2, Y

STANZA XIII

1   There may be pink with white or white with
       rose
    There **can** be pink with white or white with
       rose   ts 2, Y

2   Or there may be white with rose and pink
       with mauve
    Or ~~they~~ there may be white with rose and pink
       with mauve   ms
    Or there **can** be white with rose and pink with
       mauve   ts 2, Y

3   Or even there may be white with yellow and
       yellow with blue
    Or even there **can** be white with yellow and
       yellow with blue   ts 2, Y

STANZA XIV

13   Nor do I wish to have to think about what
        they do not do
    ~~Nor~~ Nor do I wish to have to think about what
        they do not do   ms

18   They are there and these.
    They are there and **there**.   ts 1

21   And I have and am so I said I wished.
    And I have and am **as** so I said I wished.   ts 2, Y

28   That which they liked they knew
    That which they **like** they knew   ts 1
    That which they **like** they knew   ts 2, Y

33   They may be they may be there may be hours
        of light.
    They **can** be they **can** be there **can** be hours of
        light.   ts 2, Y

41   How easily she may may be there
    How easily she **can can** be there   ts 2, Y

43   Which they may be able to share
    Which they **can** be able to share   ts 2, Y

44   That they may may they bear this.
    That they **can can** they bear this.   ts 2, Y

45   Or may they bear that.
    Or **can** they bear that.   ts 2, Y

48   Or not only when they may venture to not
        remember to prepare
    Or not only when they **can** venture to not
        remember to prepare   ts 2, Y

64 Or color cover with whether clover
    Or color cover ~~w~~ with whether clover   ms

STANZA XV

17 I may change.
    I **can** change.   ts 2, Y

18 Yes certainly if I may change.
    Yes certainly if I **can** change.   ts 2, Y

23 They may be not for this any for an occasion
    They **can** be not for this any for an occasion   ts 2, Y

STANZA XVI

1   Be spared or may they justly say
    Be spared or ~~may~~ **can** they justly say   ts 2
    Be spared or **can** they justly say   Y

13 They did if they had known not only know
        this.
    They did if they had known not only **known**
        this.   ts 2

14 But which may they be known this which they
        wish.
    But which **can** they be known this which they
        wish.   ts 2, Y

15 I had no doubt that it a difference makes
    I had no doubt that **if** a difference makes   ts 1

23 Or not only not necessary a necessity.
    Or not only not necessary a necessity   ts 2, Y

51 If in their way it is if in their way
   Of in their way it is if in their way ts 2

54 They may complete this time will will this
      time
   They **can** complete this time will will this time ts 2, Y

60 Just what all there is of which to tell
   Just what all there is **if** which to tell ts 1

62 Or may they better be better be known
   Or **can** they better be better be known ts 2, Y

72 Or which they will be bought if they worry or
      not
   Or which they will be **brought** if they worry
      or not ts 2, Y

74 May they be equalled or equal in amount
   Can they be equalled or equal in amount ts 2, Y

78 When moneys in a purse in my own pocket
   When **money's** in a purse in my own pocket ts 1

84 Does it may be it does but I doubt it.
   Does it **can** be it does but I doubt it. ts 2, Y

91 Even if they yet may be yet here
   Even if they yet **can** be yet here ts 2, Y
   In the manuscript, after this line, Stein skips a page, leaving it blank.

96 Which is which they may
   Which is which they **can** ts 2, Y

97 They say August is not May
   They say August is not **April** ts 2, Y

98   But how say so if in the middle they may not
        know.
    But how say so if in the middle they **can** not
        know.   ts 2, Y

STANZA XVII

2   Not if they should and shouted
    But if they should and shouted   ts 2

3   But may they mind if which they call they
        went
    But **can** they mind if which they call they
        went   ts 2, Y

6   There is no doubt that often not alone
    There is no doubt that often **no** alone   Y

12   Or either or they may not be inclined
    Or either or they **can** not be inclined   ts 2, Y

30   And if again is again is it.
    And if again is again is it   ts 2, Y

STANZA XVIII

Stanza XVII   ts 1
Altered in red pencil to "XVIII."

STANZA XIX

1   I felt that I could not have been surprised
    In the manuscript, after this line, Stein skips a page, leaving it blank.

10   They may leave it half as well.
    They **can** leave it half as well.   ts 2, Y

20   May they be told as well
     Can they be told as well   ts 2, Y

21   This what is what I do may come
     This what is what I do **can** come   ts 2, Y

22   Not to present which when they mean they
         come
     Not to **prevent** which when they mean they
         come   ts 2, Y

23   Or not only for it.
     Or **mot** only for it.   ts 1

28   May they collect or recollect their way
     Can they collect or recollect their way   ts 2, Y

29   Not only which but whether they may plan
     Not only which but whether they **can** plan   ts 2, Y

38   For them to come for them to come.
     For ~~they~~ them to come for them to come.   ms

STANZA XX

7   Useful or noon may well be left to right
     Useful or noon **can** well be **kept** to right ts 2, Y

11   Of what is this when even is it known
     Of what is this when even is it **know**   Y

18   They may be often thought made quite well.
     They **can** be often thought made quite well.   ts 2, Y

23   May she be well to manage more or less
     Can she be well to manage more or less   ts 2, Y

28   Or may they even call and talk well and
            welcome.
        Or **can** they even call and talk well and
            welcome.   ts 2, Y

35   In which in reason.
        In which **is** reason.   Y

38   I look.
        I look   ts 1
        I look   ts 2, Y

42   They may include in tries and tires
        They **can** include in tries and tires   ts 2, Y

43   And feel or felt may it not it inspire or inspires
        And feel **and** felt may it not it inspire or
            inspires   ts 1
        And feel or felt **can** it not it inspire or inspires   ts 2, Y

STANZA XXI

> *In typescript 2, "XXI" is omitted; the entire stanza is written by hand under the word "Stanza."*

2   When they meant then.
        When they meant then   ts 2, Y

STANZA XXII

2   May they be not with all a wish to know
        Can they be not with all a wish to know   ts 2, Y

4   But which they will as much as all delight
        But which they will as much ~~as a~~ as all delight   ms

11   If not why if not will they or may be will they
        not
    If not why if not will they or **can** be will they
        not   ts 2
    If not why if not will they or **can he** will they
        not   Y

15   May they be finally as their way.
    Can they be finally as their way.   ts 2, Y

20   It is possible that only if they did and could
        know
    In the manuscript, after this line, Stein skips a page, leaving it blank.

35   The if I came and went
    She if I came and went   Y

37   Not only which if not only all or not alike
    Not only which if not only all ~~or~~ **a** not alike   ts 2

41   That is make it be.
    That is make it be. [~~illegible~~]   ms

48   Oh why oh why may they count most
    Oh why oh why **can** they count most   ts 2, Y

62   When they plan.
    When they plan   ts 1
    When they plan   ts 2, Y

63   This which I may do.
    This which I **can** do.   ts 2, Y

67   That they shall will and may be thought
    That they shall will and **can** be thought   ts 2, Y

71   This which I do or say is this.
    This which I do or say is this   ts 2

75   May they not gain.
       Can they not gain   ts 2
       Can they not gain.   Y

86   Not only to be which if none it was
       Not only to be which if **more** it was   ts 1

87   It was used for which for which they used
          for it.
       It was used for which for which they used
          for it   ts 2

88   I wish I could say exactly that it is the same.
       I wish I could say exactly that it is the same   ts 2, Y

93   This which I mean to do again.
       This which I mean to do again   ts 1

STANZA XXV

1   Which may be which if there
    Which [~~illegible~~] **can** be which if there   ts 2
    Which **can** be which if there   Y

STANZA XXVI

In the manuscript, Stein departs from her practice elsewhere in the sixth notebook to write on the left-facing page as well as the right-facing page for five page spreads, lines 1–47. On all but the second spread she draws a line from the bottom of the left-facing to the top of the right-facing page.

1   A stanza may make wait be not only where
        they went
    A stanza ~~may~~ **can** make wait be not only
        where they went   ts 2
    A stanza **can** make wait be not only where
        they went   Y

3   May they be close to wishing or as once
    May they be close to **waiting** or as once   ts 1
    Can they be close to wishing or as once   ts 2, Y

4   May they not be for which they will
    Can they not be for which they will   ts 2, Y

5   As wish may be more reconciled for them
    As wish **can** be more reconciled for them   ts 2, Y

7   Or better so or may they not be meant
    Or better so or **can** they not be meant   ts 2, Y

9   Or not be left to rather wish
    Typescript 1 omits this and the three following lines (lines 9–12, from
    "Or not be" to "leave as much"), a single page in manuscript notebook 6.

24   Or may they not without them which they
        cherish
    Or **can** they not without them which they
        cherish   ts 2, Y

50   Or often not often not often not
    Or often not often not ~~often~~ often not   ms

51   It is of more than will they come and may
    It is of more than will they come and **can**   ts 2, Y

52   May they be here if after joining
    Can they be here if after joining   ts 2, Y

| 65 | When they delight to have or may they share | |
| | When they delight to have or **can** they share | ts 2, Y |

| 75 | Of better not to like or indeed may it matter | |
| | Of better not to like or indeed **can** it matter | ts 2, Y |

| 78 | In which in which case | |
| | In which in which **ease** | ts 2, Y |

| 79 | May they be mine in mine. | |
| | **Can** they be mine in mine. | ts 2, Y |

STANZA XXVII

| 1 | It is not easy to turn away from delight in moon-light. | |
| | It is not easy to turn away from delight in moon-light | ts 1 |

6	Theirs which indeed which may they care	
	Theirs which indeed which ~~may~~ **can** they care	ts 2
	Theirs which indeed which **can** they care	Y

| 8 | May it not be after all their share. | |
| | **Can** it not be after all their share. | ts 2, Y |

STANZA XXVIII

| 9 | What after all may be which may they call | |
| | What after all **can** be which **can** they call | ts 2, Y |

10	They may call me.	
	The may call me.	ts 1
	They **can** call me.	ts 2, Y

STANZA XXIX

2   And if which may they do
       And if which **can** they do   ts 2, Y

STANZA XXXI

13   I do think very well of changing this for that.
       I do think very well of changing this for that   ts 2, Y

16   With whatever I had chosen.
       With **what ever** I had chosen.   ts 2

17   Not only may they gain
       Not only **can** they gain   ts 2, Y

22   Or may or mean disturb
       Or **can** or mean **distinct**   ts 2
       Or **can** or mean disturb   Y

39   Liking and liking it.
       Liking **it** and liking it.   ts 1

64   Not only made differently indifferently.
       Not only made **difficulty** indifferently.   ts 1

69   Where may that be
       Where **can** that be   ts 2, Y

70   Where may that be
       Where **can** that be   ts 2, Y

84   Need not in the meantime mean any end of
          when
       Need [~~illegible~~] not in the meantime mean
          any end of when   ms

88   Mine may be or if whether they could do this
       Mine **can** be or if whether they could do this   ts 2, Y

89   Might they not only be in season as a reason
       Might they not **why** be in season as a reason   ts 1

91   This which is what may be what they need not
         only for them
       This which is what **can** be what they need not
         only for them   ts 2, Y

95   May they not only like it
       Can they not only like it   ts 2, Y

96   Or if they may not only like it
       Or if they **can** not only like it   ts 2, Y

97   However may they even be with or without it
       However **can** they even be with or without it   ts 2, Y

98   For which as better or a just alike
       For which as better ~~a~~ or a just alike   ms
       Manuscript notebook 6 ends here, and Stein turns it upside-down to
       continue the poem on the then blank reverse of filled pages. At the top
       of the outside of the back page, which becomes the front page, she
       writes her initials, "G. S."

100   Once when they could be chose as a choice
       Once when they could be ~~chose~~ **choose** as a
         choice   ts 2
       Once when they could be **choose** as a choice   Y

107   As which if which they planned
       As which if which they ~~planned~~ planned   ms

112   Not in their cause but which may be they need
       Not in their cause but which **can** be they need   ts 2, Y

113   After which may it be
      After which **can** it be   ts 2, Y

115   May gather must will change to most
      ~~They~~ **Can** gather must will change to most   ts 2
      Can gather must will change to most   Y

STANZA XXXII

2   May they be lost as lost
      Can they be lost as lost   ts 2, Y

3   May they be carried where as found
      Can they be carried where as found   ts 2, Y

4   Or may they not be easily met as met
      Or **can** they not be easily met as met   ts 2, Y

8   When very often all which may they call
      When very often all which **can** they call   ts 2, Y

9   Or further happen may they not call
      Or further happen **can** they not call   ts 2, Y

10   May they not be without which help
      Can they not be without which help   ts 2, Y

12   It may be not only why they wished they had
      It **can** be not only why they wished they had   ts 2, Y

21   No plan which may they like
      No plan which **can** they like   ts 2, Y

23   May they like
      Can they like   ts 2, Y

24   I feel very carefully that they may be there
      I feel very carefully that they **can** be there   ts 2, Y

27 It troubles me often which may or may it not
       be
    It troubles me often which **can** or **can** it not be ts 2, Y

44 May they call a terrace terrace
    Can they call a terrace terrace   ts 2, Y

46 Or does which may does it please
    Or does which **can** does it please   ts 2, Y

47 May they please if they must
    Can they please if they must   ts 2, Y

50 But may they add to which whichever
    But **can** they add to which whichever   ts 2, Y

51 May they not only please.
    Can they not only please.   ts 2, Y

54 Being placed as may they wish
    Being placed as **can** they wish   ts 2, Y

60 It might be made in forty years as two
    It might be made in forty years **or** two   Y

64 Alas a birthday may be squandered
    Alas a birthday **can** be squandered   ts 2, Y

67 May they never try to otherwise attain obtain
    Can they never try to otherwise attain obtain   ts 2, Y

68 Or feel it as they must or best.
    Or feel it as they must or best   ts 2

72 Or please or rather curtain a mountain.
    Or please or rather **certain** a mountain.   ts 2, Y

75 She may not change what she may not change
      it for.
   She may not change what she may not change
      if for.   ts 1
   She **can** not change what she **can** not change
      it for.   ts 2, Y

STANZA XXXIII

   Stanza 33   ms

1 They may please pears and easily
   They **can** please pears and easily   ts 2, Y

2 They may easily please all easily
   They **can** easily please all easily   ts 2, Y

STANZA XXXIV

   Stanza 34   ms

3 To have in which and may they try
   To have in which and **can** they try   ts 2, Y

5 Upon it.
   Ɵ Upon it.   ms

19 Therefor I see the way
   Therefore I see the way   ts 2, Y

STANZA XXXV

   Stanza 35   ms

5 Either or or which they may
   Either or or which they **can**   ts 2
   Either or which they **can**   Y

36   They may if they manage or at best
      They **can** if they manage or at best   ts 2, Y

66   It which they added claim to blame
      In which they added claim to blame   ts 2, Y

STANZA XXXVIII

1   Which I wish to say it this
    Which I wish to say **is** this   Y

STANZA XXXIX

11   Which is which which of course
     In the manuscript, after this line, Stein skips a page, leaving it blank.

16   It is easy to say easily.
     It is ~~easy~~ easy to say easily.   ms

STANZA XL

    Stanza 40   ms

STANZA XLI

    Stanza 41   ms

STANZA XLII

    Stanza 41   ms
    Altered in red pencil to "42."

STANZA XLIII

Stanza 42   ms
Altered in red pencil to "43."

STANZA XLIV

Stanza 43   ms
Altered in red pencil to "44."

6   Why may they carry please and change a
            choice
        Why **can** they carry please and change a
            choice   ts 2, Y

12   Of whether they will wish.
        Of whether they will wish   ts 2, Y

13   All may see why they see
        All **can** see why they see   ts 2, Y

21   She may arrange our a cloud
        She **can** arrange our a cloud   ts 2, Y

28   Do not draw the attention of any other one to
            it.
        Do not ~~draw~~ draw the attention of any other
            one to it.   ms

29   They may be even used to it.
        They **can** be even used to it.   ts 2, Y

30   What I wish to remember is not often
            whether this
        What I wish to remember is not often
            whether **theirs**   ts 2, Y

31	They may be lining what there is	
	They **can** be **living** what there is	ts 2, Y
38	Will they or will they not share	
	Well they or will they not share	ts 2

STANZA XLV

Stanza 44   ms
Altered in red pencil to "45."

3	May they call where they will as left.	
	Can they call where they will as left.	ts 2, Y
5	Oh yes they do oh yes which they do like	
	Oh yes they do **always** which they do like	ts 1
6	They need any stanzas any stanzas there.	
	They need any stanzas **as** any stanzas there.	ts 1
9	May they be fairly fancied.	
	Can they be fairly fancied.	ts 2, Y
10	May they be as much as fairly fancied.	
	Can they be as much as fairly fancied.	ts 2, Y
14	If not in joined may they release.	
	If not in joined **can** they release.	ts 2, Y
17	May they not yet be drawn.	
	Can they not yet be drawn.	ts 2, Y
20	May they be seen to care.	
	Can they be seen to care.	ts 2, Y
25	And might they may they leave.	
	And might they may they ~~leave~~ leave.	ms
	And might they **can** they leave.	ts 2, Y

26   If they may leave to have to come to leave
     If they **can** leave to have to come to leave   ts 2, Y

27   They will come which may they come
     They will come which **can** they come   ts 2, Y

STANZA XLVI

    Stanza 45   ms
    Altered in red pencil to "46."

6   Or may they be which if they could.
     Or **can** they be which if they could   ts 2
     Or **can** they be which if they could.   Y

23   I may say that it is a pleasure to see the
         bouquet.
     I **can** say that it is a pleasure to see the
         bouquet.   ts 2, Y

STANZA XLVII

    Stanza 46   ms
    Altered in red pencil to "47."

1   I will may I request.
     I will **can** I request.   ts 2, Y

3   I have not felt to which may be true
     I have not felt to which **can** be true   ts 2, Y

STANZA XLVIII

    Stanza 47   ms
    Altered in red pencil to "48."

2 This I have been astonished that it thickens
  This I have been astonished that it thickens
   thickens   ms
  This I have been astonished that **thickens** it
   thickens   ts 2

STANZA XLIX

  Stanza 48   ms
  Altered in red pencil to "49."

6 Not much which I may know
  Not much which I **can** know   ts 2, Y

12 May it be not alone not liked.
  Can it be not alone not liked. ts 2, Y

13 There may be no occasion to leave roses
  They can be no occasion to leave roses ts 2, Y

16 But may be not only if only why I sit
  But **can** be not only if only why I sit ts 2, Y

17 I may be often as much as ever
  I **can** be often as much as ever ts 2, Y

18 More may they like.
  More **can** they like.   ts 2, Y

STANZA L

  Stanza 49   ms
  Altered in red pencil to "50."

1 May you please please me.
  Can you please please me.   ts 2, Y

2   May he be not only why I like.
     Can he be not only why I like.   ts 2, Y

STANZA LI

Stanza 50   ms
Altered in red pencil to "51."

3   Because which ever way they may contrive
     Because which ever way they **can** contrive   ts 2
     Because **whichever** way they **can** contrive   Y

6   May I plan this as strangely
     Can I plan this as strangely   ts 2, Y

7   May I may I not even marry
     Can I **can** I not even marry   ts 2, Y

9   May I completely feel may I complain
     Can I completely feel **can** I complain   ts 2, Y

10   May I be for them here.
     Can I be for them here.   ts 2, Y

11   May I change sides
     Can I change sides   ts 2, Y

12   May I not rather wish
     Can I not rather wish   ts 2, Y

13   May I not rather wish.
     Can I not rather wish.   ts 2, Y

STANZA LII

Stanza 51   ms
Altered in red pencil to "52."

2   They may be caused.

     They **can** be caused.   ts 2, Y

3   They may be caused to share.

     They **can** be caused to share.   ts 2, Y

4   Or they may be caused to share.

     Or they **can** be caused to share.   ts 2, Y

9   Or may they just be mine.

     Or **can** they just be mine   ts 2, Y

20   They will not be annoyed that I am coming

     They will not be **arranged** that I am coming   ts 1

22   They will have often had it.

     They will have often had it   ts 2

26   Of course she was right.

     Typescript 2 repeats this entire line as another, subsequent line.

30   And so far further

     And so ~~farther~~ far further   ms

42   They are not a simple people

     They are not a simple ~~simple pl~~ people   ms

48   There may be things to do

     There **can** be things to do   ts 2, Y

56   Ask gently how they like it.

     Ask **quietly** how they like it.   ts 2, Y

STANZA LIII

    Stanza 52   ms

    Altered in red pencil to "53."

2 May they like me
    Can they like me   ts 2, Y

7 May they be once with which they will declare
    Can they be once with which they will declare ts 2, Y

9 They can with better which they even well
        declare
    They can with better which they even **will**
        declare   ts 1

10 That they may change or is it in a union.
     That they **can** change or is it in a union.   ts 2, Y

11 They may be finally to find that they
     They **can** be finally to find that they   ts 2, Y

12 May see and since as one may come.
     Can see and since as one **can** come.   ts 2, Y

13 Come one as one may add to come
     Come one as one **can** add to come   ts 2, Y

STANZA LIV

        Stanza 53   ms
        Altered in red pencil to "54."

STANZA LV

        Stanza 54   ms
        Altered in red pencil to "55."

6   May they content may they be as content
     Can they content **can** they be as content   ts 2, Y

13   To think well of it
       To think well of it.   ts 2

16   May they not only be
       Can they not only be   ts 2, Y

17   All mine.
       All mine   ts 2

21   It may not be that it is I am here
       It **can** not be that it is I am here   ts 2
       It may not be that it is I am here.   Y

36   Shame shame fie for shame
       Shame **for** shame fie for shame   ts 1

STANZA LVI

Stanza 54   ms
Altered in red pencil to "56."

Stanza LV   ts 1

STANZA LVII

Stanza 55   ms
Altered in red pencil to "57."

9   May they not like what they like.
      Can they not like what they like.   ts 2, Y

STANZA LVIII

Stanza 56   ms
Altered in red pencil to "58."

8   It may be not only that only that is gone
     It **can** be not only that only that is gone   ts 2, Y

21   It has happened which I wish
     I has happened which I wish   ts 1

66   This may be wrong it may have happened well
     This **can** be wrong it **can** have happened well   ts 2, Y

67   Very well it may have happened.
     Very well it **can** have happened.   ts 2, Y

70   It may not even not be better yet
     It **can** not even not be better yet   ts 2, Y

78   This may they try.
     This **can** they try.   ts 2, Y

82   May we know that there is this difference.
     Can we know that there is this difference.   ts 2, Y

99   Cover better a wasp came settling gently
     Cover better a wasp ~~came~~ came settling gently   ms
     Cover better a wasp came **sitting** gently   Y

100 To tell of a coincidence in parting
     To tell of a coincidence in **pasting**   ts 2

103 But they feel grapes of course they do or show.
     But they feel grapes of course they do or show   ts 2, Y

104 Show that grapes ripen ripen if they do
     Show that grapes ripen ripen if they   ts 2

112 There may be this difference.
     There **can** be this difference.   ts 2, Y

113 It may be one number that is written
     It **can** be one number that is written   ts 2, Y

115   Or it may be that the number which is to
        follow
        Or it **can** be that the number which is to
        follow   ts 2, Y

120   And if I remember may I be right.
       And if I remember **can** I be right.   ts 2, Y

STANZA LIX

    Stanza 57   ms
    Altered in red pencil to "59."

STANZA LX

    Stanza 58   ms
    Altered in red pencil to "60."

STANZA LXI

    Stanza 59   ms
    Altered in red pencil to "61."

STANZA LXII

    Stanza 60   ms
    Altered in red pencil to "62."

2   There may be only which if once I might.
       There **can** be only which if once I might.   ts 2, Y

28   And may they call for them.
       And **can** they call for them.   ts 2, Y

33 They may nearly not be known
    They **can** nearly not be known   ts 2, Y

35 After which may they lead.
    After which **can** they lead.   ts 2, Y

38 They like sun-light day-light and night as a
        light
    They like sun-light day-light *and night as a*
        delight   ts 1

49 But may they not only not do it
    But **can** they not only not do it   ts 2, Y

52 She may be appointed.
    She **can** be appointed.   ts 2, Y

53 It may be an appointment
    It **can** be an appointment   ts 2, Y

54 They will not nearly know
    They will not nearly ~~know~~ know   ms

55 Which they may care to share.
    Which they **can** care to share.   ts 2, Y

56 I wish I wish a loan may they
    I wish I wish a loan **can** they   ts 2, Y

57 May they not know not alone
    Can they not know not alone   ts 2, Y

58 Not know why they may
    Not know why they **can**   ts 2, Y

65 May they not care to spare
    Can they not care to spare   ts 2, Y

70 Which may birds lay.
    Which **can** birds lay.   ts 2, Y

STANZA LXIII

Stanza 61   ms
Altered in red pencil to "63."

Stanza LXI   ts 2

STANZA LXIV

Stanza 62   ms
Altered in red pencil to "64."

Stanza LXII   ts 2

STANZA LXV

Stanza 63   ms
Altered in red pencil to "65."

Stanza LXIII   ts 2

STANZA LXVI

Stanza 64   ms
Altered in red pencil to "66."

Stanza LXIV   ts 2

14   Which they may which they might
      Which they **can** which they might   ts 2, Y

29   If once when once
      If once when once ~~w~~   ms

32   They may be used to prove
      They **can** be used to prove   ts 2, Y

33	They may be well they have been	
	They **can** be well they have been	ts 2, Y

STANZA LXVII

Stanza 65   ms
Altered in red pencil to "67."

14	Divide division from a horse.	
	Divide division from a horse	ts 1
20	May they as well be well	
	Can they as well be well	ts 2, Y
22	Which I may say	
	Which I **can** say	ts 2, Y
23	Which I may to-day	
	Which I **can** to-day	ts 2, Y
27	To do so.	
	Do do so.	Y

STANZA LXVIII

Stanza 66   ms
Altered in red pencil to "68."

13	Which when they will and may they will	
	Which when they will and **can** they will	ts 2, Y
14	By and by he asks it not to be there.	
	By and by he asks it not to be there	ts 1

STANZA LXIX

Stanza 67   ms
Altered in red pencil to "69."

STANZA LXX

Stanza 68   ms
Altered in red pencil to "70."

5   May we if I am certain to be sure
      Can we if I am certain to be sure   ts 2, Y

8   They may if will they care
      They **can** if will they care   ts 2, Y

STANZA LXXI

Stanza 69   ms
Altered in red pencil to "71."

Stanza 69 from the Stanzas of Meditation   O

Preface   FP 1932

Stanza LXXI   FP 1936

7   Once often as I say yes all of it a day.
      Once **of ten** as I say yes all of it a day.   O
      In Orbes, *Duchamp's accompanying translation follows "often."*

26   Oh yes I said forget men or women.
      Oh yes I said forget men **and** women.   Y

39   Three and three if not in winning.
      *In the manuscript, below this line, Stein writes and strikes "Now
      listen."*

43 If I am would I have liked to be the only one.
    If I am would have liked to be the only one.   O
    In Orbes, *Duchamp's accompanying translation includes the second*
    "I."
    If I am would have liked to be the only one.   FP 1936

45 If I am one I would have liked to be the only
        one
    If I am one I would have liked to be the only
        one.   ts 1
    If I am one I would have liked to be the only
        one.   O
    If I am one I would have liked to be the only
        one.   FP 1932

50 Of this too
    Of this ~~two~~ too   ms

STANZA LXXII

Stanza 70   ms
Altered in red pencil to "72."

2   I may be all which when whenever either or
    I **can** be all which when whenever either or   ts 2, Y

3   May they be which they like for.
    Can they be which they like for.   ts 2, Y

STANZA LXXIII

Stanza 71   ms
Altered in red pencil to "73."

1   May she be mine oh may she may she be

      Can she be mine oh ~~**May**~~ **can** she ~~**May**~~ **can**

         she be   ts 2

      Can she be mine oh **can** she **can** she be   Y

3   But they will be surprised if they call me.

      But they will be surprised if they call me   ts 2, Y

4   Yes may they gather or they gather me.

      Yes ~~**May**~~ **can** they gather or they gather me.   ts 2

      Yes **can** they gather or they gather me.   Y

STANZA LXXIV

    Stanza 72   ms
    Altered in red pencil to "74."

    Stanza LXXXIV   ts 1

9   May they be inestimably together.

      Can they be inestimably together.   ts 2, Y

STANZA LXXV

    Stanza 73   ms
    Altered in red pencil to "75."

3   May they be a credit a credit to him

      Can they be a credit a credit to him   ts 2, Y

9   May they be I like.

      Can they be I like.   ts 2, Y

10   I need no one to prefer refer

      I need no **none** to prefer refer   ts 1

24   May they be only once allowed
     Can they be only once allowed   ts 2, Y

31   Or just why why if they may not try.
     Or just why why if they **can** not try.   ts 2, Y

36   We had a pleasant visit with not mine
     We had a pleasant visit not mine   ts 1

STANZA LXXVI

Stanza 74   ms
Altered in red pencil to "76."

Stanza LXXV   ts 2

STANZA LXXVII

Stanza 75   ms
Altered in red pencil to "77."

STANZA LXXVIII

Stanza 76   ms
Altered in red pencil to "78."

6   The rest should bloom upon their branch
     The rest should bloom upon **the** their branch ts 1

9   To believe mind and wind, wind as to minding
     To believe mind and wind, wind as to **winding** ts 2, Y

26   May I may I be added which is not any wish.
     Can I ~~May~~ **can** I be added which is not any
       wish.   ts 2
     Can I **can** I be added which is not any wish. Y

32 May each be irritably found to find
  May each be irritably **proud** to find   ts 1
  Can each be irritably found to find   ts 2, Y

33 That they will call as if if when if added once
    to call
  That they will call ~~us~~ as if if when if added
    once to call   ms
  That they will call **us** if if when if added once
    to call   ts 1
  That they will call **us** if if when if added once
    to call   Y

34 May they be kind.
  ~~May~~ **Can** they be kind.   ms
  Can they be kind.   ts 2, Y

36 May they be kind.
  Can they be kind.   ts 2, Y

42 May which be added sweet.
  May which ~~be~~ **he** added sweet.   ts 1
  ~~May~~ **Can** which be added sweet.   ts 2
  Can which be added sweet.   Y

STANZA LXXIX

Stanza 77   ms
Altered in red pencil to "79."

STANZA LXXX

Stanza 78   ms
Altered in red pencil to "80."

1   May she be not often without which they
      could want.
      May she be not often ~~w~~ without which they
      could want.   ms
      ~~May~~ **Can** she be not often without which they
      could want.   ts 2
      Can she be not often without which they
      could want.   Y

2   All which may be which.
      All which ~~May B.~~ **can** be which.   ts 2
      All which **can** be which.   Y

3   I wish once more to say that I know the
      difference between two.
      I wish once more to say that I know the
      difference between two!   ts 2

STANZA LXXXI

   Stanza 79   ms
   Altered in red pencil to "81."

   Stanza IV   P 1940, 1972

STANZA LXXXII

   Stanza 80   ms
   Altered in red pencil to "82."

   Stanza V   P 1940, 1972

STANZA LXXXIII

> **Stanza 81** ms
> *Altered in red pencil to "83."*
>
> **Stanza VI** P 1940, 1972

1   Why am I if I am uncertain reasons may
     inclose.
     Why ~~and~~ am I if I am uncertain reasons may
     inclose.   ms

4   Which if they may refuse to open
     Which if they ~~May~~ **can** refuse to open   ts 2
     Which if they **can** refuse to open   Y
     Which if they **can** refuse to open   P 1940, 1972

7   Everybody knows that I chose.
     Typescript 2 types and then inks out two or three capital letters (illegible) after the period.

8   Therefore if therefor before I close.
     Therefor if **therefore** before I close.   ts 1
     Therefor if therefor before I close.   ts 2, Y
     Therefor if therefor before I close.   P 1940, 1972

9   I will therefor offer therefore I offer this.
     I will **therefore** offer therefore I offer this.   ts 1
     I will therefor offer **therefor** I offer this.   ts 2, Y
     I will therefor offer **therefor** I offer this.   P 1940, 1972

10   Which if I refuse to miss may be miss is mine.
     Which if I refuse to miss ~~MAY Be~~ **can** be
       miss ~~Miss~~ is mine.   ts 2
     Which if I refuse to miss **can** be miss is mine.   Y
     Which if I refuse to miss **can** be miss is mine.   P 1940, 1972

13   Certainly I come having come.
     Certainly I come having come   P 1972

14   These stanzas are done.
     Manuscript notebook 6 ends here. Poetry *(1940 and 1972) does not*
     indent this line of the poem but does leave a blank line before it.

Printed and bound by CPI Group (UK) Ltd, Croydon, CR0 4YY

09/06/2025

14685938-0001